A REGIONAL HISTORY OF
THE RAILWAYS OF GREAT BRITAIN

General Editors: DAVID ST JOHN THOMAS and J. ALLAN PATMORE

VOLUME VII
THE WEST MIDLANDS

PUBLISHED IN THIS SERIES

Volume I : *The West Country* (fourth edition)
by David St John Thomas

Volume II : *Southern England* (second edition)
by H. P. White

Volume III : *Greater London* (second edition)
by H. P. White

Volume IV : *The North East* by K. Hoole

Volume V : *The Eastern Counties* by D. I. Gordon

Volume VI : *Scotland: The Lowlands and the Borders*
by John Thomas

———

BY THE SAME AUTHOR (WITH R. W. MILLER)

The Cambrian Railways vol 1   1852–1888
vol 2   1889–1968
The North Staffordshire Railway

Frontis: The GWR was the last railway to reach Wolverhampton through its broad-gauge line from Oxford, but it was destined to make a greater social impact on the town than any other railway company, mainly because of the work provided by Stafford Road locomotive works. For detailed notes on this 1883 scene, see

A REGIONAL HISTORY OF
THE RAILWAYS OF GREAT BRITAIN

Volume VII
THE WEST MIDLANDS

by

Rex Christiansen

WITH 32 PLATES
13 ILLUSTRATIONS IN TEXT
7 MAPS
AND FOLDING MAP

DAVID & CHARLES : NEWTON ABBOT

0 7153 6093 0

Set in Baskerville, 11 pt, 1 pt leaded
and printed in Great Britain by
Clarke Doble & Brendon Limited Plymouth
for David & Charles (Holdings) Limited
South Devon House Newton Abbot Devon

Contents

Illustrations

MAPS IN TEXT

NOTE ON FRONTISPIECE

Wolverhampton Stafford Road Works 1883. Shrewsbury line and site of the later Dunstall Park station are on extreme right. Extreme left foreground shows the corner of no 1 turntable shed, built 1860 and linked to the line to Victoria Basin. The small smithy is sandwiched between the tender shop (left middle, which was converted from the broad-gauge locomotive shed of 1854), and the erecting shop and stores—both buildings of that same year. The line on the right is headed by a Wolverhampton product of 1879—0–6–0ST no 152T, a West Midland Railway 2–2–2, no 214 (Beyer Peacock, 1861), and ex-Shrewsbury & Chester 2–2–2 no 14 (Sharp Brothers, 1848). After withdrawal in 1885 the last named was preserved at Wolverhampton until cut up for unknown reasons in 1920. Behind it lies an 0–6–0 of '322' class (Beyer Peacock, 1864–6). Left, nearest camera, is 2–4–0 no 725 (Swindon 1872), shedded at Bordesley. Behind it three more class '1501' saddle tanks. Pointing to camera is a domeless boiler 2–2–2, recently rebuilt, either 999 *Sir Alexander*, or 1121 (Swindon 1875). It was shedded at Wolverhampton to work Paddington expresses. To its right is 2–4–0 no 806 (Swindon 1873), which regularly worked Wolverhampton–Chester expresses.

CHAPTER I

Character of the Region

A few days after the first atomic bomb fell on Japan I travelled for the first time by train from Birkenhead to Paddington, getting a taste of the railways of the West Midlands. At midnight, as I lay awake waiting with schoolboy excitement to catch the early morning express from Birkenhead Woodside, all the ships in the Mersey Docks (and they were packed with them) blew their sirens. Peace had returned to the world after six weary years of war. Japan had surrendered and it was VJ Day: 15 August 1945.

My seat to Paddington, booked weeks in advance, was useless, for by Wolverhampton, where No 6005 *King George II* came on, the third-class compartment was jammed with sixteen people. That number was to be increased at Birmingham, where there seemed to be no platform, just people. We ran slowly block by block through the Chilterns, clearly seeing the trains in front, also jammed with thousands bound for the peace celebrations in London.

Since 1945 the atomic bomb has dominated world strategy. Changes on the railways have been less drastic. There are many lines on which trains run faster; there are quite a few on which they no longer run at all. More lines are under review. That became clear from an internal report by the Department of the Environment which leaked out in October 1972. It envisaged a reduction in national rail mileage from 11,700 to 7,000—possibly to 3,800. It questioned the future of passenger services between Shrewsbury and Crewe and over the former main line of the North Staffordshire Railway between Crewe and Derby. The Minister of Transport Industries explained that the report was not conclusive: it was only one of a number of options that the Government would consider.

By 1972 the West Midlands had already suffered plenty of

economies, of which the most drastic was symbolised by Birmingham's Snow Hill station, which lay in ruins—a miserable untidy car park. But the economies had been possibly no more than the region could bear, for it had always had plenty of lines. From the early days of railways the area was attractive, not only because of its expanding, firmly based and widely diverse industries (which would have been sufficient incentives in themselves for the railway builders), but because it was a region that could be easily served by lines destined for elsewhere: from Euston to Liverpool and Manchester, and to Scotland; from Paddington to Shrewsbury, Mid Wales and Merseyside; and to Bristol from Derby, the hub of the Midland Railway.

And how those promoters promoted! What companies they formed and how well and securely they bonded them into giants by take-overs and mergers!

Not that the promoters were particularly clever people who could take credit for opening up large areas by building railways, as some colleagues had done elsewhere. The history of railways in the West Midlands has a twist. Birmingham, Wolverhampton and the smoke-belching industry-producing towns of the Black Country were prosperous before railways arrived. Iron furnaces were blackening and disfiguring the Severn gorge at Coalbrookdale before railways gave them cheaper, safer and more reliable transport than barges that had to drift downstream with the current, often too gently flowing for iron masters impatient to develop quick trade.

Prosperous, too, were the Potteries before trains arrived, for industrialists and potters had built the Trent & Mersey Canal, the first trunk route through the British Isles since Roman times. Canals were exploited with the same spectacular success by the industrialists who created the Birmingham Canal Navigations, almost undisputedly the finest canal system in Britain. It fed their factories with coal and raw materials and took away their goods— often products not then being made in any other part of the country or the world, and so continually in great demand.

While the arrival of railways was the most far-reaching peacetime event in, for example, the history of the West Country (a point made by David St John Thomas in the first volume in this series), their arrival in the West Midlands was only one in a series of momentous events in evolution. But they can take some credit for expanding and increasing the prosperity of the West Midlands, and giving the region good transport for products being shipped overseas from the Mersey, the Thames, Bristol and other ports.

This is going to be a complicated book because it deals with a complicated region. To help make the text readable (by excluding many dates), yet informative (by putting them at the back), I have included a detailed Chronology of opening and closing dates of lines (stations and junctions where important), and major developments or changes. It is self-contained, providing a comprehensive history in miniature of each line.

The boundaries of my West Midlands need some explanation, for they have startled some people, mainly because they are tightly contained west and south of Birmingham, and yet reach to North Cheshire. The reason is that they have been drawn by the editors, whose job has been to dovetail them with other books in this series. To provide a potted guide to them, I pass now to a regional round-up in chapter order.

'WORKSHOP OF THE WORLD'

The hub of the West Midlands remains the City of Birmingham —'workshop of the world'—a tag it received many years ago and sustains today by its boast of being the home of 1,500 trades. That is rather more than in pre-grouping days, when the goods agent at Curzon Street from 1907, C. R. J. Woodward, noted in a 1922 return that the principal industries were, 'Hardware, Holloware, Iron, Steel, Brass, Bedsteads, Foodstuff. In Birmingham there are 1,000 different trades'.

No wonder Birmingham was the goal for many railway companies, beginning with the two great trunk routes—the Grand Junction and the London & Birmingham—followed (crosscountrywise) by the Birmingham & Gloucester and the Birmingham & Derby Junction, and, later (again on a north–south bearing), by the Birmingham & Oxford, and the Birmingham, Wolverhampton & Dudley. The lines of all but the last still feed the City.

Birmingham—and the Black Country—were not in a hurry to

have railways. The proven success of the Stockton & Darlington, reinforced by that of the Liverpool & Manchester, caused no clamour among iron and steel masters and manufacturers, but they were not blind to the value of railways. A railroad had been planned about 1808 from Walsall to Erdington by a land agent, William James, of Henley-in-Arden, a man of plans, rather than action, as it turned out. He was the author of the next known scheme, advanced in 1822, for a link between Wolverhampton and Birmingham : Newhall Hill.

James had a wider vision, as C. R. Clinker told the Dugdale Society of Warwickshire in 1954 :

> James' fantastic scheme for a railway from Birmingham to London at the very beginning of the nineteenth century would probably have entirely altered the transport map of central England and resulted in industrial development which it is not easy to visualize.

James' scheme of 1822 was followed only a year later by the formation of the company that was to link London and Birmingham. Historically, the L & B is often considered jointly with the Grand Junction because of its close associations with that company, authorised the same day, yet the two contemporary systems could have been hardly more different. While the L & B faced many natural obstacles and had to build such cuttings as Tring, tunnels as Kilsby and banks as Camden, the GJR ran through flattish country. While the GJR 'petered-out' in the sense that its northern junction was a simple end-on meeting with the Warrington & Newton, the L & B ran to a grand terminus at Euston.

ROUTES : THROUGH AND DIVERSIONARY

Both were promoted on the through route concept. The point was underlined at the first L & B directors' meeting on 31 January 1832 :

> The connexion by Railways between London and Liverpool—a new Company being formed for a Railway between Liverpool and Birmingham—which with the Manchester and Liverpool Road now in operation, and the London & Birmingham Road, will connect London by Railways with the rich pastures of the centre of England,

and the greatest manufacturing districts, and through the Port of Liverpool, afford a most expeditious communication with Ireland.

The 100 mph speeds of Inter-City expresses today is five times the average planned by the L & B. It estimated that trains doing 20 mph would reach Birmingham from Euston in 5h 38m, against 12h taken by stage coaches. The trains were to reach Rugby in 4h, Coventry in 4h 30m, while north of Birmingham, Stafford was to be reached in 7h and the Cheshire border near Crewe 2h later.

The L & B had a station of scaled-down splendour at Birmingham: Curzon Street, and almost alongside it lay the entirely separate station of the Grand Junction. The companies worked very closely, handling through coaches. For a time incoming trains from the north connecting with the L & B trains ran into Curzon Street, but a reverse arrangement was never made.

One of the first proven values of the Grand Junction was in the way it speeded mail. It was claimed that 'by its aid the letter-bags sent from London at eight o'clock in the evening were delivered before noon the next day in Manchester, and the dinner-tables of the inhabitants of Birmingham were supplied with fish purchased the same morning in Liverpool'.

The artery between north-east and south-west England with which the Gloucester and the Derby companies stabbed Birmingham's heart never matched the L & B in engineering glory.

One great merit of lines that encircle Birmingham is the variety of diversionary routes they offer. When I was in Rail House on a glorious summer's day, control reported that heat had buckled a rail on the Birmingham West Suburban route. Within minutes trains had been switched to the old Midland direct line through Camp Hill. A railway friend smiled with satisfaction. 'There is,' he stressed, 'always an alternative route in the West Midlands.'

The Midland has a strong presence in Birmingham, dating back to one of the great 'snatches' of railway history. It happened long ago when the Great Western was crusading, challenging and threatening everywhere, including Birmingham, with the broad gauge. Euston was ready to fight when it seemed that the Birmingham & Gloucester was to be swallowed by Paddington and converted. The Midland stepped in and 'narrowness' prevailed. No company was more pleased than the North Western, which showed its gratitude by allowing the Midland access to its magnificently designed station at New Street, and Derby was destined to have its own platforms there. New Street was—and is—quite a station. Originally hidden away in a deep cutting, it is now camouflaged by tall buildings. It was opened in 1854 to replace the beautiful stately terminus at Curzon Street, which was hopelessly small and almost useless from the day the L & B opened. Other companies seem to have taken the hint about building stations like that, for the GWR, while challenging the LNWR in so many other ways, never attempted to build an edifice as noble as Paddington. Snow Hill's situation in a cutting would, in any case, have prevented it.

The LNWR ancestry of the L & B and GJR established it in an unchallengable position from its formation on 1 January 1846. The MR never attempted much territorial gain, apart from taking over the Birmingham West Suburban Railway. The GWR fought stubbornly, occasionally bitterly, because it had much to gain, including large mineral and goods traffic flowing south from the West Midlands, and heavy passenger traffic.

Paddington had its successes and within a decade from 1846 it broke Euston's monopoly of traffic from Liverpool and Birkenhead to Birmingham and London, and also between Birmingham and London. Many years later Snow Hill and Moor Street (developed to relieve the pressure of suburban traffic, as was Mayfield station, beside Manchester London Road), were used as bases from which Paddington tried to open up country south towards Stratford-upon-Avon, which it tagged 'Birmingham and its Beautiful Borderlands'.

Testimony to the outcome of that campaign is to be found to this day in the green and tree-dotted fields which have survived suburban encroachment. That may have saddened Paddington hearts, but it is a source of continuing delight to those of us who love open countryside, especially near city boundaries, where it is at its greatest premium.

THE COMMUTER NETWORK

It is hard for the casual observer to realise why Birmingham as Britain's second city has so small a commuter system, while London has such an extensive one. It is because Birmingham is a city very different in character. The car-owning population has grown faster there than anywhere in Britain. To match it, a magnificent system of motorways was built right into its heart, but now there are signs that it is becoming overcrowded and people are turning to rail—possibly for the first time. Road competition is not a new phenomenon for the railways : they had to face it from the early days—a year before the Grand Junction opened two companies were running horse omnibuses to Wolverhampton and Dudley. Buses linked Vauxhall and central Birmingham until New Street was ready, one of the first known instances of road-rail coordination. When trams were introduced, it became competition. Electric trams (1904–53) and buses were quickly able to conquer the hilly suburbs and there was no call for extra railways as these spread outwards.

The railway companies were alive enough to the advantages of road transport, and between the world wars Paddington's unrivalled publicity experts noted several local golf courses served by Midland Red buses, and included them in a brochure issued to players.

The dependence of the population on private cars was emphasised in a regional study report of 1971, which stated that there was an inordinate degree of dependence on the car; in no other conurbation did so high a proportion of commuters drive to work. This was said to be partly because intensive development of the West Midlands had taken place largely within a century and a half, and the latter part of that period had seen a parallel development in the car. Problems facing both kinds of commuter—the minority who used public transport and the majority who used cars—would steadily intensify. The report felt that there would be a need to divert people to public transport, particularly rail, as the car traffic expected in the future could not be carried on the existing road system—or on any conceivable road network. The survey estimated that the region's population would grow by a little under 500,000 by the end of the century. Among new centres of development envisaged was the Earlswood area, adding 68,000 to North Warwickshire's population, and almost certainly saving that line.

The report's conclusions reflected thinking of the period, for the *Wolverhampton Express & Star* had complained only two months earlier that British Rail was showing lack of vision. Within a 40-mile radius of Birmingham more than 500,000 people would be caught in a massive tangle unless inter-district rail services were restored.

RAILS TO WOLVERHAMPTON

Wolverhampton is smaller than Birmingham, and overshadowed by it, but it is still big and it is still important. Long before railways it was a natural and strategic centre of roads and canals (with links to the Trent and Severn). The Grand Junction paid heavily for misjudging the status of Wolverhampton. Apart from Stafford and Warrington (not, of course, its own northern terminal), the Grand Junction really had little do to with towns. Rarely has such an important line run so far and served so few places of population. Perhaps its avoidance of central Wolverhampton, and its decision to serve it with nothing more than a puny station at Wednesfield Heath, may have been genuine oversights. It lay more than a mile to the east of the centre and that so infuriated local merchants and manufacturers that they called for competing lines with, most important of all, an alternative route to London and the south. Whether these strong-minded folk would have done so had the Grand Junction met their every demand is a question that history has left unanswered. But one may assume that they would still have wanted other lines, for their creed was competition in all forms of trade and transport.

Wolverhampton was eventually to have three strings to its Birmingham bow: the Grand Junction, the Birmingham, Wolverhampton & Dudley (from Snow Hill), and the Stour Valley, a route which Euston developed as far better, yet totally complementary to the GJR. It was more direct and served more places. When modernisation came, the Stour and GJR routes were natural ones for electrification, while the BW & D, the poor 'piggy-in-the-middle', was simply overwhelmed.

One way and another, Wolverhampton broke a few railway hearts. It humiliated the Grand Junction. The Shrewsbury & Birmingham's hopes of reaching Birmingham were shattered there, as were Paddington's dreams of 'Broad Gauge to the Mersey'. Besides the BW & D, a second mixed gauge line served Wolverhampton, built by the only sizeable company to name the town in its title—the Oxford, Worcester & Wolverhampton.

With the hindsight of history, it is easy to see how the GWR's multi-pronged drives from Oxford and Worcester were bedevilled by broad gauge complications and considerations.

The GWR was further hampered by its long feud with the OW & W and its battles along the border to reach Chester and Merseyside, using the West Midland as a springboard.

Wolverhampton had a modern railway, in effect a by-pass, in the Kingswinford branch, not completed until 1925. At the southern end lay Stourbridge, quite historic because of its loco-motive building industry as well as its lines. It was, loosely, the home of the Shut End Railway (sometimes spelt with two ts), built to carry coal from Shut End, north of Kingswinford, to the Ashwood Basin on the Staffordshire & Worcestershire Canal. It was conceived as a tramroad by the prominent local coalowner, Lord Dudley and Ward. Ignoring claims by the canal owners that they had the construction rights, he built the line with his own men. It opened in the summer of 1829. There were inclined planes at each end and an interesting middle section, level for 2 miles, which was operated from the start by a steam locomotive called *Agenoria*. Its designer was J. U. Rastrick, one of the founders of a locomotive firm at Stourbridge called Foster & Rastrick.

Rastrick is better remembered as a surveyor of important rail-ways, but his design of locomotive stood the test of time. Those who research the history of early locomotives soon come across *Agenoria* because her feats were legendary. It is recorded that she pulled a 131-ton train at nearly $3\frac{1}{2}$ mph. That was almost twelve times her own weight of no more than 11 tons. She worked the line for 35 years and is now preserved, officially in the Science Museum at South Kensington, London, but actually, for a long time, in the Railway Museum at York.

Another example of the firm's work has found a resting place in an American museum. It comprises parts of an 0–4–0 built a little earlier than *Agenoria* and called *Stourbridge Lion*, only the second locomotive seen in America; she reached New York about a fortnight before the Shut End Railway opened. She had been ordered by a prominent American engineer, Horatio Allen, who visited England following the success of the Stockton & Darlington Railway, as a buyer for the Delaware & Hudson Canal Company.

Later, the Shut End system was connected to another of Lord

Dudley's lines, the Pensnett Railway, which ran from his Round Oak steelworks. The Pensnett was among the most complex of private systems and its memory has been well captured in an excellent short history.

The Stourbridge routes lay on the western fringe of the Black Country, no longer the grim area I remember depicted in colour plates in my school geography books. Today one can swiftly sweep through a goodly slice of the area by electric express between Birmingham and Wolverhampton amid scenery no worse than any place where industry is deeply rooted.

THE GREAT BIRMINGHAM CUT-OFF

The terms cut-off or by-pass have been popular since the advent of motorways, but the concept is not new. It was practised with superb effect in the Trent Valley, through which a line was driven between Stafford and Rugby to carry the main line to the north clear of Birmingham, Wolverhampton (Coventry, too) and their congested lines. The line itself was unimpressive but its result was. There was a useful shortening, more in time (2h) than distance (8 miles), and it was possibly a vital factor in the races to Aberdeen in 1895. Without it, the North Western could never have won.

The Trent Valley's creation was mixed up in politics, chiefly those of the L & B and the Grand Junction; but it also became the instrument of peace, for it ended bitter rivalry and allowed the formation (with the Manchester & Birmingham) of the LNWR. Originally, the L & B saw the Trent Valley plan, advanced by the rather isolated Manchester & Birmingham company, as the means of achieving its heart's desire: a route between London and Manchester independent of the GJR. It tried hard to secure the Trent Valley, but the GJR stepped in and gave the company powers to subscribe a large part of the capital and have full running powers. For the L & B, friendship with the GJR was the only answer.

While the Trent Valley carried many expresses clear of Birmingham and so slightly diminished the city's importance as a railway centre, there was no great concern, for the area was large enough to support a major network of its own, and demand London expresses to meet its needs.

The story of the Trent Valley is told in Chapter VIII, together with the railway background of several important towns, notably Nuneaton, Rugby and also Coventry, which had one of the most *un*eventful railway histories a city of its size has ever known. The reason was straightforward—Euston's dominance.

When the London & Birmingham line reached Coventry, the town had a population of under 30,000. Today it has more than ten times that number. In some ways it is remarkable how the LNWR managed to keep out its rivals, except for the Midland, to which it granted limited access. Lines projected to Coventry between 1845 and 1910 combed the area like a salvo of torpedo tracks, but none hit. Coventry's present-day image as mainly a car town dates from immediately after the Kaiser's war, but before then it had undergone a mini-revolution caused by the demand for the bicycle. As a writer noted in the late 1890s: 'Coventry, no longer the city of Godiva, but the city of the cycle! The full force of the boom burst upon the trade in the summer of 1895, but '96 was *the* year. Night and day worked Coventry.'

The urgency of delivery was met easily by the LNWR and the MR, which could handle cycles, crated and carried to goods depots by horse and cart, more conveniently than cars, although car railheads were established on the Coventry loop in 1971.

CHARM OF NORTH SHROPSHIRE

From Coventry a railway ran to Leamington Spa—as did several others until this small town had far more than it ever deserved. The same was true of smaller towns and villages of Shropshire, a county with few lines left open and few stations on those that have survived. Railways had a distinctive flavour throughout Shropshire. They were mostly mineral lines in mainly rural surroundings—totally different to the Potteries, where purely mineral lines were developed by the North Staffordshire Railway in industrial backgrounds. The Shropshire lines north of the Severn did not have quite the appeal of some of the more remote rural lines on the Welsh border, like the Bishop's Castle, but they had a character that set them apart from the mundane.

On the secondary line from Wellington to Nantwich, special arrangements were necessary to maintain and guard the four paraffin vapour lamps used on the two platforms at Hodnet station, Western Region operating instructions laying down in 1954 :

> Guard of 8.52 pm ex Crewe to extinguish Up platform lamps and convey them to Peplow. Guard of 9.25 pm ex Wellington to extinguish Down platform lamps and convey them to Tern Hill. Lamps to be returned to Hodnet by first train next morning.

The LNWR was perhaps more keen on standard, matter of fact efficiency than the GWR, but somehow the branch it built to Coalport, to prevent the GWR 'getting away' with all mineral traffic, absorbed the Shropshire charm as it plunged through short tunnels, twisted in and out of wooded cuttings and slid down steep banks.

Elsewhere in Shropshire the giants met on more social and equal terms through joint ownership of the Shrewsbury & Birmingham route between Shrewsbury and Wellington. The line from there to Stafford was purely LNWR, the company in early days having staked a strong claim of right of access to Shrewsbury. The joint line and that to Stafford was the child—the only child —of the Shropshire Union Railways & Canal Company, which fell far short of its original objective of converting dozens of miles of canals into railways.

Market Drayton became the junction for a quite charming single line running east to the Potteries. A little north of Market Drayton lies the boundary of Cheshire, a county chock-full of mature lines—the Grand Junction, Manchester & Birmingham, Chester & Crewe, Shrewsbury & Crewe and the Cheshire Lines Committee, which lay farthest of all from the heart of the West Midlands. No part of Cheshire lies within that region, now Government defined since the formation of an economic planning council in 1965.

INTRODUCING THE NORTH STAFFORDSHIRE

But Shropshire does lie officially within the region and so do the Potteries, birthplace of a railway that made astute use of canals. The North Staffordshire Railway was the most independent of all those in the region. Once created, it came to friendly terms with its chief rival—the Trent & Mersey canal, which was serving the most important areas of the industrial complex. Relations between the NSR headquarters at Stoke and Euston were not so warm. To the North Western, the NSR was what one can pardonably call a 'Knotty' problem, taking the cue from the company's nickname (one of the most distinctive in British railway history), which was quite genuine and historically correct. For its emblem was that of the County—the nicely twisted Staffordshire Knot. For years Euston disliked having to rub shoulders with a small company, especially one so obviously successful, with the glorious mesh of lines, some no more than a mile long, yet all making handsome profits—for mostly they carried minerals, not passengers.

Anyone who has studied the NSR cannot regard it except with affection. I am now trying to bring out its character in a wider context than in the book I wrote with R. W. (Bob) Miller. There were—and are—two very different areas of North Staffordshire, but most people know only one : the five towns (in reality, six) of Arnold Bennett. Their legacy of black pit heaps, flooded clay-pits, derelict factories and mines and rows of back-to-back houses, is vanishing. It is no credit to a go-ahead city like Stoke, or governments dedicated to improving the environment, that ruins like those of California Locomotive Works and the famous Stoke Roundhouse survived long past the day when electric inter-city expresses began carrying millions of travellers through the Potteries rather than along the more pleasant West Coast main line only a few miles to the west.

The NSR's independent spirit, drawn from that which had imbued the early potters, iron founders and coalowners, enabled it not only to maintain a highly profitable network locally but to reach out and, by using running powers, send trains, often headed by their own engines, deep into rival territory. They ran as far as they could without running out of steam—literally. When the NSR got access to Llandudno—one of the most popular of Pottery seaside resorts—it had no locomotives capable of working such a distance, so it built them, making sure tenders were large enough to carry coal and water for the round trip.

The NSR operated, although a little reluctantly, the only major narrow gauge line mentioned in this book : the Leek & Manifold Valley Light Railway, a late child that was always ailing and died in early manhood. A valley gave the Manifold its character.

Hills were the backbone to the Cromford & High Peak, which served the Pennine region with far greater success and for far longer. It was promoted earlier than most in the 1820s, not to compete against canals, but to complement them. The object was to transport minerals being discovered in Derbyshire, Nottinghamshire and Leicestershire to the Manchester area by conquering hills over which it was impossible to build canals. Later, the C & HP became part of a route that the LNWR developed between Ashbourne and Buxton, tourist centre of class rather than mass. Nowadays Buxton is the centre of the Peak National Park, an area so designated for people to visit and enjoy: but not by train. The Ashbourne line is now a walker's trail and the C & HP has been similarly converted.

Many regarded the C & HP as a 'heavenly' line. Certainly it gave endless scope to the effusive Victorian travel writers, one of whom said: 'The gradients remind us of King David's description of the effect of a storm at sea. "They mount up to the heavens, they go down again to the depths," and the curves whereof were equally acute.'

Apart from the High Peak and the Manifold, the rail passenger through the West Midlands gets (or got) little value for his fare by looking out of the carriage window. Dramatic views of the countryside just are not there, though they lay not far away—the Peak route between Derby and Manchester comes especially to mind. The rural scenery of the region was pretty uniform—flattish with occasional hills like those at Whitmore, where the Grand Junction crosses the Trent and Mersey watershed.

Yet it would be hard to cut a slice out of the railway map of Britain and find a more varied cross section than the one defined in this book.

CHAPTER II

Birmingham : 'Premier' Lines

GRAND JUNCTION

Navvies' picks and shovels, skill and brawn, gave Birmingham an extensive network of railways within a few years. Promoters scrambled and men raced to tear away earth to lay rails through the heart of what was then the greatest industrial area in Britain. First to arrive was the Grand Junction, whose achievements remain overshadowed by those of the London & Birmingham, authorised on the same day, 6 May 1833, which made it one of the most momentous days in Britain's railway history.

The GJR was radically different from its predecessors in two significant ways. Besides being the first of the great trunk routes to be constructed in Britain, it was by far the longest line to be completed and opened at the same time, instead of in sections. Much of the GJR lies north of Birmingham, but its story is told in full because it was the route as a whole that influenced the development of railways in Birmingham.

The GJR's ancestry can be traced back to a scheme to link Birmingham with Birkenhead (as the Mersey ferry-head for Liverpool) that reached Parliament in 1824. It was vigorously opposed by land and canal owners in central Cheshire and the plan was thrown out, a process repeated two years later. During initial surveys, George Stephenson was horrified when he learned from landowners near Nantwich that canal agents had intimidated farmers by saying that the locomotive was a frightful machine with a 'breath' as poisonous as the fabled dragons of old.

Such an atmosphere killed the next scheme, promoted in two sections : from Birkenhead to Chorlton, near Whitmore (a hamlet prominent in early schemes for railways to and through the Potteries), and from there south to Birmingham. It failed to get

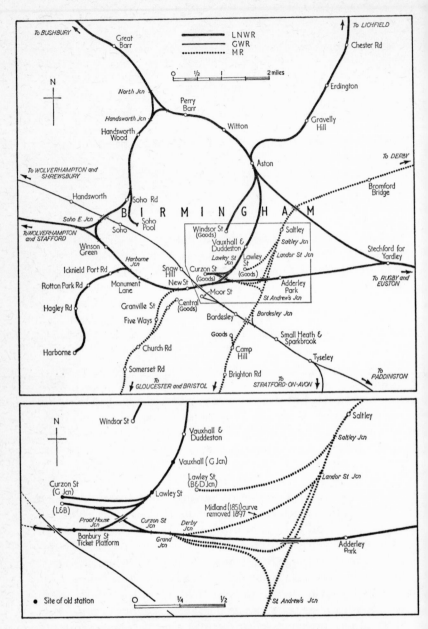

Birmingham, ringed by LNWR lines; bisected by those of the GWR and the Midland Railway. *Inset*: the original terminal stations

Parliamentary sanction, and when its promoters were forced to think again, they favoured Liverpool rather than Birkenhead as the northern terminus, to avoid ferrying goods and passengers across the Mersey. They realised that Liverpool could be reached as easily as Birkenhead by striking north from Whitmore to Warrington, where the Mersey was narrow, and joining the Liverpool & Manchester at Newton via the Warrington & Newton Railway, a 5 mile branch from that line.

As the L & M neared completion, George Stephenson, with the support of the board, got Joseph Locke to survey what became the Grand Junction route. It was proposed as an alternative to one advanced by the W & N, surveyed by Robert Stephenson as engineer. It met strong opposition from the South Cheshire landowners, as it aimed at Sandbach, one of the larger villages.

The Grand Junction route was to be a modest $82\frac{1}{2}$ miles and have the advantage of giving access to both Liverpool and Manchester. 'Grand Junction' was an obvious title, and construction was straightforward in physical but stormy in human terms because of George Stephenson's jealousy of Locke and his ambition to be sole engineer. As a compromise the route was split at Chorlton, Stephenson taking on construction of the northern section, and Locke the southern. It was a job to which George Stephenson was not suited temperamentally and Locke's competence in such work exposed his poor and sluggish performance. In August 1835 Stephenson withdrew and Locke became chief engineer for the whole project.

A young Cheshire land agent and surveyor, Thomas Brassey, who had worked under Telford on the Holyhead road, tendered to build Dutton viaduct, near Northwich. His price was too high but he got a contract for a stretch of the line near Penkridge. So began his distinguished career as an international railway builder.

Embankments and cuttings were of no special merit, but the gradients were engineered more steeply than those of the L & B. Those across the watershed between the Trent and Mersey at Whitmore varied between 1 in 180 and 1 in 260 over 6 miles. They were legacies on which locomotive men were to sweat and curse for more than a century until diesel and electric locomotives arrived.

George Stephenson was quick to claim praise for his own work on the Dutton viaduct, for he is said to have written anonymously in 1838 :

> The most important work upon this line is a viaduct near North-wich with 20 arches, each a 60ft span and about 60ft high. It is built over the river Weaver, and is a very fine specimen of masonry and bridge building. It is one of Stephenson's finest designs.

The GJR cost £18,846 a mile, cheap compared with the London and Birmingham's average price of more than £53,000 a mile. Because of the easy lie of the land between Warrington and Birmingham, and because it was carried clear of two important towns—Walsall and Wolverhampton—construction of the 78 miles was quick and straightforward. The last section completed was a twenty-eight arch viaduct at Lawley Street, Birmingham, leading to its terminal alongside Curzon Street. The Act of 16 June 1834 also authorised a short junction line with the L & B outside the stations.

The Grand Junction used a temporary terminus at Vauxhall from the opening on 4 July 1837 until early in January 1839, when the new terminus (not called Curzon Street until 1852) was brought into use. Vauxhall fell out of passenger use on an unknown date. Part was converted into a goods depot, and another section was adapted as an extension to the L & B loco-motive depot.

The GJR was neither flamboyant in design or opening : the occasion, late in the reign of William IV, friend of Nelson, was marked with little celebration. The entire Staffordshire Con-stabulary lined the route to keep people off the track, but few spectators turned out. The largest crowd was at Stafford—the only intermediate station of importance—where the Mayor fired a 21-gun salute with an ancient cannon at the approach of the first train to Birmingham, which was made up of the locomotive *Wildfire* and eight named first-class coaches.

WHY THE NEWSPAPERS WERE WRONG

The lack of bands, displays, banners and distinguished visitors to grace the opening did not escape notice, for a newspaper reported :

> It was remarked as somewhat singular, that there was, even throughout the day, a comparatively small attendance of the leading

merchants and manufacturers of Birmingham, which is attributable
to none of the latter having been placed on the direction of the
Grand Junction Railway. Indeed, the directors are entirely limited
to the bankers and merchants of Liverpool.

But the papers were wrong. There was no leading Birmingham
figure on the board because local people showed almost complete
lack of interest in the company, and few subscribed to it.

On completion, the GJR was not a passenger line of importance,
for the population along its route was estimated at only 150,000.
The largest centre of population anywhere near was that of the
Potteries, some 7 miles east of Whitmore. According to contemporary guides, Whitmore was the thirteenth station, though
perhaps that was lucky, for soon it became one of the busiest,
where stagecoaches made connections for the Potteries and several
other areas. There was little coach traffic at a station called Crewe,
a hamlet of 184 people lying amid the fields of the rich farming
plain of south Cheshire, on the estate of Lord Crewe. The story
of its development will be told in Chapter X.

The GJR was originally laid with double-sided rails invented by
Locke, who made them reversible so that they could be turned
over when worn. This proved impracticable because the rails
became dented along their base, where they pressed into the
chairs. But if the track idea was not successful, the company was,
and shares, worth £90 during construction, doubled in value once
it opened. The company retained its profitability, and its dividends
were among the best returned by early companies, because of its
comparatively cheap construction. In the first half of 1840, the
GJR paid $15\frac{1}{2}$ per cent, against the Liverpool & Manchester's
then standard figure of 10 per cent, and 8 per cent paid by the
L & B.

The GJR quickly lost some of its original importance when the
section between Birmingham and Wednesfield Heath on the
outskirts of Wolverhampton was duplicated by the direct Stour
Valley route (Chapter VI). Passenger traffic between Wolverhampton and Birmingham over the GJR was never intensive and
it suffered when passenger services were withdrawn between
Willenhall Bridge and Bushbury from 1 January 1873, bringing
about the closure of Portobello and Wednesfield Heath stations.
Passenger trains were reintroduced over part of the route when
the LNWR began a link between Wolverhampton and Walsall on

1 March 1881, made possible by the opening of a curve from the Midland at Heath Town to Portobello, and the 'Pleck' curve. There were no demands to reopen the two stations.

The GJR merged into the LNWR as the senior partner because it was much bigger than the other constituents, having absorbed the Chester & Crewe and railways in Lancashire, including the Liverpool & Manchester.

Until electrification, little of moment happened to the GJR in the Birmingham area. What changes did take place were minor and resulted from wider considerations, as in the mid-Victorian years, when poverty prevented the working classes from travelling much. To encourage local travel, the LNWR drew attention to local amenities by supplementing station names, no matter how ponderous. In the winter of 1878 Witton station had 'for Aston Lower Grounds' added to its name board. The addition was not included in working timetables.

LONDON & BIRMINGHAM

How can a 30 mile section of the L & B be detached and considered virtually in isolation from the substantial whole? The task of writing about the route between Birmingham and Rugby, the only part in the West Midlands, would have been difficult but for the geographical accident that made Rugby something of a frontier. Between Birmingham and Rugby the L & B route ran through rolling country, easily conquerable; but south of Rugby the more rugged terrain led to much heavier engineering works. Once the line was extended from Curzon Street to New Street station, both sections had a common quality: gradients that were gentle for most of the way, yet severe at either end—on Camden bank and through the tunnels into New Street.

The first scheme of William James (1771–1837) was loose and bound up with his proposals, made about 1808, for a General Railroad Company with a capital of £1 million to build a national network of railways. This was about the time that he suggested a line from Walsall to Erdington. Later James surveyed other routes through the West Midlands, including Birmingham–Manchester (through Derbyshire) and Wolverhampton–Birmingham. This latter scheme dated from about 1822, and soon afterwards he surveyed a London–Birmingham route via Oxford.

Page 33　(above) Mid pastures green : the Grand Junction Railway station at Newton Road, West Bromwich, in the year of opening, 1837. A drawing made in stone by E. Bifsell; (below) Sutton Coldfield 1862, on the opening of the branch from Birmingham, which, according to the *Birmingham Post*, was responsible for turning the community 'from rural sleepiness to bustling activity'. Tank no 334 at the head of a train of four-wheel coaches, with diminutive one at far end

Page 34 (above) London & Birmingham glory : Wolston viaduct between Coventry and Rugby. Lithograph by Bourne. Railway architecture gave added interest to the flattish Avon valley; (below) Despite its inadequacies for coping with passenger trains, the L.N.W.R. was keen to show off Curzon Street

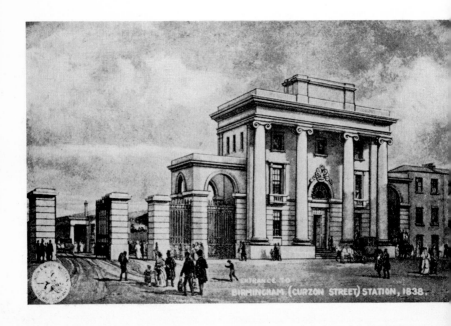

The scheme was premature but the route was sound, much more so, it turned out, than the first seriously considered one to link London and Birmingham. That was a plan of 1 April 1826 by Sir John Rennie, and its main fault was that it by-passed Coventry, running via Southam, 2 miles to the south. To be fair, Coventry was then suffering a heavy decline in its traditional industry of cloth weaving and being overtaken as the capital of the region by Birmingham. Rennie's plan fell victim to a credit squeeze and no further initiative was actively taken until 1829, when more widely spaced alternatives were considered.

Francis Giles, an engineer for some 20 years, mostly with Rennie, surveyed a line through Coventry, while Rennie favoured one via Oxford. The position was resolved when groups promoting rival lines merged on 11 September 1830. One group, consisting of Coventry men, had consulted Robert Stephenson, who had advocated a route with their interests in mind. Soon afterwards Robert and his father were appointed joint engineers of the L & B. A Bill that went before Parliament on 20 February 1832 was strongly opposed by landowners who wanted a better price, and after receiving a majority of only twenty-one, it was rejected by the Lords. A second Bill promoted the next year received the Royal Assent on 6 May 1833, but only, it was said, after opponents had been bought out by offers giving them treble the value of their land.

Despite many obstacles, the L & B was constructed in workmanlike fashion and suffered from none of the financial troubles of the kind that were to hit many companies in later years. Robert Stephenson reported on 17 February 1838 that a single 'permanent road' had been laid between Rugby and Birmingham, and that a second, with the exception of 150yd in Church Lawford cutting, was well advanced.

> Though laid, however, the road is not in a fit state throughout to be travelled upon by engines and trains; for on some of the principal embankments it requires to be raised and adjusted. But this is a work, which with the proper number of men, can easily be completed before those other points. At Birmingham station the large turnplate in the locomotive engine-house is completed, and the necessary rails fitting it for the reception of engines will be laid in a few days. The lines of rails in the passenger sheds are laid and the requisite sidings will be completed in a fortnight.

C

A line from the Liverpool and Manchester Railway near Newton, to London, by way of Birmingham, will unite the two greatest sea ports in the kingdom.—

It will connect with them and with each other, all the principal manufacturing districts; viz. the iron manufactories and potteries of Staffordshire, the cotton and silk manufactories of Lancashire Cheshire, Derbyshire, &c. the woollen manufactories of the West Riding of Yorkshire.—

It will connect the metropolis and the counties which lie to the South of it, or on either side of the Line, with the great provincial towns of Birmingham, Manchester, Leeds, Liverpool; and, by way of Liverpool, with Dublin, Belfast, and Glasgow.—

It will afford increased facilities of intercourse to upwards of seven millions of people.

The proposed Railway from London to Birmingham forms part of this great national line. Its precise direction and the towns near which it will pass, will be best understood by inspection of the map which accompanies these observations.

Its length will be about 111 miles. Its planes will not vary from the horizontal level more than 16 feet (or one on 330) in any one mile.

The cost will be £2,500,000. The sufficiency of this sum has been ascertained by Committees of the Houses of Lords and Commons, on the testimony of Mr. Stephenson, confirmed by that of other eminent Engineers.

The Railway will probably not be used to convey coals, lime, and other cheap and heavy articles which compose the chief traffic of canals; but it has been found by very accurate inquiry that the returns for passengers, the lighter and more costly kinds of merchandize, agricultural and other produce, will ensure an income, at low Railway prices, of from six to seven hundred thousand pounds per annum.

The cost of constructing the Liverpool and Manchester Railway greatly exceeded the estimate; and the expense of maintaining and working it, is more than was anticipated; but still it pays between eight and nine per cent. on the whole sum invested, and £100. shares sell for nearly £200.

It is quite unnecessary to enlarge upon the beneficial influence of every great improvement in the means of internal communication, on the progress of national prosperity. All the advantages which England has derived from good roads and an extensive system of inland navigation, cannot fail to be greatly increased by the more powerful and more perfect machinery of Railways.

The reduction of time and expense in travelling, and in the conveyance of merchandize, must afford great and immediate benefit to the mercantile and manufacturing interests; and it should be borne in mind, that one half of the whole population of the kingdom, and a much greater proportion of the inhabitants of the districts through which this Railway will pass, derive their means of support from manufactures.

The facilities which the Railway will afford for travelling to Irish families, and especially to Irish Members of both Houses of Parliament, are obvious.

The same advantage, in a degree proportionate to their distance from London, will be afforded to English families similarly circumstanced.

The Landed Interest will be benefited—

1. By having a new and improved conveyance of every species of agricultural produce, and especially butchers' meat, dairy and garden produce, to the principal markets of the kingdom : for example, from Northamptonshire to London or Staffordshire in three or four hours.

2. By the expenditure of upwards of two millions in labor, during the construction of the Railway, and the constant employment of from one to two thousand persons upon it when completed.

3. By the amount of poor's rates assessed upon it through its whole length, and

4. By the enhanced value of estates.

Above all, the public must derive a benefit which cannot easily be estimated, from the power the Railway will give for the rapid transmission of Intelligence, Bullion, Troops, and Military Stores. In connexion with the steam boats, *it will reduce the time of passing between London and Dublin to four and twenty hours.*

A major section of the prospectus of the London & Birmingham promoters of 1833

The first regular trains ran from Birmingham to Rugby on 9 April 1838, and the remainder of the line was opened a few weeks later. The company advertised the first limited service of through trains between London and Birmingham from Sunday, 24 June 1838. The line was still single for part of the way, including Kilsby Tunnel, south of Rugby, into which the last brick had been ceremonially inserted on 21 June. The *full* service started on 17 September—the much quoted completion date—and road coaches were then withdrawn between Denbigh Hall, near Bletchley, and Rugby.

The only intermediate station of first-class status on the section was Hampton, soon to become a junction. Hampton lies on the edge of the Shakespeare country and there was happy inspiration, one would like to feel, in the elaboration of its name in 1886 when it became the much prettier Hampton-in-Arden, although the utilitarian title was retained in timetable footnotes.

The other two original intermediate stations were Brandon and Coventry, the latter a miserable affair; the story will be told later of the price successive owners had to pay for that *faux pas*. The original Coventry station did have one distinction. It had, with Birmingham, Rugby and several stations further south, waiting rooms with female attendants.

SUBURBAN BRANCHES

Birmingham grew so fast in Victorian days that companies had constantly to extend or improve their systems, though capital spending was restricted in periodic times of depression. Because of having diverse industries, the region never suffered as badly as other parts of the country. One quite sustained depression occurred in 1861, just after Richard Moon had taken over as LNWR chairman, following the death of Admiral C. R. Moorsom. Moon blamed the depression for, among other things, a half-year drop of £5,000 in revenue from Birmingham.

> Gentlemen connected with the district, which may be considered the centre of our system—South and North Staffordshire—are aware that those districts have been almost shut up. The superintendent at Wolverhampton told me a short time ago that he had only two days' work a week there.

Trade picked up only slowly and it was 2 years before dividends were increased.

The last year of Moorsom's chairmanship had included the establishment of a Central District based on Birmingham to control 148 route miles on ten lines between Rugby and Stafford. It formed part of the LNWR's Southern Division.

SUTTON COLDFIELD BRANCH

The district was soon extended by the opening of several branches, the first being that to Sutton Coldfield, a scheme which had been in the air for a long time. The Birmingham, Lichfield & Manchester, engineered by John Robinson McClean, of whom more later, was authorised on 27 July 1846, from the GJR at Aston to the Trent Valley at Lichfield. Its ambition to reach Manchester does not appear to have been strong, for the company's title was designed to do no more than keep it in the mind of other promoters considering a link between the West Midlands and Manchester. The plans were short-lived, being abandoned a year later when the LNWR received powers for a more compact Birmingham & Lichfield Railway. It was planned over a slightly different route, but it became still-born through lack of money and it was not until 12 years later, on 8 August 1859, that the LNWR got a fresh Act for a line shortened to Sutton Coldfield, with a north spur at Aston to create a triangular junction. When the line was completed in 1862, Sutton Coldfield was an exclusive area and the railway was regarded by some as an unwelcome intrusion. It was said that police were kept busy 'controlling the indecent behaviour and depredation by visitors'. But the line pleased its promoters, and 7 years later, in 1869, the *Birmingham Post* stated that the railway was responsible for the community passing 'from rural sleepiness to bustling activity'.

More than 20 years were to pass before the route was extended to Lichfield, and then only after the LNWR had stepped in after the failure of schemes advanced by the Birmingham & Sutton Extension Railway and the Birmingham & Lichfield Junction. The LNWR received powers on 29 June 1880, and Lichfield City, and intermediate stations at Four Oaks, Blake Street and Shenstone, were opened $3\frac{1}{2}$ years later—34 years after plans had first been made.

Public clamour for the extension from Sutton Coldfield to Lichfield was never matched by need. The Cathedral city grew only slowly and the Trent Valley line also made little impact on development.

The suburbs between Birmingham and Sutton Coldfield are fashionable, well populated areas, and when the line was dieselised in 1956, the attraction of the new trains brought a spectacular increase in annual passenger returns, which rose from about 750,000 to 2,500,000 in two years. The country between Sutton Coldfield and Lichfield remains unchanged, although dominated by the tall television mast, and so half of the locals terminate at Four Oaks. Birmingham commuters, like those elsewhere, travel only 5 days a week and so the line is heavily subsidised. It was selected for a modification of services in the Beeching Report.

When a scheme to modernise six stations was announced, BR stated : 'It should be emphasised that at all these places, the staff amenities are being improved'. Such a statement was felt necessary, no doubt, so as not to discourage the recruiting of railwaymen in a region where industry, notably that of car manufacture, paid high wages.

A terminal for summer motorail services to Scotland and the West Country was established in the former goods yard (closed 1 May 1967) at Sutton Coldfield. The passenger station retained its buildings, including its tiled gents' toilet, and a second was built and labelled 'Gentlemen, Motorail passengers', which I suppose could be interpreted as a direction—or a tribute! No matter, the terminal closed in the autumn of 1972 and Crewe was developed as a motorail terminal for the north-west from 20 May 1973. It was said to have good catering and other facilities, and greater development potential than the 'rather isolated' car loading points at Sutton Coldfield and Newton-le-Willows.

HARBORNE RAILWAY

Another line conceived to serve Birmingham's growing suburbs was the Harborne Railway, which planned a single line from the LNWR near Monument Lane and the GWR near Soho. West of Harborne the line was to join the projected Halesowen & Bromsgrove Branch Railway at Lapal, near Halesowen. The extension was dropped because of opposition that also led the promoters to withdraw, with GWR consent, the link between Monument Lane and Soho. This left a route of just under $2\frac{1}{2}$ miles, which the Harborne Railway Company was authorised to build on 28 June 1866.

There were no local directors on the board, which may have been one reason why no attempts were made to begin construction. The project was kept alive by a 3 year extension of time, granted from 1870, and by an agreement made with the LNWR by which the Harborne company contributed towards an improved junction at Monument Lane, facing New Street station, almost $1\frac{1}{2}$ miles to the south. The LNWR worked the branch for 50 per cent of the gross receipts from the opening (to passengers and goods) on 10 August 1874.

The Harborne Railway, which had its offices in London, became an extremely lucrative investment for shareholders, who refused three LNWR offers to buy, and the company remained independent until 1922. It was by far the best-paying suburban line in Birmingham and in its heyday during 1914 had twenty-seven trains each way—a tremendously intensive service for a little branch. They began at 5.35 am from Harborne and finished with an 11.15 pm from New Street. A fast lunchtime service between New Street and Harborne, omitting Icknield Port Road, enabled city workers to get home for a meal.

As bus competition increased over a shorter and more direct route into the city centre, branch fortunes declined, but it struggled on until the depression of the 1930s, when the LMS felt the need for economies. Harborne was an obvious case and it closed to passengers on 26 November 1934. Buses had not been the only handicap : mainline trains between Birmingham and Wolverhampton had always taken priority on the congested section between Monument Lane and New Street, and the Harborne locals often suffered delays that passengers were not prepared to tolerate when there was a good alternative.

The railway, though, was held in some sort of affection by local people and the farewells were elaborate. During World War II— in 1943—two readers wrote to the *Railway Magazine* suggesting passenger services should be restored to relieve bus congestion, but the next passenger train to reach Harborne was an enthusiasts' special in June 1950. Freight continued until 4 November 1963.

The fortunes of the line might have been different had those of the railways projected to join it been more successful. The Birmingham West Suburban Railway, incorporated in 1871 along a roughly parallel route about a mile to the south, was authorised to join the line at Harborne but, as will be noted, never did so. In the same year the Birmingham & Halesowen Junction Railway planned a link from the BWSR terminus near Granville Street in central Birmingham to Harborne Junction. As it would have run parallel to the Stour Valley line, it would not have been popular with the LNWR, but the scheme collapsed before any action was necessary by Euston.

THE SOHO LINE

Few, if any, lines developed after the main system were to be as valuable as the short link between Soho and Perry Barr, opened by the LNWR to goods in 1888 and passengers a year later. Powers of 16 July 1883 had also provided for quadrupling from Harborne Junction to Winson Green and a short branch to a goods depot much below rail level at Soho Pool. It opened from Perry Barr North Junction to coal and mineral traffic in 1887. The Soho line, with double-facing junctions at either end, relieved traffic pressures over a wide area and allowed more freight to pass clear of New Street station. Widening between Aston and Vauxhall followed in 1891.

NEW STREET STATION

History has repeated itself on the London–Birmingham route. A casual traveller of 130 years ago must have been struck by the majesty of Euston and Curzon Street. Nowadays New Street has much the same airline-terminal appearance of the rebuilt Euston. The new Euston is, of course, an 'original', while New Street is a substitute, since it originally replaced Curzon Street. The LNWR got authority for an extension from there to the site of New Street on 3 August 1846. The Act stipulated that as the station was to obliterate King Street (one of the main roads in the city centre), a footpath, open to the public at all times, must run through the station. Like the footpath, the station was to be for passengers only. The Act was the outcome of conflicting claims put to a Commons Select Committee that considered schemes for several railways, including the Stour Valley and the Birmingham, Wolverhampton & Dudley. The verbal battle hinged on the merits of New Street or Snow Hill as the best site for a station, assuming only one was to be built. Robert Stephenson, surveyor of the Stour Valley, said New Street would be an exact model of that of the Manchester & Leeds Railway at Manchester, 'which had the largest traffic in the world'.

Birmingham councillors voted 16–6 in favour of New Street, and a former mayor, Alderman Weston, contended that while New Street would be central and have easy approaches, those to Snow Hill would be steep and narrow. A general merchant, John Lord, said that banks, the Post Office, the news-room, the contemplated exchange, and all buildings of any note, were in the neighbourhood of New Street. Business was continually leaving the Snow Hill area.

The headmaster of Birmingham Grammar School, the Rev James Prince Lee, said the development of New Street station would cause the removal of a number of very objectionable houses at the back of the school, which was a very handsome building. The houses were a nuisance to the school.

Charles Shaw, a magistrate and large ow & w shareholder, claimed that New Street was the most dangerous spot in Birmingham. Two policemen were kept there for the protection of life and property. There were a good many pickpockets. Pleadings on the merits of both stations reached such a pitch that at one point the chairman of the Select Committee commented: 'I suppose all the inhabitants in the neighbourhood of Snow Hill are in favour of Snow Hill station?' And counsel answered 'Yes'.

The L & B (Birmingham Extension) Bill provided the infant LNWR with a line of just under a mile from Curzon Street at a modest cost of £35,000. Engineered by Robert Stephenson it included a tunnel of 273yd.

New Street was formally opened on 1 June 1854 and was used by the Midland from 1 July when Curzon Street was closed to regular passenger trains. The latter station continued to be used for Sutton Coldfield excursions until 1893, the last train running on Whit Monday, 22 May. There was plenty to impress travellers about New Street, and one of the first to record his impressions was George Borrow, who passed through en route for Chester to begin the holiday in which he was to write *Wild Wales*. He observed pithily : 'That station alone is enough to make one proud of being a modern Englishman'. The Midland had access by virtue of the original Birmingham & Gloucester Railway Act, which gave the company access to Curzon Street and any future terminus of the L & B.

The first major changes were foreshadowed in the 1884 edition of the *Guide to the Midland Railway* :

> We are surrounded by the bewildering bustle of a station which, although one of the longest in this country, and indeed in the world, is about to be considerably enlarged.

The work led to the Midland platforms being brought into use on 8 February 1885, and in October north to west expresses began using the Midland side, while those northbound ran into LNWR platforms. That arrangement lasted until 1889, from which year the expresses were exclusively handled by the MR. Eight years later—from 1 April 1897—New Street became a joint station under both companies.

Few contemporary railway writers could afford to ignore the continual growth of the station, Pendleton noting in *Our Railways* in 1896 :

> New Street Station presents the most vivid picture of the swift go-ahead life of that city. The traffic has grown so rapidly that it has become absolutely necessary for the London and North-Western Railway to improve the approaches, to double the south tunnel, and to put down additional lines. What improvements and extensions will be necessary in the next quarter of a century it almost passes the wit of railway engineers to conceive. The crowd of restless humanity gets greater every year. It was big when John Bright spoke in Bingley Hall; it was bigger when the Queen visited Birmingham in 1887; and there was considerable crush into New Street when Mr Gladstone spoke in the town Hall in 1888. But New Street Station, congested and bewildering to its utmost, though the traffic is carried on with care and skill, must be seen when the great multitude is surging to the Onion Fair, or the Cattle Show, or on some night when the great muscular crowd from the Black Country invades the city intent on the delights of the pantomime.

Improving the approaches meant raising the main line between Vauxhall and Proof House Junction to carry it clear of the

Curzon Street approaches. The work was finished in 1893, trains using the new stretch from 7 May.

The LNWR never made much fuss about New Street in the historic sketches of the system in the *Railway Year Book*, but it recorded, under important engineering works, that the roof had a span of 209ft and a length of about 840ft.

The New Street that the LMS inherited was no wonder station —at least not in the view of one person, who noted in 1923 :

> It is on a cold, wet night that the station reaches its most repulsive. It is ill-lit by a faulty gas system, devoid of adequate seating, the roof leaks in countless places, the lavatories proclaim their presence.

German bombs were to make New Street worse, as were years of use and heavy traffic, especially during wartime. Sir Arthur Smout, a former president of the city's Chamber of Commerce, was quoted as saying in 1964 : 'I know of no station in this country, Europe or the United States, which for filth, muck and general dishevelment compares with New Street'.

The rebuilding of the station was the biggest work of its kind during the West Midland electrification and modernisation. Twelve through platforms replaced eight through roads and six bays, and for the first time in Britain private developers were sought to help in the £4,500,000 project, which embraced more than the station itself. The three-tier structure has the platforms at its lowest level, under the concourse, which it sandwiched between platforms and a spacious covered shopping centre, with fountains as a feast for the eye and canned music for the ear. You can listen to a military band as you buy a ticket—using a credit card if you wish. There is music, too, in the shopping centre above, which continues the public right of way across the station, which had to be preserved because of the original Act.

Birmingham Corporation did not contribute towards the station construction, but it leased part of the site and built a block of twenty-one storey flats called Stephenson House. New Street has plenty of new features, not least ticket barriers, which brought to an end New Street's distinction as one of Britain's few open stations. Surveys about passenger's habits during the design stage found that most of those arriving left without looking at book-stalls or going to refreshment rooms; that hardly a third of departing passengers had prebooked tickets; and that 60 per cent of travellers looked at indicator boards.

Officials waxed poetic once the venture was complete, pointing out that 'trains which radiate from New Street to all points of the compass, justify its claim to be the finest rail inter-change centre in the country. Birmingham now has a station befitting the Second City. A station of which its citizens, and British Rail can justly be proud'.

The giant concrete structure is not a thing I can love, but I do admire its functional design. It ran into one snag : it was found necessary to build small shelters on the platforms for passengers, who, while kept dry by the huge roof, often almost froze on windy days when it became a tunnel through which gusts were blasted.

THE LNWR NETWORK TODAY

With Snow Hill banished, New Street station is the unchallenged hub of local and inter-city passenger services covering a far wider area than this book. It also remains the hub of the old LNWR system, so much of which was embraced by electrification which came fully into operation on 6 March 1967 as the last section of the London–Manchester–Liverpool project. The work included putting under the wires the GJR and L & B, besides the Stour Valley and the Soho Loop. Bescot became the freight hub after the closure of several smaller yards. Complete conversion was not necessary at Bescot, for many West Midland freights are diesel-hauled.

The North Western made Birmingham a district headquarters; in 1972 British Rail announced that it was to be upgraded from a divisional to a regional headquarters, for one of eight new 'territories' to replace its five regions and twenty divisions throughout Britain.

Birmingham is so big a city—yet its commuter network is so small. This fact tends to be overlooked now that the West Midlands Passenger Transport Executive has taken control of lines around it, and also those in the Coventry and Wolverhampton areas, for the PTE strategy rests on the development of wider inter-town links, besides shorter commuter lines. In January 1973 a £3 million a year contract was signed for BR to provide trains over lines on which the Executive will fix the frequency and timing of them, and also fares. The operation of trains remains with BR, which is reimbursed for any loss. Other losses are recovered by the Executive in grants from the government. British Rail welcomed the agreement because it recognised the vital part railways have to play in public transport in city regions.

The Executive plan to develop services from Birmingham (New Street and Moor Street : there was no suggestion of reviving Snow Hill), to Coventry, Derby, Kidderminster, Leamington Spa, Leicester, Lichfield, Redditch, Stratford-upon-Avon (via Solihull and the North Warwickshire lines). Other services that received renewed grants in 1973 were those from Birmingham to Wolverhampton, and Worcester (via Barnt Green and Kidderminster), and between Stourbridge Town and Stourbridge Junction. By far the largest subsidy (£597,000) was given by the government to maintain Wolverhampton–Chester locals.

The two routes between Birmingham and Walsall continue to be subsidised, but only while under further review.

During the planning stages, electrification, and the extra speed it would give to train services, were seen as the panacea for many ills. The conversion of the short link from Bescot to Walsall was designed to draw ties with Birmingham still tighter. Hourly non-stop expresses were projected to supplement local trains using both routes—via Soho and Aston. That idea was soon scrapped in favour of a semi-fast link with better revenue potential, but even the locals were soon running heavily in the red.

The critical financial position into which these and local passenger services nationally had sunk became clear in the late 1960s, when the Labour government began giving publicly stated grants to keep open individual routes. Two large subsidies were immediately necessary for the Walsall electrics : £177,000 was paid in 1970 to sustain the Aston route, and £105,000 to maintain the direct route via Soho—a total of more than £250,000 a year. No wonder that one of the first recommendations to the West Midlands PTA after its creation was that the Walsall services should be replaced by buses, no more than nine additional ones being needed.

The problems of ailing lines are well known to transport experts but they are not always as clearly defined for the man in the street as they are at Lichfield, where the two stations lie some distance from the main residential areas. The city's third station,

Trent Valley High Level—closed when trains between Birmingham and Burton-on-Trent via Sutton Coldfield were withdrawn in 1965—seemed ideally situated for a new housing area and light industrial estate that was developed in the subsequent five years. Staffordshire County Council suggested it should be reopened and used by the Birmingham diesels, whose route was to be extended just over a mile from City station, but a survey showed that revenue would not match the cost of reinstating the station and the extra train mileage. The Council said it could not contribute, so High Level remained empty and local roads crowded.

A rapid transit system for Birmingham has been under consideration for several years. Consultants who reported in 1971 suggested a 16 mile rapid transit route along the 'A38 corridor' from Longbridge to Four Oaks, utilising much of the Birmingham West Suburban and Lichfield branches, with a 3 mile underground link in the city centre between Aston and the University. Cost was estimated at about £50,000,000, with another £6,000,000 for an extension to Redditch New Town. The consultants felt the commuter system needed pulling together, and their report came at a time when Manchester was considering something similar and Liverpool was about to extend the Mersey underground.

A station costing £2,500,000 is to be built by British Rail to serve the National Exhibition Centre, which is to be sited beside the main line near Elmdon Airport. Five platforms will serve the seven exhibition halls. Faced with strong opposition from London interests, Birmingham had used electrification to strengthen its claim to have an unrivalled site for a national centre.

Curzon Street's original building remains a problem child, and in 1970 a storm broke out when seven preservation societies opposed demolition. The *Birmingham Post* asked : 'Worthy relic —or picnic box?' The headline was prompted by a BR statement that the building was used by only one railwayman 'to leave his sandwiches there while he does his work'. Birmingham Public Works Committee opposed demolition, but BR retorted that it would rather spend the money needed for preservation on stations still open. If, as had been suggested, it might become a railway and steam museum, another organisation must meet the cost.

CHAPTER III

Birmingham: The 'Midland' Makers

BIRMINGHAM & DERBY JUNCTION

The two companies that built the north–south route through Birmingham soon merged to form the LNWR. Two that constructed the cross-country artery from north-east to south-west were destined to merge into the Midland Railway. Both were incorporated three years after the GJR and the L & B. The Birmingham & Gloucester was authorised on 22 April 1836 to build a line from the L & B at Aston to Cheltenham, via King's Norton. The Birmingham & Derby Junction was incorporated, without much initial opposition, on 19 May, to construct a route surveyed by George Stephenson. It was also to stem from the L & B, this time at Stechford, almost 4 miles south of Birmingham, and run to Derby. Tamworth and Burton-on-Trent were to be the main intermediate stations.

The Derby line was to form, with the North Midland Railway, a through route between Birmingham and Yorkshire, and its promoters were mainly businessmen of Birmingham. This made it one of the few trunk routes developed on mainly local initiative. Its early pattern was greatly influenced, much to its detriment as it turned out, by a war between two companies incorporated in the same Parliamentary session. The Midland Counties Railway of 21 June 1836 was to link Derby with Nottingham and also (and this was to be the bone of contention) build a branch to the L & B at Rugby to provide a direct route between Derby and London. The route, which ran through Leicester, was to be extended to Leeds by the North Midland, authorised a few days later. The NM's ambition was to reach London independent of the MCR, and it sought to exploit part of the Birmingham line to reach the L & B. It wanted to keep the north-south route as short as possible and persuaded the B & DJ to build a branch of 6 miles between Whitacre and Hampton to save its trains having to run via Birmingham's outskirts at Stechford.

THE STONEBRIDGE RAILWAY

Attracted by the prospect of revenue from the through traffic, the B & DJ went ahead with the Stonebridge Railway, which name it acquired because of its promotion as a separate line. Its Bill went before Parliament at the last minute, after the MCR had suddenly revived a branch to Pinxton, a move regarded by the B & DJ as being competitive. With the authorisation of the Stonebridge Railway, the Birmingham directors decided to delay construction of the western stem from Whitacre to Stechford. Resources were concentrated on the branch for two main reasons. Besides providing the NMR with its through route, it could still enable trains from Derby to reach Birmingham by reversing on to the L & B at Hampton. The formal opening between Hampton and Derby on 12 August 1839 provided a roundabout journey between Euston and Derby of 139 miles.

The NMR reached Leeds on 1 July 1840, and at the same time the York and North Midland Railway was extended from Normanton to York. These important extensions would have brought extra traffic and badly needed income to the B & DJ had it not been for the completion on the same day of the Midland Counties to Rugby. For a short time this line's terminus lay at the north end of Rugby viaduct, but once the line had joined the L & B, 11 miles was chopped off the mileage to Derby—no mean saving in the days of early operating. The unhappy B & DJ tried to overcome the mileage handicap by cutting fares, charging through passengers only 2s between Hampton and Derby, a quarter of the ordinary fare for local passengers. At the instigation of the MCR, the Attorney General began an action to restrain the B & DJ from charging the lower fare, but the Lord Chancellor refused an injunction, saying he thought it was an experiment that was not likely to be repeated. His award was made with costs to the B & DJ.

In some quarters the B & DJ was not regarded as a very important line. When L & B shareholders met in the summer of 1840, Captain Watts, R.N., asked the chairman, Glyn, to denounce insinuations that they supported the B & DJ against the MCR because of tolls for handling through traffic between Hampton and Rugby. Watts was sure that the directors would not lend themselves to 'petty rivalry of minor lines'. Glyn replied that his co-directors had stated their policy of strict neutrality in a resolution handed to the Birmingham directors.

No such neutrality was observed by the NMR, which as early as 1838 had secretly agreed to use the Midland Counties route the moment it was completed. The B & DJ got wind of the agreement and had it declared illegal. The result was not entirely satisfactory, for it increased the antagonism of the other two companies, which were obstructive in every possible way.

The L & B's *claim* to be neutral about B & DJ disputes arising from through traffic did not extend to the Derby through trains of the B & DJ between Birmingham and Hampton. It made the hapless company pay heavy tolls, and after preventing the company engines from working through, handled traffic in a dilatory manner.

Such frustrations caused the B & DJ hastily to seek its own route into Birmingham. The original section planned to join the L & B at Stechford would obviously be no better, and so powers were obtained in 1840 to abandon it in favour of a line continued through the Tame valley to a separate terminus at Lawley Street. This line, through the wide and shallow valley, was the best approach the railways ever achieved to central Birmingham, for the Birmingham & Gloucester, the LNWR and later GWR routes were all restricted by deep and narrow cuttings and tunnels.

Yet while the approach was good, the situation of Lawley Street was a disaster. Built in the fork of the converging GJR and L & B lines, it lay 40ft below their level. Connections were authorised but never built, and the only link between the B & DJ and the L & B was a rather comical and highly inefficient wagon hoist.

The line opened on 10 February 1842 and, besides Whitacre, there were stations at Forge Mills (for Coleshill), Water Orton and Castle Bromwich. B & DJ goods trains continued to Curzon Street via Hampton for 2 months until the opening of an inclined spur between Lawley Street and the GJR. Passenger trains and London mails of the B & DJ were compelled to use Curzon Street

Page 51 (*above*) Two eras at New Street: Birmingham's new 'Grand Central Railway Station' on its opening in 1854; (*below*) More than half a century later, the LNWR side about 1911 with (draughty) signal frame over footbridge

Page 52 Station designs: (*above*) Coventry after rebuilding, c 1865. It was to prove inadequate for many years; (*below*) Donnington, one of the few stations built by the Shropshire Union Railways & Canal Company. Neat squat building with ornate chimneypots. Platform raised slightly and extended towards Wellington

until the expiry of a Post Office operating agreement on 1 July.

The Stonebridge Railway then lost all its strategic significance and was soon singled. It was the first main line to be demoted in the country, but not the last, even in an area so congested as the West Midlands. It closed to passengers as a wartime economy in 1917, and soon after grouping Coleshill was renamed Maxstoke so that Forge Mills on the L & B main line could become Coleshill, even though it lay further away from the district. Regular through goods services were withdrawn in 1930, though a local service was maintained on the northern half to Maxstoke until 1939, when the section became a crippled wagon store. A derelict bridge had split the line 4 years earlier. Two miles of the southern section from Hampton were reopened during World War II to handle sand from local pits, which was used for airfield construction. The line was lifted in the autumn of 1952.

FORMATION OF THE MIDLAND

Any chance of the Stonebridge Railway being needed to defeat fresh rivalry between companies disappeared with the creation of the Midland Railway on 10 May 1844 by the amalgamation of the NMR, the MCR and the B & DJ. The Birmingham & Gloucester was to join a little later.

The Midland Railway was born of the warfare and discontent that had weakened all its constituents, and out of the fear of the broad gauge reaching Birmingham from the west. The danger was clear to people who had shares in several companies. The Bristol & Gloucester had been conceived as a broad gauge route and there was concern that the complementary Birmingham & Gloucester would be swallowed by the GWR interests.

The Midland's creation upset the power struggle between the advocates of the gauges, and tilted opinion in favour of the narrow, because the Midland became the largest railway in the country under united management. Among the architects of its early success as a company were two men who moved from the B & DJ : Matthew Kirtley, who had been locomotive foreman at Hampton, and a clerk, James Allport, who was now set for a career that was to earn him a knighthood as general manager.

The Midland's expansion in the West Midlands was helped by

D

friendly relations with the LNWR. These were strengthened by two connections to the B & DJ route: a link at the inter-section point at Tamworth was established in 1847, and 4 years later (1 May 1851) the Midland was able to close Lawley Street to passengers by diverting trains to Curzon Street over a spur from Landor Street Junction to Derby Junction. In 1897, the spur was removed as redundant.

Lawley Street was—and is—an important goods depot. Goods lines were laid between there and Saltley in 1876, underlining the predominance of freight in the company's traffic throughout the area. Heavy mineral traffic developed from pits near Tamworth, and a triangular layout was put in at Kettlebrook, $\frac{1}{2}$ mile west, to give access to Amington Colliery, which was also connected to the Trent Valley.

Nearer Birmingham, the Kingsbury branch of almost 5 miles was authorised on 28 July 1873 to serve Birch Coppice Colliery and Baxterley Park, another pit linked to the Trent Valley. Opened on 28 February 1878, it left the main line at Kingsbury, about $\frac{1}{2}$ mile south of what became the junction of the cut-off to Water Orton, built to eliminate the sharp mainline curves at Whitacre. Opened in 1909, the cut-off was nearly 4 miles long. Whitacre and Kingsbury stations were closed to passengers in March 1968, having lost their freight facilities a few years earlier. The tiny building on the up platform at Kingsbury, demolished in November 1962, was original B & DJ. Some of the important junction status that Whitacre lost when the Stonebridge Railway was demoted in 1842 was restored after the MR revived plans for a direct link between Birmingham and Leicester (See Chapter VIII).

Visual proof of road transport's domination of the West Midlands is to be found in several places, notably the junctions at Bescot, and between Washwood Heath and Castle Bromwich, where the spacious mainline layout is overpowered visually by the London motorway carried on stilts parallel to the line for several miles.

Washwood Heath yard was improved to handle extra traffic generated by the modernisation of the Bristol routes, but this never developed to the estimated level and plans were in hand in the early 1970s for its reduction to a subsidiary yard.

BIRMINGHAM & GLOUCESTER

While the B & DJ was a constituent of the Midland Railway, the B & G was destined only to be incorporated into it. But first it had an eventful life as an independent company with quite historic roots. They sprang from Bristol interests, which originally gave strong financial support to a half-hearted scheme in 1824. That scheme soon collapsed and it was not until 1832 that a route was completely surveyed—by Isambard Kingdom Brunel, who favoured one much to the east of that chosen in the following year via the Lickey Incline. This was one of two presented by Captain William Scarth Moorsom (brother of the Admiral, LNWR chairman until 1861), who succeeded Brunel when he left the B & G in 1832 to join the GWR.

The Lickey Incline was not the only drawback to the route chosen by the B & G; some felt it would have been more profitable to serve towns like Stourbridge, and possibly Dudley. But the promoters had not the financial resources to buy land, much dearer in those prospering towns than in the country. As it was, it took years to raise enough money to make the scheme a reality, but Parliament did approve the plans at first submission.

The lack of capital was afterwards reflected in the slow progress in construction. The line was built in the direction opposite to its title—from Gloucester to Birmingham. The first section opened was the 31 miles between Cheltenham and Bromsgrove, on 24 June 1840, followed by an extension north to a temporary station at Cofton Farm on 17 September via stations at Blackwell and Barnt Green. On 17 December a further section was opened with stations at Longbridge, Lifford, Moseley and Camp Hill. The link with the L & B was achieved on 17 August 1841. The seventeenth day of the month seemed popular with the directors! Gloucester Junction, as it was aptly named, was built on the site of what later became Grand Junction.

B & G trains then ran to Curzon Street, Camp Hill becoming a goods station, as it remained until closure in 1966.

The B & G fought most of its major battles outside the West Midlands, notably at Gloucester, which became a gauge frontier when the broad-gauge Bristol & Gloucester was opened on 8 July 1844. The creation of the Midland strengthened opposition to any broad gauge extension to Birmingham, but it did not remove the threat, for at that time it was not known which gauge might be favoured by the Commission the government had set up to examine the gauge question and the conflicting claims. The infant MR remained remarkably alert to the outcome considering the many other problems it was then facing.

Its method of seizure of the Bristol route is a classic story of railway tactics, one which surprised its opponents by its brilliance. It came about when the Midland's deputy chairman, John Ellis, chanced to meet two B & G directors on a journey to London and learned that amalgamation was pending between the GWR, the B & G and the Bristol and Gloucester, but that the smaller companies were quibbling over terms. On his own initiative Ellis made a slightly improved offer to rent the line from Birmingham to Bristol at 6 per cent of the capital of the two independent companies, which stood at £1,800,000. The agreement, which included option to purchase, was signed by Hudson, the Midland chairman, on 8 February 1845.

That is the most widely told version of the racy story, but it is not the whole, for the L & B chairman, Glyn, revealed to shareholders on 13 February 1846 that he had been approached by the Midland, which suggests that its plans for the Bristol takeover were not quite off-the-cuff and had been under consideration for at least a short time. Answering allegations made by the GWR chairman, Charles Russell, Glyn stated:

> Now, gentlemen, this is the first time I ever heard that we were connected with Mr Hudson in the purchase of the Birmingham and Bristol line. I perfectly remember the fact of the purchase, because an honourable friend of mine, who is connected with the Midland Railway, called on me to ask whether I thought the London & Birmingham Company would be concerned in it, and I told him that I was not prepared to advise that they should.

The agreement between the MR and the Bristol companies was stated to have been made 'under the conviction of the absolute necessity of a uniformity of gauge between the northern and manufacturing districts and the Port of Bristol'. It was made a year ahead of the Gauge Commissioners' Report of 1846, which opposed any extension of the broad gauge.

BIRMINGHAM WEST SUBURBAN RAILWAY

No railway slips more comfortably from country to city than the Birmingham West Suburban Railway. I thought it one of the most ineptly named of lines one summer's eve when I came north over the Birmingham & Gloucester, with the Malvern Hills as a sunset backcloth, climbed Lickey, and dropped through Bournville. Beside the carriage window lay the Worcester & Birmingham Canal, with tranquil tree-shaded reflections that seemed a hundred miles removed from the Birmingham soil from which they sprang. Change of mood was accomplished quickly and painlessly as we plunged through the deep cuttings and tunnels leading to New Street. Under its concrete roof, the country seemed far away.

The character of the Birmingham West Suburban has changed completely for it is an important main line—quite the opposite to a branch, the form in which it was conceived by a local company. From the start it had potential and it was quickly developed by the MR, which extended it to provide a loop to avoid reversal of expresses at New Street and save minutes in an age of strong competition on long-distance passenger routes.

The final shape of the BWSR was rather different from that for which private promoters received their authorisation in 1871, and it probably underwent more changes than any other line in the region. Originally, it was to be no more than single, stretching from the MR at Lifford to a terminus in central Birmingham at Albion Wharf, cut back during construction to Granville Street to avoid making a costly crossing of the Worcester & Birmingham Canal. In this simple form the line opened on 3 April 1876, having in the interim become part of the MR. There were stations at Church Road, Somerset Road, Selly Oak (passing loop), and Stirchley Street (Bournville was added to its title in 1880). A station was opened at Lifford on 1 June and the locals, worked from the start by the MR, ran to Kings Norton.

During construction, the MR obtained authority for extensions and improvements: in 1874 a branch was authorised to the Worcester & Birmingham Canal at Lifford, and soon the obvious extension of the line into New Street was discussed. An Act of 1881 authorised doubling and a connection to Church Road Junction near Granville Street terminus, which was closed and replaced by an alternative station at Five Ways. A new junction was built at Lifford, where the station was resited for a third time and put back on the Gloucester line.

Conversion began in 1883, the contractor being Joseph Firbank, whose biography, *The Life and Work of Joseph Firbank, J.P., D.L., Railway Contractor,* was published in 1887 by a barrister, Frederick McDermott :

A system which was good enough for a local service consisting of nine trains a day each way was, however, far from ready for the heavy business of a great line like the Midland, and, before the West Suburban could be exalted to a part of a great system, it had to undergo widenings, straightenings, deviations, and a multitude of other operations, which finally converted it into practically a new line. Like many other contracts which Mr Firbank carried out, the mileage on this section was but small—viz., $5\frac{1}{4}$ miles—but the actual work done, and its cost, was greater than would have been involved in the building of many miles of road through an ordinary country. To begin with, there were three tunnels of 225yd, 184yd and 88yd. The first of these carries three lines, and all are under public thoroughfares, with tramways and all the underground complications of a large town. Then there are some heavy cuttings, out of one of which 120,000 cubic yd were taken, and embankments. In carrying out this work, 1,100 men were employed, with sixty horses, seven locomotives, seven steam cranes, and ten portable engines, whilst 30,000,000 bricks were used, mainly in the retaining walls 50ft high, which had to be built in some parts. The greatest trouble was, however, met with in dealing with the canal which had to be tunnelled three times within a distance of 80yd.

This would have proved a sufficiently delicate operation under the most favourable circumstances, but in this case the difficulty was greatly increased by the fact that the canal is, at this point, carried at a height of 70ft above the level of New Street Station, on an embankment of loose material. Whilst, therefore, the tunnelling operations were in progress, the waterway had to be carried in wooden troughs, large enough to allow of the free passage of the canal boats. These troughs were necessarily of immense strength, and when the tunnels—one of which is for a road, another for the West Suburban line, and the third forms the approach to the Midland Company's new goods yard—were completed, and the water at this part of the canal was pumped out, for ten days over 100 men were engaged, night and day, in removing the massive timbering, in 'puddling' the bottom of the canal near the tunnels, and in rebuilding the canal

walls where interfered with. It is difficult to realise the administrative
skill and grasp of details required in planning and carrying out such
a work as this; it could, indeed, only be executed by the help of tried
assistants, and a reliable staff. In return for such services, Mr Firbank
did all in his power, on this as on other contracts, for the comfort
and welfare of his men, many of whom had worked for him for twenty
years—some could, indeed, at the time of his death, claim to have
been associated with him for forty years of active service.

Nothing was wasted and the section between Church Road
and Granville Street was extended to give access to the Central
goods depot that the MR opened in 1887 on the opposite bank of
the Canal. In contrast to the original BWSR plan to bridge the
waterway to reach Worcester Wharf, the depot's title until 1 June
1892, the Midland tunnelled under on a gradient of 1 in 80.

Midland express services were switched via Bournville from
1885.

DIRECT LINE AND LIFFORD CURVE

Until 1885, Derby–Bristol expresses used the 'direct' line between
St Andrews and Landor Street Junctions, portions to or from
New Street being marshalled at Camp Hill or Saltley. The direct
link was authorised in 1862 and opened in the first half of 1864;
no accurate date is known. The line, no more than $\frac{3}{4}$ mile long,
gave a head-on connection between the two historic routes
stretching away from Birmingham.

In 1892 a triangle was completed at Lifford so that a circular
suburban service could be run.

To Birmingham trade was everything. Pendleton in *Our Railways*, 1896, described the great trade and traffic of the Midland
on the south-western section :

> The bulk of traffic at the great goods station every day is enormous.
> At Worcester Wharf and at Lawley Street the huge warehouses are
> congested with goods, and the lines and sidings busy with traffic . . .
> At Worcester Wharf, and in the long range of cellars devoted to
> bonded stores, the electric light is used. Probably, however, in no
> place will its usefulness be so thoroughly demonstrated as at the
> company's chief Birmingham depot at Lawley Street. Here large
> warehouses, destined to provide many acres of floor-space, are in rapid
> construction. On one side of the yard stands a fine building devoted

to hydraulic power, while on the opposite side is that for the electric lighting machinery. As at Worcester Wharf, the offices, yards, warehouses and sidings will be worked under the fullest advantages, provision being made for the employment as required of some six to eight machines for arc lighting.

THE MIDLAND SYSTEM TODAY

Once diesels conquered the Lickey Incline, the immediate development became possible of Derby–Bristol as a trunk artery on which north-east–south-west traffic could be concentrated. Reasons for its selection were detailed in BRB's plan, published in February 1965, for *The Development of the Major Railway Trunk Routes*. It showed that in the previous year the B & G carried by far the heaviest freight traffic between the West Midlands, South Wales and the South West—90,000 tons a week, compared with 70,000 tons via Worcester and Hereford, and 60,000 tons via Stratford and Gloucester.

Future traffic flows were estimated at forty-five trains a day between the West Midlands and Bristol, and a similar number to South Wales. Line capacity was calculated to be about 140 trains a day running at speeds between 35 mph and 70 mph. Concentration on one route was expected to produce large savings in running costs. The concentration was achieved in the spring of 1965 and it allowed closure of the Stratford-upon-Avon & Midland Junction line, which for so long, especially during World War II, had been a by-pass of the congested West Midland system for some mineral traffic to and from South Wales.

The Shrewsbury & Hereford route also suffered, losing through expresses between the North West and West of England, which were diverted via Birmingham, gaining access to New Street over the ever-important BWSR, which retains two stations—Selly Oak and Bournville. They are served mainly by peak-hour locals to Redditch and one or two of the direct expresses between Birmingham and Worcester, a link maintained more intensely by locals via Stourbridge Junction and Kidderminster.

Suburban services on the 'direct' line via King's Norton ceased more than 30 years ago, stations between there and New Street being closed as a wartime economy in 1941. When the return of peace brought no demand for reopening, closure was rubber-stamped as permanent in 1946. On nationalisation, the Birmingham–Gloucester line passed to the Western Region, but the section north of Barnt Green was transferred to the London Midland in February 1958.

In the mid-1960s a railhead for the delivery of cars made at the 'Austin' works at Longbridge was established at King's Norton, but the start of some services was delayed for a short time while fears of redundancies were resolved among car-transporter drivers. The depot was extended in August 1971 to handle three weekly trains carrying some 600 cars to Bathgate.

In the summer of 1964, when diesels were still a novelty, the LMR timetable distinguished lines operated by diesels and those still served by steam. It was hardly necessary, for the only steam line shown was the B & G south-west from Saltley.

East of Birmingham, only two local stations remain open on the B & DJ between Birmingham and Tamworth : Water Orton and Wilnecote served by Derby locals. The 'Leicesters' run non-stop between Birmingham and Nuneaton, and most through expresses have no booked calls between Birmingham and Tamworth or beyond.

CHAPTER IV

Birmingham : Broad and Narrow Gauge

The broad gauge squeezed into the West Midlands by the skin of its teeth, for the Birmingham & Oxford Railway and the Birmingham, Wolverhampton & Dudley Railway were authorised on 3 August 1846 during the short period between the Gauge Commissioners' Report and legislation by Parliament to put their recommendations into effect by prohibiting, with certain exceptions, any broad-gauge extensions. Both lines were conceived to break the L & B monopoly with alternative routes to London.

Its position at Birmingham was first challenged when the GWR established a northern bridgehead at Oxford, reached by the broad gauge from Didcot on 12 June 1844, and revived schemes for lines to Rugby, Worcester and Wolverhampton. Forced to retaliate, the L & B put forward the London, Worcester & South Staffordshire Junction Railway from Tring via Banbury, the Vale of Evesham and Dudley, to Wolverhampton, with one or two embellishments.

The rival Oxford, Worcester & Wolverhampton Railway was better because it was designed to open up a new area to railways rather than to duplicate a route. Some MPs were sceptical that even if the L & B did build a second line, it would use it in preference to its more direct and excellent main line. The chairman, Glyn, tried to pacify shareholders over what he called

> . . . the extraordinary circumstance of the GWR company trying to find themselves in South Staffordshire. When you look at a map it certainly seems a little out of their course; but they had offers made to them to carry a Railway through the districts, and we do not find fault with them for accepting that offer [sic], which they no doubt thought promised to result in benefits to their proprietors.

The GWR's crusading zeal was strengthened by the self-seeking tactics of the Grand Junction and, in particular, its astute and ruthless secretary, Mark Huish. He astonished many people by advocating that narrow-gauge companies should adopt mixed gauges, and said the GJR was prepared to allow broad-gauge rails to reach Liverpool and Manchester, letting Paddington realise what was then its dream of broad gauge to the Mersey.

His (now famous) circular of 11 June 1845 asserted that it would be highly dangerous if the L & B controlled the entire area between London, Bristol and Birmingham, by buying, leasing, amalgamating or reaching agreements with other railways and canals. He claimed the L & B was aiming also to gain entire control of the area from Birmingham to Manchester and Holyhead.

Several noted authorities, including MacDermot, have doubted that the GJR intended to allow the broad gauge north of Birmingham. Rather were Huish's words interpreted as a political move —one he later admitted—to bring about amalgamation with the L & B and the Manchester & Birmingham to weld together a system strong at every point and in every direction.

Another Huish ruse to intimidate the L & B was a threat to build a line to the GWR at Oxford and have an independent route to London. Huish found ready allies in the iron masters and manufacturers of the Black Country, aware of the financial advantages and facilities they would get from competition. The L & B monopoly was doomed by the authorisation of the OW & W on 4 August 1845. 'A very severe blow,' admitted Glyn to shareholders three days later. They had lost the battle because Parliament had adopted the principle of competition for the first time. He did not find fault 'with those opponents of ours, the iron masters of Staffordshire who took advantage of the principle laid down, in order to obtain that which they thought would be a substantial benefit to themselves'.

He attacked the action of the GWR and the GJR, but his comments concerning the latter were soon forgotten, for on 7 November the L & B, GJR and M & B agreed to form the LNWR from the new year. As preparations went ahead, the GJR tried desperately to forget the Birmingham & Oxford concept, but the iron masters saw the LNWR proposal as nothing more than the L & B in a new guise, and promoted a Bill which would give their company powers of lease or sale to the GWR. Huish tried many ways to get this clause deleted, but without success.

THE BIRMINGHAM & OXFORD

Shortly before the incorporation of the B & O the GWR chairman, Russell, gave what he called a brief but accurate statement of its origin :

> The Oxford & Birmingham was not of our seeking. It was suggested to us, and was repeatedly urged upon us by the Grand Junction Company, and as repeatedly refused by us. The Grand Junction Company said to us, 'The London and Birmingham Company have obtained a Line to the North independent of us. Is it not just that we should obtain this line independent of them to the metropolis?' We replied: 'Whatever may be your views, gentlemen, it concerns you and not us,' and we steadily, resolutely, and perpetually refused to have any connection with that Line.
>
> It was not until the Birmingham Company joined with Mr Hudson in purchasing the Birmingham & Bristol Line that we consented to have anything to do with it. But when the Birmingham Company had sought to carry their Line down to Bristol we thought the time had arrived when we were justified in seeking to carry our Line up to Birmingham. We then consented to act with the Grand Junction Company.

The L & B and LNWR attempts to defeat the B & O turned all the more sour when its authorised route stemmed from a junction at Birmingham with the LNWR (*officially* constituted only a few days earlier). The southern terminus of the B & O was to be with the GWR's projected Oxford & Rugby line at Knightcote, near Fenny Compton. There was also to be a link to the OW & W's Stratford branch.

The Birmingham Extension Act of the same date authorised a short line from the B & O at Adderley Street to Great Charles Street, including a station at Snow Hill. The section between Moor Street and Monmouth Street was to be covered by a tunnel to preserve valuable land, and the railway was to be amalgamated with the B & O by virtue of the passing of the Act. The Oxford capital was authorised at £700,000 and the Extension at £300,000.

THE BIRMINGHAM, WOLVERHAMPTON & DUDLEY

The Extension had a more important function : to link between the B & O and the BW & D, promoted shortly after the B & O in

1845, by the same interests and for the same reasons. It had the support of the OW & W, which it was to join at Priestfield, Wolverhampton, at the northern end of its route, authorised from Monmouth Street, Birmingham, so as to duplicate the B & O for a short distance to give the companies equal rights over the site of Snow Hill station.

The gauge question had generally remained in the background when the BW & D presented its case to a Select Committee, although the engineer, John Robinson McClean, stated that he had designed tunnels to the broad width of 30ft. Neither Act mentioned gauge because under the Gauge Act, then before Parliament, the broad gauge was to be virtually outlawed; but like the B & O, the BW & D was conceived broad gauge because it was to join the Oxford branch of the GWR. The only major difference in the Act was that the BW & D was not given powers for lease or sale.

Its role as part of a through route between the Black Country and London was soft-pedalled in Committee, being presented as a line purely local in concept and intent. McClean stressed that he planned it to serve as many works and collieries as possible.

Annual expenditure was estimated at 40 per cent of gross receipts—an often quoted figure for schemes of the period.

Part of the BW & D's case had rested on its superiority to the Shrewsbury & Birmingham Railway, then seeking a Birmingham and Wolverhampton route identical with the Stour Valley. Counsel said the S & B would cost £1,200,000—or £500,000 more than *its* estimated cost. While the S & B approach to Birmingham would cause the demolition of much property in the centre, its own route would cause little loss. While it would not serve Darlaston (a growing town, population 8,244), it was argued that unless the line was sanctioned, opponents would be left with one of the greatest and most overpowering monopolies ever constituted by the cupidity of companies coalescing for the purposes of profit. Unlike the S & B, it would serve Walsall, Bilston and Dudley.

It was claimed that Robert Stephenson had tried to remedy defects of the Stour Valley by proposing to unite with the OW & W —a line which he abominated and spurned, and one which the SVR promoters believed would not be made.

The BW & D line would be the freest, the most independent and the best; it would not be under the influence of a council sitting at Euston Square, which could have no interest in the district. Several witnesses claimed that any amalgamation between the S & B and the L & B would produce the greatest monopoly in existence. At the same time, they contended it would be all right for the BW & D to amalgamate with the GWR.

One witness called by the BW & D was William Matthews, a Staffordshire and Worcestershire county magistrate and a director of the B & O and South Staffordshire Railways. He admitted receiving 300 shares from the GWR for his advocacy of the broad gauge on its behalf, and agreed he had once said that he would rejoice to see the day when the broad gauge would be extended from London to Liverpool—and had no doubt that that would be the case. He totally departed from the Gauge Commissioner's Report as to the difficulties caused by a break. While he would rather have continuity of gauge, he did not think the disadvantage so great as had been represented by commercial men.

One witness claimed he had changed his allegiance to the BW & D; George Muntz, a Birmingham MP, and a relative of the Oxford chairman, P. H. Muntz. He said he had done so when he found that the S & B promoters would not be an independent body outside the control of any other railway or canal company. He felt that nothing but competition would compel the L & B to act rightly towards the public.

The concept of an independent competitive route appealed to iron masters like John Barker of Wolverhampton, who employed about 1,300 people, using 150,000 tons of coal to produce 25,000 tons of iron a year.

More antagonism against the S & B was provided by the BW & D chairman, Lord Hatherton, who petitioned against it because it proposed to take lands that he held in trust for competing lines. The L & B had not been the slightest advantage to South Staffordshire, and if the S & B and GJR amalgamated, it would mean a great and permanent evil and the most extensive monopoly that Parliament had yet sanctioned.

Another BW & D director, John Askew, a past High Bailiff of Birmingham, said that while Snow Hill would accommodate passengers and goods, New Street would be only for passengers. He advocated a junction with the L & B. While the S & B route to Wolverhampton would involve no break of gauge and be shorter, the BW & D would go through more picturesque country!

Charles Shaw, the Birmingham magistrate and critic of New Street, said he had devised a plan in 1835 for a route similar to the BW & D and had become a shareholder. The main advantage of the present plan was that it would serve areas which its rivals did not. He had planned a terminus at Newhall Street, Birmingham, because he did not dare ask shareholders for the capital needed for one at Snow Hill, which he would have preferred.

Cross-examined, Shaw admitted he had some property in Snow Hill but said it was not of much importance to him; he would not have the slightest objection to parting with it if it was needed for a station. Shaw said he had been connected with the L & B but had lost sympathy because it had increased fares.

'AS PRETTY A MOVE . . .'

Soon after the B & O and BW & D were incorporated, they agreed on amalgamation followed by lease or sale to the GWR, the proposal immediately winning the support of that company. But a battle developed when Oxford shareholders revolted against sale to Paddington, favouring negotiations with Euston. The directors managed to restrain the shareholders, but Huish, by now general manager of the LNWR, saw his chance and began buying a controlling interest in the B & O. In 1847 Euston managed to acquire four-fifths of the 50,000 Oxford shares, and planned to take control by enlarging the board from twelve to eighteen directors by adding six of its own. The move was too late, for the B & O had agreed a lease with the GWR, and to make sure it did so, the GWR appealed to Parliament, which appointed a committee of inquiry. The GWR also sued the B & O for breach of contract. The LNWR action to enlarge the board was held to be 'ultra vires', and the B & O slipped out of Euston's hands, the lease being confirmed to the GWR.

The row between Paddington and Euston left Birmingham with a scar that remains to this day. It was born of difficulties which arose over plans for a link of just over $\frac{1}{2}$ mile between the North Western and the B & O. The junction, planned in the original Act, was to be near Curzon Street, but it had to be moved because the LNWR would have crosssed the B & O on the level. The GWR

G. W. R.

WOLVER-HAMPTON

---

(30) L. & N. W. Ry. **TO PAY.**
Parcel Tattenhall Road
from

To _____

                              s.   **d.**
Paid on..............   :
Carriage..............   :
                          £

G. W. R.

BIRMINGHAM
(SNOW HILL.)

Destinations of memory

promoted a Bill for a connection nearer New Street. Ever-suspicious, Euston sensed several sinister motives, fearing mainly that its rival would gain access to New Street and so obtain a station in Birmingham without having to build one. It also feared the GWR would gain access to the Stour Valley.

Brunel needed only 14 chains of land for the link, but while the Commons agreed, the Lords disagreed. The B & O fell back on its original plans and work started on a viaduct at Duddeston. The LNWR refused to surrender land and so the viaduct was completed only to the GWR land boundary. Both companies then agreed that neither wanted the junction, so the viaduct remained —and remains—uncompleted, a miserable monument to pig-headedness.

THE GWR TAKES CONTROL

The B & O was safely lodged in the GWR fold on 31 August 1848, together with the Birmingham Extension and the BW & D. There was no immediate threat of competition to the LNWR because, having secured its ground, the GWR bided its own time for construction. Almost 4 years later (June 1852) it obtained a $3\frac{1}{2}$ year extension for all lines, but in fact the B & O was virtually finished and the Extension was opened on 1 October. The stations included Leamington, Warwick, Hatton, Knowle, Solihull and Acock's Green. Eight more were to be added in later years, and Snow Hill (not known as such until 1858) was to have two radical rebuilds. The first was in 1871, when the wooden structure used since opening was moved to Didcot as a carriage shed. Snow Hill assumed its final form in reconstruction that began in 1909 and took 3 years because traffic was so heavy. Rather more modest in concept than New Street, Snow Hill eventually had two magnificent island platforms, long and wide, with bays at the Wolverhampton end. Downhill stretches through tunnels at either end made starting easy, and goods trains used two central through roads.

Euston's suspicions that the GWR would have liked to use New Street were not unfounded, for Paddington attempted to reach Wolverhampton via the Stour Valley rather than by building the BW & D. Negotiations failed, possibly because they were ill-timed. The approach was made when the LNWR was determined to block in every possible way GWR aspirations of reaching Mersey-side.

Construction of the BW & D eventually started in 1851. There were few noteworthy works and only three short tunnels, and while the work continued, the S & B used the SVR under an agreement that was to end when the Shrewsbury & Birmingham amalgamated with the GWR on 1 September 1854. The BW & D was confident of the completion by then, not only of its own route but also that of the Wolverhampton Junction Railway, dealt with in the next chapter.

The first inspection of the BW & D was made by Captain Douglas Galton a week before its proposed opening on 1 September—the deadline. The next day a tubular bridge between Soho and Handsworth fell into a road just after a locomotive and two ballast wagons had passed over it. Brunel condemned five of McClean's bridges as being too weak and the GWR was allowed to continue use of the SVR during the two months it took to replace or strengthen them. Eventually both sections—the BW & D and Wolverhampton Junction Railway—opened on 14 November. The double track between Birmingham and Cannock Road Junction, Wolverhampton, was mixed gauge. Despite its modest length of only 11 miles, the BW & D added quite a number of places to the GWR map: Hockley, Soho, Handsworth and Smethwick, West Bromwich, Swan Village, Wednesbury, and Bilston.

Bradley & Moxley station, which was added in 1862, was destined to have a limited life, being closed temporarily on 1 May 1915 and permanently from the beginning of 1917. It was demolished to allow the building of new loop lines between Wednesbury and Bilston.

This was only two years before the decline of the broad gauge set in, a purely narrow-gauge passenger service being introduced on the BW & D from 1 November 1864. More sweeping conversions from 1869 involved the OW & W, the Victoria Basin branch at Wolverhampton, and the lines from Bordesley to the Midland and from Wednesbury to the LNWR. Two years earlier, what was virtually another spur—the line between Cannock Road Junction and Bushbury—had been taken out of passenger use.

The BW & D's existence was uneventful for the rest of its life. It became a useful, though not scenically attractive, part of the main line between Paddington and Birkenhead, and was the most northerly part of the GWR used by *King* locomotives, prohibited north of Wolverhampton for many years.

A station, quaintly named The Hawthorns, was opened at Smethwick Junction on Christmas Day 1931. It had four platforms (two on the Stourbridge line), and was substantial. It was not for the use of ramblers, as one may perhaps be forgiven for thinking, but for soccer fans going to watch West Bromwich Albion.

DECLINE AND DECAY

The London Midland Region take-over of Western Region lines in the Birmingham area from January 1963 as a prelude to electrification was part of a far wider change. It also involved the S & B and Cambrian lines, since the LMR controlled their feeder routes.

Despite reduction of some services, Snow Hill remained busy, a worthy 'runner-up' to New Street, as 1964 returns showed:

	Passenger trains	Passengers
New Street	175,000	10,250,000
Snow Hill	130,000	7,500,000

By then the Snow Hill passenger locals had been dieselised. The Western Region had put suburban services on a regular interval basis in the winter of 1954, running an extra 3,000 miles a week. The pattern incorporated expresses making stops at Leamington Spa, Snow Hill and Wolverhampton Low Level. Most services had been dieselised from the summer of 1957 and had attracted an extra million passengers in a year. The LMR converted most suburban routes from 17 November 1958 and lifted passenger figures from 7,500,000 to well over 8,000,000.

Rising costs made some routes hopelessly uneconomic, and several methods were tried in vain attempts to stem the losses. In 1961 cheap weekday fares were issued before 9.30 a.m. from stations within 8 miles of central Birmingham, and off-peak fares reduced. Neither was a success and in March 1962 further economies were made by rationalising Birmingham passenger services and withdrawing ten little-used locals.

A 'pick-me-up' a month later was more novel: a Western Week from 9–14 April covering the area from Banbury to

Wellington. The aim was to get the public to understand the railways' problems and to use trains rather more. Half-crown diesel trips were run from Snow Hill to rail installations at Wolverhampton and Tyseley. Public forums were held in several towns, with railway officials explaining why they had to increase fares, reduce services and close branches and stations.

The Western was more of a *railway* to its supporters than a region and its death was sad and bitter. Ten years afterwards older railwaymen still talked of its take-over with bitterness, though not malice. LMR officials sometimes mused that with more willing cooperation from their new colleagues from the Western, problems might have been solved quicker; Western men resented changes they considered unnecessary.

CLOSURE OF SNOW HILL

The bitterest blow to Western pride was the virtual closure of Snow Hill in 1968—something regarded by many as inconceivable only a short time before. In 1961 a railway friend had shown me, with pride, the station's power box, which was opened at platform level on 11 September 1960. It was the prototype for a four-character train-describing system for the Region and it replaced 50-year-old boxes at both ends of the station.

Once electrification was finished, Snow Hill was doomed and the withdrawal of the Paddington–Birkenhead service was marked by steam specials, although there were no longer any *Kings* to haul them—all having gone in 1962.

Snow Hill clung to life by retaining two local services that became celebrated for their longevity : the routes along the BW & D to Wolverhampton and to Langley Green. The LMR tried hard to close them. In 1969 it proclaimed : 'Some days one taxi would be sufficient to take all the intending passengers'. The West Midlands Economic Planning Council protested that extra hardship would be caused and the withdrawal of the one-coach diesels would add significantly to the time it took passengers to get to work, and also add to already considerable road congestion.

The Minister of Transport, Mrs. Barbara Castle, refused their withdrawal, but she did agree to the switching of south Birmingham services to New Street to enable the closure of the southern approach tunnel to Snow Hill, and also of Dunstall Park Station on the s & b route. These economies took effect from 4 March 1968.

GWR pride was evident among people interviewed by the *Birmingham Post* about their memories of Snow Hill :

> It is a better station than New Street. The platforms are longer and wider. I remember when people queued up all night for trains the next morning to take them on holiday, and they'd be all the length of one platform and round into another. I've had many happy years here, part in the 'thirties. There was a comradeship then, and you don't find it now, except among the older men.

The mood of the station—and its users—was caught in the *Sunday Mercury* by a writer who captioned a photograph :

> In the days when steam was a king: a freight train roars through Snow Hill with a majesty that everyone thought would last for ever.

A 1969 report suggested the demolition of the ornate front and the construction of a department store and shops, offices, an exhibition hall, a bus terminal and a park for 500 cars. The station lingered into the 1970s, mainly as a ruin, partly demolished, partly converted into a car park and partly—though only just—as a station. No, it was an unmanned halt, for guards issued tickets.

Visitors wondered how progressively minded Birmingham could allow the ruin of Snow Hill to blotch its heart. The City Architect's outline redevelopment proposals of 1972 included a complex for the projected Rapid Transport System, using the trackbed. Whatever happens, Snow Hill will be remembered by a semicircular mural (one of the finest I have seen), tracing its history. It lies, under the station's shadow, inside a traffic roundabout at St Chad's Circus. It had been finished by the time the last 'ordinary' train ran. The final chapter in the local services began with a public inquiry by the West Midlands Transport Users' Committee in the summer of 1971. It reported firmly against withdrawal of the trains, pointing out that alternative bus services were in difficulties at peak hours. While closure would cause hardship, there were no ways of alleviating it. The PTA refused financial support and both services ended from 6 March 1972. The cost of maintaining them had been estimated at £240,000 in the ensuing year—BW & D £179,000; Langley Green

£61,000. Revenue would reach only £10,000 on the BW & D, £3,000 on the complementary service, and £90,000 would be saved in running costs and £22,000 needed for renewing signals and telecommunications. The track was retained while rapid transit and other studies were completed.

The proposals covering closure included The Hawthorns Halt, though this had been closed since 27 April 1968. After the end of passenger services, most of the BW & D was closed completely. Two sections remain : the $2\frac{1}{4}$ miles from Wednesfield to Bilston, reached from the South Staffordshire; and just over $\frac{1}{2}$ mile at Handsworth, from the Junction to Queen's Head, retained for steel and cement trains. Access is from Smethwick West.

BIRMINGHAM & NORTH WARWICKSHIRE

Shakespeare's County has been further opened up by the completion of the GWR line known as the Birmingham & North Warwickshire Railway. This is the final link in the Great Western route between Bristol and Birmingham, although the 'Forest of Arden' Railway would perhaps more correctly describe this line.

This statement, in GWR *Holiday Haunts*, 1921, left no doubt about the main purpose of what was the only major addition to the company's system in the West Midlands from the completion of the initial network until grouping; the Kingswinford branch was to come afterwards. The subsidiary value of the B & NW, which was to be its main one in reality, was to serve pleasant, if empty, country dotted with small villages like Earlswood Lakes :

This district, which is only nine and a half miles from Birmingham, has become a very favourite resort for those wishing to enjoy the beautiful lanes of leafy Warwickshire. Most of the cottagers provide for the 'creature wants' of the townsman.

The initiative for the line came first from a private company formed by landowners and others who wanted a direct link between Birmingham and Stratford-upon-Avon. The GWR opposed the scheme, though not strenuously, but Parliament approved and it was incorporated on 25 August 1894. It was to run 24 miles from Moor Street, Birmingham, to Stratford, with connections by the Alcester branch at Aston Cantlow and at Stratford with the GWR and East & West Junction Railway.

The GWR had feared the B & NW could easily become part of a through route to London, 16 miles shorter than its own, being plotted by the Manchester, Sheffield & Lincolnshire Railway. This company wanted to work the B & NW and close the gap between its London extension, then in the planning stage, by using running powers for 22 miles over the E & WJR from Stratford to a junction projected at Moreton Pinkney. The bankrupt E & WJR welcomed the plan, and the B & NW got further powers on 4 August 1896 to increase its capital to double the E & WJR. The MS & L agreement collapsed when the Great Central, as it had become, agreed terms with Paddington to improve its London approach.

The North Warwickshire was destined never to be constructed by its original promoters, and not to reach its projected length. By Act of 9 August 1899, plans for an independent line between Birmingham and Stratford were abandoned and the company, the Birmingham, North Warwickshire & Stratford-upon-Avon Railway, settled for one leaving the GWR just south of Tyseley, so making it dependent on that company for access to Birmingham. When there was no inflow of capital, the GWR stepped in and took over on 30 July 1900. It got further time for completion and a year later authority for a second revision of the route, to run from Tyseley to its Stratford line at Bearley North Junction. In this form the B & NW opened to goods on 9 December 1907 and to passengers, using trains from Snow Hill, from 1 July 1908. There was a closely packed chain of ten stations within the 18 miles.

THE ROUTE TO BRISTOL

On the opening day, the GWR ran its first express from Birmingham to Bristol, underlining the B & NW's strategic importance; but it lost that importance once the route was duplicated by the development of junctions at Bearley and Hatton, which provided a route only slightly longer. The GWR first projected the Birmingham–Bristol route in reply to competition from companies wanting a direct link between Birmingham and Southampton. The Andoversford & Stratford-upon-Avon Railway of 1898 had the support of the Midland & South Western Junction, which also wanted to work the B & NW. The idea was rejected when the GWR undertook to build a line between Honeybourne and Cheltenham. It was felt that by joining the two lines, and providing a through route, this section was preferable to the Andoversford route. The Honeybourne line opened 2 years ahead of the B & NW on 1 August 1906, and it was later doubled.

One of the more important and imposing of the B & NW stations was that at Henley-in-Arden. It was purely for passengers because goods were handled at a depot established at what had been the terminus of a short branch from the Birmingham & Oxford at Rowington Junction, near Lapworth. Plans for a Henley railway dated from 28 June 1861, when a scheme was projected for a mixed gauge branch of just over 3 miles. Half the line was constructed and it lay semi-derelict until the route was completed under GWR influence, on 6 June 1894, by the Birmingham & Henley-in-Arden Railway, which the GWR was to absorb on 1 July 1900—a month ahead of its take-over of the North Warwickshire company. The passenger service survived until 1 January 1915, and two years later the branch closed and most of the track went for war use.

The GWR exercised its inherited B & NW powers to build a terminus at Moor Street to overcome the congestion that threatened Snow Hill even after reconstruction and extension. Moor Street opened in 1909, but freight was not handled for 5 years. Its design emphasised the scarcity of land, which troubled all Birmingham railway builders. To keep it compact, the terminal was built without run-round loops, being fitted instead with two locomotive traversers for engines up to the size of *Castles*. They were taken out of use on 17 December 1967.

'BEAUTIFUL BORDERLANDS'

The GWR lost no time in advertising the beauty of the North Warwickshire countryside—and trying to riddle it with houses to produce commuter traffic of Paddington proportions. *An Up to Date Property Register* covering *Birmingham and its Beautiful Borderlands* was published quarterly and its lavishness in an age before the firm establishment of the Public Relations Officer was matched by its lyrical language. It dealt with suburbs on the main line to Leamington as well as on the Stratford route. It seemed the GWR never dreamed that Birmingham's pride might be wounded if the campaign was based on London criteria.

Birmingham, like London, extolled the *Register*, is singularly blessed in its borderlands :

> Within 15 minutes of leaving Snow Hill, the busy toiler, either in his brains or his hands, can alight among the green fields of Shirley, Solihull or Knowle. Recent extensions of railway communication have obviated the necessity for the shopkeeper or employee to reside in the immediate vicinity of his daily vocations. Snow Hill is only 2 or 3 minutes' walk from the centre of Birmingham, every part of which is easily accessible by tramway.

'Accessible by tramway . . .' How the GWR recognised competition—and used it to its own advantage.

Such was the case presented in issue no 5, covering the months up to the summer of 1914. Soon war was to shatter more than the rural peace of Warwickshire. Suddenly, it no longer mattered that the rent of houses in the country was cheap—between £12 and £40 a year—for those rents soon rose beyond recognition, and the postwar depression that stretched into the 1930s meant there was little development in the area. The GWR did what it could to encourage passengers, and provided a stop at Whitlock's End in 1936; it was a small halt, because there was no demand for anything more.

Planning controls and green belts introduced after World War II restricted development, and few estates have been built near the North Warwickshire line. The introduction of DMUS, which could easily breast its long banks, brought some increase in passengers, but nothing like that necessary to make the line pay. A deadline was set for the withdrawal of passenger services : on 5 May 1969—the start of the summer timetable, but five local authorities took the case for retention to the High Court and prevented closure. Pressure groups were set up, and BR management responded to suggestions—but the public did not. Little interest was shown even when day returns were issued during rush hours from inner suburban stations. As the *Journal* of the Branch Line Society lamented in May 1971 : 'The rush hour service is good so what more can BR do?'

The freight outlook seems brighter, for the B & NW has easier gradients and can handle longer trains than the Birmingham &

Gloucester, and in recent years extra freight has been diverted via Stratford to relieve pressure on the Lickey passenger artery. Plans current in 1972 to close the Honeybourne line as a prelude to motorway development south of Stratford were reported to have been shelved. This will enable the B & NW to be retained for weekend passenger diversions.

As a commuter line, the North Warwickshire had been given a reprieve late in 1970 when the West Midlands PTA subsidised it as far as Grimes Hill & Wythall, leaving the rest of the subsidy to be found by the Government. It was a stopgap measure to allow the PTA time to consider the line's long-term future.

The rural atmosphere of the North Warwickshire rubs off a little on Moor Street, the most important GWR passenger legacy left in the Birmingham area. Its smallish concourse—with flower baskets—enables it to retain something of the air of a country station, even though it is dominated by the tall buildings of the new Birmingham—buildings whose height is exaggerated because they tower from the top of the ridge on which the city centre stands, while Moor Street lies at its foot. Passengers can walk to New Street through pedestrian subways.

CHAPTER V

Wolverhampton : GWR Lines

SHREWSBURY AND BIRMINGHAM

Wolverhampton's development as an important railway centre was shaped from the strife and bitterness of rival companies fighting for routes from the West Midlands to Merseyside. It became the storm centre when the ambitions of the Shrewsbury & Birmingham Railway were cut back to Wolverhampton and the route to Birmingham was given to the Birmingham, Wolverhampton & Stour Valley Railway. They were, of course, in the opposing camps of the giants : the GWR and LNWR.

The Grand Junction assured Wolverhampton of its status as a town of note on the railway system, but no junctions were originally envisaged. They came from promoters striking west towards the Welsh coast to capture traffic from Ireland. A geological map published by a London firm in 1838 showed a projected route from Shrewsbury to the Lleyn Peninsula : the line was to reach Shrewsbury along the lip of the Severn Valley, passing to the south of the Wrekin mountain and approaching the town from the south-east, roughly along the route of what is now the A458 road from Bridgnorth.

Local interests which promoted the S & B years later favoured going north of the Wrekin. They quickly formed an alliance with the London & Birmingham, which was then at war with the GJR because of that company's advocacy of the broad gauge. Equally offensive was the GJR claim to Shrewsbury as part of its territory, an outpost to be reached from Stafford. This was a plan much ahead of the Shrewsbury & Crewe. The S & B intended to join the L & B at Birmingham, and, if that was rejected, a connection was contemplated at Worcester with, according to the board minutes, the GWR : there was no recognition of the OW & W. The

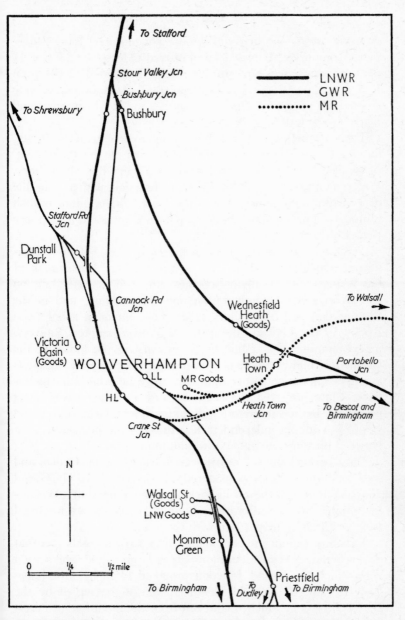

Wolverhampton: The original Shrewsbury & Birmingham spur
from Stafford Road Junction to the LNWR was closed for more than
a century, from 1859 until restored for electrification in 1966

plan was soon forgotten when the L & B plumped for an independent route to Merseyside, and offered to lease the s & B at 4½ per cent guarantee, plus surplus profits. By mid-1844 Sir John Rennie estimated the cost at £800,000. Two branches were mooted: from Shiffnal (as spelt until 1869) to Ironbridge and Dudley to Stourbridge.

The L & B urged the Shrewsbury company to extend to Chester, but the Grand Junction got the bill thrown out by Parliament. A similar fate befell a GJR inspired scheme—the Shrewsbury, Wolverhampton & South Staffordshire Junction, with a main line over virtually the same route as the s & B, with a minor branch of under ½ mile at Shrewsbury. Capital was proposed at no more than £660,000.

The s & B scheme was much preferred by the Dalhousie Committee, which reported in 1845 to the Railway Department of the Board of Trade about schemes projected between London and Worcester, Wolverhampton and Birmingham, and in the Birmingham and Shrewsbury areas. They included a line from Rugby to the Oxford, Worcester & Wolverhampton Railway. The Committee felt a line to Shrewsbury in the hands of the Grand Junction would be used to protect that company's interests against competition rather than encourage lines beyond Shrewsbury. They preferred the s & B because its scheme was being promoted by a substantial and independent local party, and would provide an independent line through the prosperous area between Birmingham and Wolverhampton.

Plans revived the following year failed Standing Orders and the formation of the LNWR scattered them to the winds. The Grand Junction at once withdrew its backing of the Shrewsbury, Wolverhampton & South Staffordshire Junction, while the L & B refused to have anything more to do with the s & B.

The most significant part of the SW & SSJ proposals was that the terminal at Wolverhampton was to be at a low level station with which the Grand Junction proposed to replace the hopelessly distant Wednesfield Heath. It was to be served by the Portobello Loop, which was to run from the main line at Portobello and rejoin it at Bushbury. The OW & W was to have a quarter share in the SW & SSJ, and the station idea had the support of 1,600 residents, but the Grand Junction was forced to scrap its plans when the OW & W objected to the loop crossing its own line on the level. In turn, the s & b had to abandon a fork to the station and switch to a high level connection with the Stour Valley Railway. In casting off the sw & ssj, the Grand Junction was careful not to damage its Shrewsbury aspirations, which it kept alive through the Shropshire Union Railways & Canal Company, its ally.

Left out in the cold by the creation of the lnwr, the Shrewsbury promoters pressed ahead with plans for a main line between Shrewsbury and Birmingham, with branches to Coalbrookdale and further south to Dudley, and from Smethwick to Stourport via Stourbridge. The estimated cost had now risen sharply to £2,200,000. The scheme was among sixteen for the area considered by a Select Committee in June 1846. The route had been surveyed by Robert Stephenson and William Baker. Counsel pointed out that there would be no steep banks that could possibly be avoided, for Stephenson was 'wedded to easy gradients'.

While the s & b would be an integral line under single control, its rivals—the sw & ssj and the bw & d—would have to form alliances with existing companies, including the ow & w. Witnesses presented a convincing case for a line between Wolverhampton and Shrewsbury. A Shrewsbury lead merchant, Birr, said local trade was interrupted when canals ran short of water. A direct link between Shrewsbury and London would greatly increase trade and bring back to the town the trade of lead manufacturing.

The magistrates' clerk at Shifnall, Osborne, said three-quarters of the local people backed the s & b, since the rival scheme would cause great residential upheaval. Its station would be a quarter of a mile from the market-place, while that of the s & b would be only 100yd away.

The s & b scheme was favoured by factory owners because it would serve Darlaston, which rivals would miss. A Birmingham land surveyor, Fowler, said it would serve seventy-six works between there and Wolverhampton, but its rival only thirty-four. While the Shrewsbury line would run parallel to the canal, the rival would have to cross it at right-angles fifteen times.

The chairman of the Birmingham Canal Company, Scott, said he and others had drawn up the s & b scheme, once the intentions of the ow & w had become plain, because they felt the s & b would serve Wolverhampton far better.

A Tipton iron master, Richard Bradley, said the s & b would

give him cheap and direct links to his main markets in London, Birmingham, Manchester and Liverpool. Between 9,000 and 10,000 people lived near the station proposed at Tipton. The sw & ssj would have only a goods station there; the nearest for passengers would be at Dudley.

Lord North's mining agent at Dudley, Smith, said that if the s & b was not sanctioned, people going from Dudley to Birmingham would have to use four different railways.

ROBERT STEPHENSON V BRUNEL

Some of the fiercest controversy surrounded the siting of stations at Wolverhampton, especially when it was found that the s & b and the bw & d had earmarked the same land. That was resolved by the companies dividing the site, taking the canal as their boundary. Brunel and Locke favoured a low level station and bw & d counsel claimed that Robert Stephenson's case for one at high level had been 'shattered to pieces'; instead of having the 'absorption of momentum', Stephenson would not have acceleration from one at high level, which would form a sort of pinnacle highly objectionable in every way. The s & b did not want a high level station to suit the district but so it could construct a line to pour all its traffic from Shrewsbury on to the Birmingham canal.

A Wolverhampton banker called Hill caused laughter when he hoped that the ascent people would have to make to the s & b station would not be anything so bad as that to the room in which they were sitting. Wolverhampton street commissioners voted 15–10 in favour of the bw & d at a meeting described as 'stormy —like most Wolverhampton ones'.

The ow & w claimed the s & b route was parallel to its own and, therefore, unnecessary. The Grand Junction contended that it had a better line, as did the sw & ssj, although it did not bother to present its case. It was supported by the gjr and the ow & w and it had links with the Trent Valley & Midlands Railway; during the Committee stage these bodies arranged to split the projected schemes, the tv & m taking lines south of Walsall, including that to Dudley, a move welcomed by the bw & d.

The s & b had many opponents, including several iron and coal masters who said it would interfere with mineral workings, and Surveyors of Highways at West Bromwich, Halesowen,

Rowley Regis, Tipton and Sedgley. Birmingham Water Works Company felt the line would affect pipes and mains, and the Trustees of the Park Street Burial Ground, Birmingham, said it would cross the ground in 'an improper manner'. When time for presenting Bills to the current Parliamentary session was about to expire, the s & b renewed attempts to reach agreement with the bw & d. The response was cool, the bw & d stipulating that any talks must be on the understanding that the Birmingham and Wolverhampton line must remain independent of the London & Birmingham to give local people the benefit of competition. The bw & d offered to surrender its Dudley branch if the s & b gave up the Tipton–Wolverhampton section 'since the population and traffic of the district did not require it'. The idea was described by the s & b counsel as 'the most niggardly he had ever heard'. If the section were conceded, the area would be bound hand and foot to the gwr.

A group of iron masters objected to any agreement preventing the sw & ssj continuing its Tipton–Dudley line to Wolverhampton. After two days of discussion without firm proposals from either side, the Select Committee announced that it favoured two stations at Birmingham and Wolverhampton.

The future of the railways of Wolverhampton was largely shaped by several Acts of 3 August 1846, including the previously mentioned bw & d Act. The s & b authorisation of that day was for a much truncated line of no more than $29\frac{1}{2}$ miles between Shrewsbury and Wolverhampton, of which the 10 miles from Shrewsbury to Wellington were to be shared. The appointed partner was to be the gjr-encouraged Shropshire Union Railways & Canal Company (the sur as we shall know it). It was an amalgamation of three canals, of which the Ellesmere & Chester Canal Company changed its name to the sur & cc from 3 August 1846, and absorbed the other two. The sur incorporation, therefore, dates back to 1793. Like the Cambrian, it had the plural 'railways' in its title.

The s & b was also given a quarter share and running powers over the Birmingham, Wolverhampton & Stour Valley Railway to reach Birmingham. Later it built a branch to Coalbrookdale (Chapter VIII).

F

DELAYS IN CONSTRUCTION

From politics to construction: it began soon after the S & B received its Act and in the first year 'considerable progress' was reported in boring Oakengates Tunnel (to broad-gauge dimensions). The tunnel was only 471yd long, but it was thought necessary for navvies to work day and night. The mainline contract was estimated at not more than £500,000, with Shrewsbury station and a Brassey contract for a Severn bridge costing another £80,000. The financial prospect was regarded as bright and capital adequate, since the S & B were meeting only a quarter of the cost of Shrewsbury station and sharing the cost of the line to Wellington.

Later such optimism was shaken by events, reflected in a report by Robert Stephenson as consulting engineer, and William Baker, who was also the SUR engineer, of 21 August 1848:

> In our report of February we stated that the tunnel at Oakengates and Shiffnal embankment were the most backward. Unfortunately this is still so owing to unseasonable weather during the last few months. The engineers were unable to cover time lost, but they are working day and night.

Some ten months of work were needed before the 13¼ miles between Shrewsbury and Oakengates, including the entire joint section, could be opened, together with the Wellington–Stafford line of the SUR, on 1 June 1849. The target date for the rest of the S & B was 1 October, but only by 'great exertions' was the line opened on 12 November, and then only to a temporary station at Wolverhampton.

The line was important, and its early territorial visions were not confined to Merseyside, since one plan was to make it an important part of a route between Shrewsbury and Eastern England. Shareholders attending the first meeting on 19 September 1846 learned that the engineer was to survey extensions from Wolverhampton station to the GJR at Willenhall as the first steps in a scheme to provide a route to several places, including Walsall and Lichfield. This scheme would replace defunct ones for branches at Show Hill and Portobello. Just under a year later shareholders heard that the company had received powers to run over the LNWR to Willenhall, providing, with the South

Staffordshire and North Staffordshire Railways, a route to the east.

The political history of the s & b up to the time it was swallowed up by the GWR was closely allied to that of the Shrewsbury & Chester Railway, whose story falls outside this volume. The close relations that developed between the two companies were due largely to the early formation of a Through Traffic Committee to exploit Merseyside traffic at the expense of the LNWR. The exuberant activities of the Traffic Committee were responsible for the s & b skirmishing with the Birkenhead Railway, but its main battles were fought on its doorstep.

FORCING PASSAGE SOUTH

The s & b directors knew as well as anyone the limited potential of a line running through little but fields; but the system had little else once the LNWR refused point-blank to complete the Stour Valley line over which the s & b was to use its built-in running powers to reach its real goal of Birmingham. Faced with this opposition, the directors showed the same determination and ingenuity they had demonstrated after being cast off by the London & Birmingham on the formation of the LNWR. The position was further complicated by the LNWR having joint ownership with the s & b of the last $\frac{1}{2}$ mile of the approach to Wolverhampton High Level, for this was the only section that ran beside the Birmingham Canal and where transhipment was possible.

Victoria Basin, close to High Level, was constructed for this purpose. Battles, physical and legal, began from the moment the s & b attempted to lay a pathway of planks down the railway embankment to transfer goods from train to barge. The LNWR showed complete contempt for the legal position, since the s & b access to Birmingham contained in the Act of Incorporation had been safeguarded when Euston leased the sVR.

The first major clash was tagged as the 'Riot at Temporary Station' by the *Wolverhampton Chronicle* of 7 July 1850, when 300 navvies employed by Hoof, Hill and Moore, the Stour Valley contractors, met those of the s & b, who were identified by large pieces of red tape tied round their arms. As a riot developed, police and soldiers (with fixed bayonets) marched to the scene, where the mayor read the Riot Act. Later the same day several wagons were overturned further along the line and after stone throwing, police drew cutlasses and charged to disperse the rival navvies.

A Chancery injunction ended the violence and later the s & b was able to transfer its traffic to the canal at Victoria Basin. The s & b looked for a new way to Birmingham, seeking, with the Shrewsbury & Chester, closer ties with the GWR.

COURT OF INQUIRY

A traffic agreement signed by the companies in 1851 brought violent reaction from the LNWR secretary, Captain Huish. He acted in much the same way as he had done when faced with opposition by the Birmingham & Oxford, and attempted to take over the s & b. Having acquired some shares, the LNWR 'packed' the next shareholders' meeting at Wolverhampton. A Court of Inquiry was called for, and it was chaired by Robert Scott, whose report attacked the s & b's attitude towards the LNWR. It was announced that the s & b had reopened negotiations and reached a preliminary agreement for leasing to the LNWR for 21 years. Shareholders were to get dividends of up to 3–4 per cent, paid from the traffic receipts of the line, which meant they would get nothing more than they were already receiving. The Scott Report attacked the s & b for launching an omnibus service between Oakengates and Wolverhampton, which had lost £2,000 :

> This was not a friendly act towards the LNWR who had promised you the monopoly of the s & b traffic. After the opening of a tempopary station at Wolverhampton and having a valuable agreement with the LNWR, you, the directors of the s & b, united with the s & c in competition for traffic from Birmingham and London to Liverpool, but the Chester & Birkenhead company being unfriendly to their southern neighbour, placed every impediment in the way of this through traffic and your directors had even more difficulty in approaching the Mersey than Birmingham. In fact, they are still without a terminus either at Birmingham or Birkenhead. The Committee must express their opinion that the time, manner and circumstances under which competition with the LNWR for Liverpool traffic has been carried out by your board is open to serious question and they recommend for your consideration whether an entire change of policy be not essential to the prosperity of your affairs. Instead of fostering and looking after the valuable local traffic of Shropshire and Staffordshire, their attention has been devoted to the tactics of two leviathan

railway companies and the trade of the ports of London, Liverpool
and Bristol. Nor have Ireland and Scotland escaped their attention.
All kinds of conveyance have shared their patronage, from the
omnibus at Oakengates to flatboats on the Dee and the Mersey and
steamers to Ireland. No undertaking is too great for them. They hint
at a new line from Chester to Birkenhead, they prepare for large
stations in Birmingham and they are willing to work the Chester &
Holyhead as well as the Oxford, Worcester & Wolverhampton Railway. They take offices and hire agents in Liverpool, Birmingham and
London to book passengers and collect parcels and goods and
distribute 20,000 handbills to passengers entering Euston station.

Matters simmered for a month until a special meeting considered the proposed agreement with the LNWR. It dragged on
for the ridiculous length of 4 days and at one stage, Ormsby Gore,
who was forced to stay in the chair, pulled a nightcap out of his
pocket and went to sleep. Virtual deadlock existed between two
rival factions within the s & B. Both welcomed a take-over offer
by the GWR for both the s & B and the s & c. The offer forced
many shareholders to reconsider Euston's proposals, and the next
day influential members of the s & B agreed to amalgamation
with the GWR and s & c.

Euston made little attempt to stop the s & B falling into GWR
hands, but it fought hard against the s & c amalgamation. This
was not to take place for another 3 years (not until 1 September
1854), but since it was virtually a *fait accompli*, the LNWR became
even more determined to prevent either the s & B or the GWR
getting access to Birmingham. It refused, using one ruse or
another, to open the Stour Valley, and it was not until February
1854, when the BW & D was nearly complete, that relations
improved sufficiently for the s & B to be allowed at last to run
trains to New Street. The service, much in keeping with the
chilly political temperature, was poor—three trains each way on
weekdays only, an intensity more akin to a rural branch than a
main line. The s & B concentrated its passenger traffic and closed
its small station at Stafford Road sometime in March.

S & B : THE BREAK-THROUGH

Once the BW & D opened 6 months later, there was nothing more
the LNWR could do to impede the Shrewsbury traffic, and gradually it became more friendly with the GWR. In 1858, the GWR

built a goods station at Herbert Street, adjacent to Victoria Basin, to replace its temporary one at Stafford Road. The following March it sold its half share in the original joint station at High Level to the LNWR and transferred the original S & B goods depot. The spur between the LNWR and GWR lines was severed and Herbert Street was then served by a branch that ran for nearly a mile from Stafford Road Junction.

The GWR brought peace and orderliness to the S & B system, and stability of employment if we take the case of Evans, appointed stationmaster at Codsall in 1856. His family held the office until after grouping, two sons having succeeded their fathers.

An important marshalling centre was developed at Hollinswood in separate sections : one served a group of private sidings, and the other was used to marshal trains. There was no public goods depot at the sidings, which held more than 500 wagons. Before grouping there were plans for extensions to handle trains from the north and the Crewe line, and to relieve occasional congestion at Oxley yard. Hollinswood dealt with traffic rather more varied than was found in some yards. Mainly it consisted of heavy minerals : iron, steel, coal, bricks, chemicals, roadstone and rail ballast : Large quantities of limestone and ore were marshalled for local blast furnaces.

The S & B's strategic role through the years has remained unchanged, since it remains the artery between the West Midlands and Shrewsbury, north and mid-Wales, and acts as a subsidiary line, gradually diminishing in importance, to Chester and Birkenhead. Its position was once challenged unsuccessfully by the ambitions of the Bishop's Castle Railway, which sought to extend to Newtown and provide a link between Paddington and Aberystwyth rather shorter than the roundabout haul via Shrewsbury. Faced with loss of mileage revenue, both by shortening its own route and paying fees to the BCR, the GWR remained totally unenthusiastic.

The S & B served the Severn Valley line, and its future to Ironbridge is assured by the power stations in the valley.

The Shrewsbury line passenger service was never heavy, local trains being reinforced by Paddington–Birkenhead expresses. Local services were badly hit as buses became reliable. There was local agitation in 1911 for a station at Waterloo Bridge to serve parts of Oakengates, Ketley and Hadley, but it was never pressed with vigour; indeed Oakengates was 1¾ miles away. When the GWR again considered the proposal in 1924 it was noted that 'recent inquiries do not appear to warrant the provision of a Station, having regard to the development of road motor traffic'.

Recently there have been recommendations that a station to serve Telford New Town should be built by 1975 on the site of the old GWR goods depot at Hollinswood. There has been talk of withdrawing local trains between Wolverhampton and Shrewsbury, where the town council has called for the electrification of the route. Local authorities claimed the local trains were busy with daily commuters to Wolverhampton and Birmingham who might have to find other jobs or move if they were taken off. The news came as work was in progress on modernising the station at Wellington, much reduced in track layout since it ceased to be a junction for either Nantwich or Stafford.

The Nantwich line had been used by freight trains between Crewe and the Oxley marshalling yard, which closed in March 1967, after the traffic had been switched via Stafford, and handled by the newly modernised yards at Bescot and Crewe.

Electrification embraced a small part of the S & B, the spur from Wolverhampton High Level to the Shrewsbury route being relaid in preparation for the closure of Snow Hill. The stabling of coaches and dmus, which had taken place at High Level and Walsall Midland, was concentrated at Oxley, where the sidings were realigned, and the section to High Level electrified in 1972. This was the first section of the GWR to go under the wires.

WOLVERHAMPTON JUNCTION RAILWAY

Probably the least known of the mixed gauge lines was the Wolverhampton Junction Railway, for which the GWR received powers in 1852. It ran for no more than ¾ mile but it was the vital link needed to give the company access to the S & B. Its course between Cannock Road Junction and Stafford Road took it through part of the locomotive and carriage works the S & B had established at Stafford Road in 1849. Although the buildings were new, several had to be demolished to make way for the line, which opened with the BW & D in 1854.

Running powers were given to the ow & w, and the completion of the wjr as a mixed gauge route led to the need for a final stretch of conversion, which involved a third rail being laid over the s & b between Stafford Road Junction and Victoria Basin. The shunting limit for trains worked over the wjr was established about ¾ mile west of Stafford Road Junction, and this was to be the 'end' of the gwr's dream of broad gauge to the Mersey.

The gwr used Herbert Street as a transhipment centre for goods between north and south until the local demise of the broad gauge in 1869. It continued as an ordinary goods depot.

The wjr passed into history once the s & b trains were switched to High Level on electrification, and it was quickly lifted. The trackbed can be easily traced from the carriage window.

OXFORD, WORCESTER & WOLVERHAMPTON

The Grand Junction may have got to Wolverhampton first, but it was really a gwr town, though never a divisional headquarters, except for locomotives. From 1855 the company's Northern Division, stretching from Birmingham to Chester, was controlled from Shrewsbury. The headquarters moved to Chester in 1861, following the creation of a new division for the Birmingham area, including Wolverhampton. The boundary was established just north of Wolverhampton. Besides being the southern terminus of the Shrewsbury & Birmingham, and the northern one of the Birmingham, Wolverhampton & Dudley, it was also the terminus of the swashbuckling ever-independent company that gave the town due recognition in its title: the Oxford, Worcester & Wolverhampton.

The 'Old Worse & Worse' failed to realise its promoters' hopes in more than gauge, and it took 9 years to cleave its way of no more than 89¼ miles from north of Oxford to a Low Level station at Wolverhampton, some 30ft below the s & b station at Queen Street, as it was first known. The ow & w was authorised on 4 August 1845, from the Oxford & Rugby at Wolvercot Junction to Worcester, Stourbridge, Dudley and Wolverhampton and a junction with the gjr. Branches were to include lines to Kingswinford and Tipton Basin. Its birth came during the gauge controversy, and as some concessions were felt necessary the the section north of the Birmingham & Gloucester at Abbot's

Wood, near Worcester, was designated as mixed, including the Kingswinford branch.

Although the OW & W was to provide a route south from Wolverhampton independent of the London & Birmingham, local iron and coal masters were never over-enthusiastic about it; preferring the more direct schemes of the B & O and BW & D. For one thing, the OW & W line of approach to Wolverhampton was on a level too high to allow access to some already established ironworks.

The OW & W's early friendship with the BW & D was to bring a quick result, for soon after it had bought Dudley shares worth £100,000, the Oxford company found a chance to sell them—at a profit of £23,000, much welcomed by the struggling promoters.

One reason for the slow construction of the OW & W was Parliament's ban on the broad gauge continuing north of Wolverhampton. Money was also short. Brunel's original estimate of about £1,500,000 proved wildly inaccurate, almost £1 million short of the sum required.

In the year after the company's incorporation some work was carried out around Wolverhampton, including the start of excavation on a tunnel at Dudley. By the end of 1846 work was in progress south of Tipton, but nothing was done further north because of plans (eventually authorised on 14 August 1848), for a $2\frac{1}{2}$ mile diversion of the northern section to Wolverhampton Low Level, to be built jointly with the S & B and BW & D. It was agreed that if the S & B was sold, leased or transferred to the LNWR, as then seemed likely, its share was to be absorbed by the other partners. The Act also switched the junction with the GJR from Wednesfield Heath to Bushbury.

Provision was made for another £1 million in capital, but the depressed state of the money market made that impossible to raise. A year later a committee appointed to investigate the company's affairs, found that another £1,500,000 was needed. It recommended that the line should be completed as narrow gauge—not mixed as authorised—between the Midland at Abbot's Wood and the Stour Valley at Tipton.

When no further construction took place, the Railway Commissioners called for a report, since the original Act contained a clause (disputed, of course), that the GWR was willing to complete the route 'in case of need'. The findings of Captain

Simmons (27 November 1849) were that a great deal of work remained to be done at each end of the route, although the Stourbridge–Dudley section was nearly complete, apart, that is, from stations and track! While Dudley tunnel had been finished, Stourbridge viaduct had hardly been started. This wooden structure was destined to be replaced in 1882 by a ten-arch brick and stone structure.

The Commissioners ordered the GWR to complete the OW & W at once, but the GWR was far from willing, and the Commissioners began a High Court action that dragged on over 2 years, when it was dropped, because the line was nearly finished. Treadwell's were the contractors between Worcester and Tipton, and Peto & Betts between Tipton and Wolverhampton.

Completion was due to the initiative of John Parson, a London solicitor who became legal adviser to the OW & W in 1850, and soon announced that he was probably the largest shareholder. An agreement with the LNWR and the MR, signed on 21 February 1851, provided for these companies to complete the line and work it. The GWR took its wrath to Chancery, had the agreement declared void and offered the OW & W one in similar terms.

Once the lease took effect, the OW & W became truculent towards the GWR and friendly towards the LNWR, proposing to abandon its authorised approach to Wolverhampton and join instead the Stour Valley at Tipton. Parliament was dragged into the row by the GWR, which feared it would be kept out of Wolverhampton unless it built a line of about a mile to give the BW & D access from Priestfield.

Parliament refused to sanction such a line, but safeguarded GWR interests by threatening the OW & W with heavy penalties unless the mixed gauge reached central Wolverhampton by September 1853 and ran $\frac{1}{2}$ mile beyond to what subsequently became Cannock Road Junction. The OW & W did not give concessions readily, and it was almost a year before the GWR got running powers between Priestfield and Cannock Road. The threat of penalties also made the OW & W act quickly, and the line was finished well within the time limit. Droitwich–Stourbridge opened on 1 May 1852, and Stourbridge–Dudley followed later in the year (goods on 16 November, passengers on 20 December). The haste with which sections were opened meant the line was single for a time between Brettell Lane and Dudley. Besides

Dudley, there were stations at Brettell Lane, Brierley Hill, Round Oak, and Netherton.

The section north from Dudley to the Stour Valley at Tipton, where there was a narrow-gauge spur, was finished in July 1853 but remained closed until 1 December because of doubts about the safety of several bridges, and the location of mines beneath the track. The double-track section was laid narrow gauge, with a broad-gauge rail for part of the distance.

There were doubts, too, for a time about bridges between Tipton and the s & b at Stafford Road Junction, and although the link was opened to goods in April 1854, passenger trains were not allowed until 1 July. There were three intermediate stations—Daisy Bank (a name that brought rural freshness to an industrial area), Bilston and Priestfield. About the same time, the last mile was completed to the LNWR at Bushbury and opened to goods. Passenger trains followed in October.

Wolverhampton Low Level was purely for passengers, the ow & w goods depot being opened at Walsall Street in October 1855, adjacent to the Monmore Canal basin.

In its original form Low Level was one of the worst examples of station design. It was dangerous because the two main lines crossed each other twice, in the middle of the platforms and at the mouth of the tight-bore tunnel just south of the station. About the time of gauge conversion in 1869 the station was remodelled with separate platforms, bisected in the middle by a level crossing for luggage; this crossing was much used by passengers until lifts and a footbridge were built. Many years later the overall roof was removed.

The station lost all but its Birmingham local service when the through route between Paddington and Birkenhead was severed in 1967, but it received a new lease of life as a parcels concentration depot, opened on 6 April 1970 to serve an area from Lichfield to Kidderminster. A fleet of nearly fifty vans handles some 8,000 parcels daily. Railway vans are shunted in and out of the depot over the sharp, steeply graded spur to the Midland at Heath Town Junction. The depot proved successful and soon extra sidings were laid.

Modernisation has wrought change and destruction on the ow & w between Stourbridge Junction and Priestfield. Local passenger services between Wolverhampton and Stourbridge were withdrawn on 30 July 1962. The bridge carrying the line over the Stour Valley near Bloomfield Junction, Tipton, was severed on electrification and most of the line to Priestfield lifted and stations demolished. A short section near Bloomfield is retained as a store for crippled wagons being handled by the South Staffordshire Wagon Company, which is connected to the Stour Valley line.

The OW & W between Stourbridge and Dudley has an assured future as the sole access to three major developments—Dudley Freightliner depot; the Pensnett Trading Estate, reached from Kingswinford South Junction; and Moor Lane Steel terminal, established in 1966 in the fork between Blowers Green Junction and the Old Hill branch. The Dudley Freightliner depot, the first in the area, opened in 1967 on the site of Castle Street goods yard. In 1972 about half a mile of the line between Stourbridge and Brettell Lane was diverted on to a high, semi-circular embankment round an extensive area of opencast mining.

THE KINGSWINFORD BRANCH

The grouping years were more distinguished for line closures than for the development of new lines, but in 1925 the GWR brought to fruition the legacy of the Kingswinford branch, providing mainly a Wolverhampton by-pass for heavy freight traffic between South Wales, Worcester and the north.

The area west of Wolverhampton was penetrated originally by the OW & W, which opened a branch of $1\frac{1}{2}$ miles from Kingswinford Junction to the busy Bromley canal basin in November 1858. It was extended north some years later in desultory (and historically obscure) circumstances to the Pensnett Railway (see p. 112), and there was a further extension to what became Baggeridge Junction. Early in the present century the GWR revived plans for a link from Wolverhampton to Bridgnorth and the Severn Valley line.

Authorisation in 1905 came as Wolverhampton and the surrounding areas were expanding—a trend that was to double the population to about 160,000 in the first half of the century. The branch was to run from the Oxford line near Stourbridge Junction to Dunstall Park, near Oxley sidings. There were powers to abandon part of the OW & W. Primarily the line was a springboard for the Bridgnorth line, which was to branch across country from Trysull, near Wombourn. The route was surveyed but no step was taken towards construction because of the growing impact of bus competition—including the service the GWR had inaugurated between Wolverhampton and Bridgnorth in 1904. A line to Bridgnorth would have reduced the rail distance from Wolverhampton from almost 35 miles via Ironbridge to a mere 14.

A comprehensive picture of the construction of the Kings-winford branch has been given in a useful work of local scholarship, *By Rail to Wombourn*, published in 1969 by J. Ned Williams and students of Wulfrun College of Further Education, Wolverhampton :

> Although constructed in the first quarter of this century many of the stories about the construction of the line are typical of the tales told about lines built in the nineteenth century. The line to Wombourn seems to have been built by the sweat and toil of large numbers of men and horses, with only mechanical help from the 'steam navvies', and the contractors' light railway. The contractors employed over 200 men. The men worked a 56½ hour week, working six days. They were paid 5½d per hour if they were a ganger or navvie, and lads could earn 3d an hour assisting them. Many a local boy looked forward to leaving school and earning 14s a week on building the railway. If you came straight from school you were probably first employed as a 'drummer-up'—a tea boy to one gang of navvies. Later you might work with the horses used to shunt the wagons carrying spoil, or try the dangerous job of 'spragging'.
>
> At one time the work seems to have been sufficiently intense to justify working at night, by the light of oil lamps. (The contractors' locomotives also carried lamps.) The public houses opened at 6 a.m. to refresh the navvies who had worked through the night, and, in Wombourn, stories are told about fights between drunken navvies.

Drunk or not, the men worked hard, but in 1914 work was brought to a halt, first because of a shortage of materials and then through lack of men. When construction resumed in 1919, it was carried out by the GWR. Delays were caused by subsidence, and later the GWR advised gangers to walk on the sleepers if the ground underneath disappeared.

Such methods now seem a little primitive but they were standard before the Kaiser's war, and were used to build the GWR's new Birmingham line and the Birmingham & North Warwickshire, as well as others.

The Kingswinford branch was opened to all traffic on 11 May 1925, when the *Wolverhampton Chronicle* caught the local mood with its headlines :

ALL STATIONS TO BRETTELL LANE !

NEW GWR SERVICES OPEN UP LOVELY COUNTRY.

FIRST TRAIN SENDS RABBITS AND HARES SCAMPERING.

The line's characteristic as a through route was not conducive to passenger traffic, though plenty of efforts were made to attract them, nine halts being packed into 12 miles. But the route was against the geographical grain and the passenger trains were withdrawn in 1932.

With GWR thoroughness a triangular junction was laid at Oxley with double-track spurs—also useful for turning locomotives. The branch continued to have a healthy freight service and was intensively worked during World War II, only to fall victim of economies two decades later. It was then completely closed, in 1965, between Oxley and Baggeridge, which meant it reverted to the length to which it had been built by the ow & w.

It was the only 'pure' GWR line in the Wolverhampton area, since it was the only one not originally conceived by an independent company.

STAFFORD ROAD WORKS

Apart from private works, there were three big locomotive building and repair centres in the region : Crewe, Stoke and Wolverhampton. It was at Wolverhampton that the S & B established workshops about 1849. They were much decimated, as noted, by the Wolverhampton Junction Railway and major changes took place once the GWR took over the two Shrewsbury companies. It extended to Stafford Road the policy evolved at Swindon of making its own locomotives and spares. It transferred carriage and wagon work to the former Shrewsbury & Chester works at Saltney, near Chester, and Wolverhampton took over the locomotive repair work done there.

The first locomotive built at Stafford Road in 1859 was a 2–2–2, designed by Joseph Armstrong, who had been locomotive superintendent of both the Shrewsbury companies. Stafford Road became the headquarters of the GWR Northern Division for locomotive purposes, and it was comparable to Swindon until it decided to concentrate development there after losing the broad-gauge battle. Wolverhampton dealt with the narow-gauge stock of the Shrewsbury companies and the West Midland, and also broad-gauge locomotives working north of Oxford. One of the reasons behind the extension of Swindon was the difficulty of acquiring extra land at Wolverhampton.

Soon after the take-over, the GWR carried out major improvements to adapt the works to handle locomotives of both gauges. A forge, smithy and extra shops were added. Now came boom-time at Stafford Road, and up to April 1908, when all locomotive building was transferred to Swindon, the works turned out 794 locomotives and 102 rebuilds so extensive that they could be classed as new engines. In addition, engines were made for six railmotors. The last locomotive built was a small 2–6–2 T, which became no 4519. Another of the same batch, no 4507, was destined to be the last Wolverhampton-built locomotive to remain in service, not being withdrawn until October 1963. These engines were fitted with standard GWR safety valve covers originally designed at Stafford Road, features that gave distinction to all GWR locomotives.

The gap in importance between Swindon and Wolverhampton had grown wide even before the end of locomotive building, and land bought at Dunstall Hill in 1900 for works extensions was not used until new erecting, machine and other shops were opened in 1935 to replace obsolete machinery.

Stafford Road's status altered little after nationalisation. Repair work continued and locomotives up to the size of *Kings* and *Castles* were temporarily stripped of their glory. Once BR began the hasty conversion programme to diesel and electric, the works were doomed, though few people realised at that time how soon they were to close. The change was heartily welcomed initially, an internal report stating :

> The modernisation programme in its furtherance of the progress of the Railways will make its mark felt in Stafford Road Works as the steam locomotive is replaced by the Diesel, Hydraulic and Diesel Electric Locomotives. These changes will, in time, bring a different class of work and repair to Stafford Road and to meet this change, proposals and plans are being formulated for these Works to undertake the maintenance of Main Line Diesel Locomotives in the future.

It was not to be, for fewer diesels needed meant fewer workshops, and Stafford Road was not the only works to close. In 1959—one of the middle years between nationalisation and closure—310 locomotives and 183 boilers were repaired. Gradual run-down followed and the last locomotive handled, 2–8–0, no 2859, was shopped-out in February 1964. Closure followed in June.

More than 500 men, including 200 craftsmen, lost their jobs. Some had worked there all their lives. Boy apprentices had to be transferred but their resettlement was not a big problem since a railway career no longer had the appeal of years earlier and the railways had to advertise to try and fill apprentice vacancies.

The final payroll was only a third of the size it had been during the works' heyday in late Victorian years. Enthusiasts remember Stafford Road with affection as one more homely in size and different in atmosphere from Swindon; as one where small tanks, quaint and old, chugged in from remote lines in the Welsh borders to rub shoulders with *Stars* and *Saints*.

Equally a part of the GWR scene at Wolverhampton were the locomotive sheds at Stafford Road, and Oxley, opened 1907 for goods engines. Stafford Road was much the more historic, being opened originally as a four-road broad-gauge depot. It was extended to take narrow gauge engines in 1860.

ROAD COMPETITION

Tram and bus operators did not have things all their own way in the district. An omnibus service introduced in 1890 as a feeder between High Level station and Wolverhampton tram terminus lasted no more than a few days.

More successful was the GWR bus service between Wolverhampton and Bridgnorth. Control passed to Wolverhampton Corporation in 1923 and the service became heavily used when the RAF established a large training camp at Bridgnorth—one I reached by this route, as well as over the Severn Valley line from Shrewsbury.

Wolverhampton lost its electric trams in 1928 as bus routes spread. Their impact was shown in a GWR report of 1924 about Albrighton station :

Road Motor Buses from Wolverhampton run through the district and are materially affecting the receipts at the Station, there being a decrease of 5,000 passengers in 1924, compared with 1919.

Page 101 Mainline steam : (*above*) greatest of West Midland trunk routes was the West Coast, through the Trent Valley and north to Crewe and Scotland. The climb over the Trent and Mersey watershed at Whitmore often demanded double heading of heavy expresses. LNWR no 1527 *Raleigh* and Claughton no 1085 with an up Liverpool; (*below*) to see the signals drop and a King round the bend—unforgettable to those privileged to remember. Lapworth on a summer's day, no 6022 *King Edward III* with an up Birkenhead—Paddington, 16 August 1959

Page 102 (*above*) Rugeley was one of the most decorative stations in the Trent Valley, with tall eaves, ornate chimneys and canopy. Early shunting signals in foreground. The long Up platform dipped in the middle; (*below*) Cannock station 1969, before demolition. A typical LNWR branch station, substantial, functional, adequate, and, with ridge tiles and distinctive chimneys, slightly ornate

CHAPTER VI

Wolverhampton : LNWR and MR

BIRMINGHAM, WOLVERHAMPTON & STOUR VALLEY

The GJR section between Bushbury and Bescot is the only major stretch of mainline electrification not used by regular passenger trains. The reason is that it by-passes Wolverhampton, so much better served by the direct line engineered by the Birmingham, Wolverhampton & Stour Valley Railway, incorporated on 3 August 1846 as a 'fragment' of the original scheme of the Shrewsbury & Birmingham promoters, who, as noted, had a quarter stake in the new line. The Stour Valley was promoted as a main line from Birmingham New Street to the GJR at Bushbury or Show Hill, about 1½ miles from Wolverhampton. There was to be a branch from Dudley Port to Dudley, already an important industrial centre of the Black Country.

'Stour Valley' crept into the title because of a projected line from Smethwick through the Valley of Stourbridge and Stourport. As it was never authorised, the tag was always superfluous, yet even today it is the line's distinctive label. The SVR was not promoted in competition with other lines : its concept of joining the L & B and GJR meant that it was firmly in Euston hands from formation.

Capital came from two other sources besides the company itself and the S & B, equal shares being allocated to the Birmingham Canal Company, whose main line ran parallel, and local interests. The arrangement frustrated the ambitions of Euston, which wanted control of the line to improve its own network without interference, and also as a political weapon to delay GWR interests from creating a through route to the Mersey. Euston acquired control in two stages—by a closer financial and working agreement with the Canal company, and then by leasing the s vr in 1847.

It put the need to delay the gwr-inspired plans first at the cost of doing without the line itself. It could afford to delay construction because the line was to be, in effect, a duplicate one between Wolverhampton and Birmingham. Construction was undertaken in three sections: from Birmingham to Winson Green, near Smethwick, including an 845yd tunnel near New Street station; from Winson Green to Dunkirk, near Oldbury; and from there to Bushbury. Work began from Birmingham, and initially progress was brisk, Robert Stephenson and William Baker reporting in August 1847 that the Birmingham tunnel was more than one-third complete. Difficulties in acquiring land were delaying the section near Bushbury.

Eventually the line, stretching through the new High Level station at Wolverhampton, initially named Queen Street, reached the inspection stage in 1851.

A bitter fight between the lnwr and s & b began when Euston made no attempt to open the completed line. The s & b announced it would try to secure its legal right to use running powers by seeking Parliamentary authority to open the route, failing action by the owners. When they named 1 December 1852 as the opening date, the s & b stated it would run trains through to Birmingham. Euston retorted that the s & b no longer had access because it had amalgamated with the gwr. The s & b went to Chancery and won—but the North Western postponed the opening, claiming that there would be risks to the public if a hostile attempt, as it termed it, was made to use running powers. The danger would arise from trains colliding.

The s & b publicly announced that it was about to extend trains to Birmingham. It was an ill-considered move for its powers did not extend to New Street, which stood on the lnwr Birmingham Extension line, between the Stour Valley and the station. Then, fed up with legal deadlock, the s & b tried the use of force. In a well publicised attempt to reach New Street it dispatched a train from Wolverhampton High Level. A short distance away it came buffer to buffer with an lnwr locomotive, *Swift*, blocking the line. Hundreds of people watched. Police marched and troops were alerted, but this time things were more peaceful and lawyers took over from the police and issued writs. The lnwr agreed to review the position and the s & b agreed not to try and exercise its powers for a month.

The s & b had plenty of local sympathy, including that of Wolverhampton town council, and it launched a bill for authority to open the line itself and run into New Street. It received the unanimous approval of the Commons Committee despite opposition by the LNWR, but the situation changed when Euston opened the Stour Valley to its own goods traffic in February 1852, and to passengers 5 months later. It was a route with good traffic potential, having seven intermediate stations— Smethwick, Spon Lane, Oldbury & Bromford Lane, Dudley Port, Tipton, Deepfields, Ettingshall Road & Bilston.

Once the line was opened, the s & b withdrew plans for taking action itself and its access to New Street was legalised by Parliament.

LEGAL BATTLES DRAG ON

Euston accepted arbitration on several issues, knowing that it would drag on for months. It contended that it would be dangerous for s & b trains to use the Stour Valley, and to make sure they did not get access it introduced its own half-hourly local service from 1 March 1853. At the same time LNWR expresses using the GJR between Birmingham and Wolverhampton stopped calling at Wednesfield Heath and passengers had to change at Bushbury, which was even more inconvenient.

Privately, the LNWR directors passed resolutions of self-pity, complaining that Wolverhampton was still deprived of the advantage of the Stour Valley line. Yet really they cared not a hoot that the main victim of their power games was the man in the street, whose miserable standards of living could be improved as railways grew. The s & b was not blameless, but it was less blameworthy, for it was so easily, and wrongly, crushed when it sought to give the area the sort of railways that Parliament had considered necessary.

The s & b eventually accepted an arbitration award that fixed a heavy rent for the use of New Street from 4 February 1854. The injustice of the rent was later recognised by an Appeal Court, which set it aside. Something like 3 years had elapsed between the time s & b trains from Shrewsbury might have run through to Birmingham and the day they began. There must have been moments when the ordinary traveller questioned the view of iron masters and merchants that competition was the only means of providing a good rail service.

The Stour Valley was not a popular route for the early travellers, for there were no through bookings from Birmingham to s & b stations and no connections were made at Wolverhampton with Shrewsbury trains.

Omnibuses were used to take passengers between New Street and Snow Hill, one of the earliest known examples of rail–road coordination.

As the LNWR made life difficult for the s & b, a side issue led to a long drawn-out row. It concerned the construction of Wolverhampton High Level. Both companies had construction powers for the station, which they agreed to build jointly, and appointed a joint committee of six directors to manage it, and the line to Bushbury. The agreement was the legal instrument which gave Euston control of the line beside the canal near Victoria Basin when the s & b attempted to tranship goods. The agreement included an arbitration clause and this was invoked by the Shrewsbury company when Euston called for High Level station to be divided into separate sections—a move quite contrary to the Act. The s & b objected that costs would rise. Litigation followed the usual pattern, with the case going initially in favour of the bigger company, only to be reversed on appeal.

Relations between Euston and Paddington remained tender at Wolverhampton for years : for instance, after the races in 1872, Paddington complained that the North Western had put a temporary booking office in a position to intercept GWR passengers going to *Low Level* station.

WOLVERHAMPTON & CANNOCK CHASE RAILWAY

The Kingswinford branch was not the only line mooted locally in the present century, for another had been incorporated 4 years earlier : the Wolverhampton & Cannock Chase on 17 August 1901. It had powers for an 8 mile line from the GWR at Bushbury to the Cannock branch at Great Wyrley, and to join the LNWR at Bushbury and Heath Town. An extension of time was obtained in 1903, and in 1910 the company got a Light Railway Order and a further 4 year extension. Five years later the Light Railway

Commissioners ordered powers to be transferred to the LNWR and the company wound up.

WOLVERHAMPTON & WALSALL RAILWAY

While the LNWR and GWR dominated Wolverhampton, the Midland was there as well—though with the friendly consent of the LNWR. The Midland influence in the Birmingham area was strong from the earliest days and it had a respected place alongside the LNWR and GWR, if such were possible! It was second in seniority, with the GWR in third place. At Wolverhampton the Midland's standing was relatively minor; it got its foothold from schemes conceived during the period of peace that followed the final settlement of quarrels between the larger companies. It was then that companies began making improvements and filling gaps without having to put elaborate cases to Parliament. Noticeable gaps lay between Wolverhampton and Willenhall, a busy manufacturing town 3 miles to the east, and its more prominent neighbour, Walsall.

The promise of an end to tedious passenger journeys came with the incorporation of the Wolverhampton & Walsall Railway on 29 June 1865. The route of 8 miles took 7 years to build. Four intermediate Acts were necessary for modification or time extension, and one switched the junction at Wolverhampton from the GWR to the Stour Valley, mainly because the LNWR and Midland planned to work the W & W individually (not jointly) from its opening (1 November 1872). Stations were North Walsall, Bentley, Short Heath (Clark's Lane), Willenhall (Market Place), Wednesfield and Heath Town, where the line crossed the GJR tunnel.

The LNWR bought the W & W in 1875 and sold it a year later to the Midland, which had reached Walsall from the opposite direction with a line from Castle Bromwich, built by the Wolverhampton, Walsall & Midland Junction, authorised on 6 August 1872. Although the company was nominally independent it had strong ties with the Midland and an agreement of December 1872 led to the small company's absorption 2 years later.

There was a loud public outcry when people realised that the line was to run through part of Sutton Park. This was one of the earliest recorded objections to the desecration of natural beauty by ordinary people; usually they had come from wealthy land-owners anxious to keep railways out of sight of their stately homes. The objectors, however, were not dedicated to their cause, for they withdrew their case when it was found that the line would give them cheaper coal.

The Midland bought a 2 mile long strip in the Park for £6,500 and the result, claimed a local historian writing in the early 1970s was 'a horrible scar on the face of Sutton Park, only softened by the passage of time during the growth of many fine trees along its course'. But conquering Sutton Park was not the most costly part of the line.

'TROUBLE AND ANXIETY'

The contractor, Joseph Firbank, originally estimated the cost at £175,000, but it eventually doubled. The reasons were related by his biographer, Frederick McDermott:

> The works were so largely increased as operations proceeded that the ultimate cost was over £400,000. The aqueduct to carry the canal at Daw End was an awkward bit of work, but none of the operations were of a really serious nature. Mr. Firbank used, however, to say that, of all his contracts, this one gave him the most trouble and anxiety, on account of the vexatious and unnecessary interference of the Engineer—not one of the Midland Company's permanent officials —and his assistants, who, instead of doing all in their power to assist him in his labours—as other chief and resident engineers did—took every occasion to make suggestions, which were totally unnecessary, and added very heavily to the cost of the works. This conduct ultimately led to litigation, but, unfortunately, a clause in the specification appointed the Engineer sole arbitrator, without appeal from his decisions. The case could not thus be fairly gone into, or tried on its merits, and Lord Esher (then Lord Justice Brett), in the Court of Appeal, stated that, as long as men were foolish enough to sign a specification containing such a clause, it was useless for them to come to him for assistance. Mr Firbank was not, however, daunted by this rebuff, being firmly convinced that the right was on his side, and that justice would be done him if he could get the facts carefully and impartially looked into. This was finally done, and a compromise arranged, which, if it did not give him his due, fully cleared him in the eyes of the Midland Directors, whose good opinion he valued very highly.

The Midland opened the ww & m from Castle Bromwich to Walsall on 1 July 1879. Five intermediate stations—Penns, Sutton Coldfield, Sutton Park, Streetly and Aldridge—were served by trains between New Street and Wolverhampton High Level. They reversed in and out of Walsall, though through running, avoiding the station, was possible over a stretch opened at the same time between Lichfield Road and North Walsall junctions. From 1 January 1909 Midland trains were switched to the LNWR route between Walsall and Wolverhampton, and some LNWR services began using the Midland via Willenhall to avoid reversal.

The LNWR had opened its Wolverhampton–Walsall route on 1 March 1881 after the completion of two important curves—between the GJR and South Staffordshire line via Pleck, and between the GJR at Portobello and the Midland at Heath Town Junction (see p. 81).

The official *Midland Guide* dealt briefly with the Wolverhampton route, but it also noted the changing face of the town centre following the demolition of a number of small, tightly packed streets in the early 1880s.

> The town contains few public buildings of any importance, and its streets are as a rule somewhat narrow; but during recent years great improvements have been made in this respect and a fine new thoroughfare, leading from the Railway Station to Queen's Square, has been made.

BROWNHILLS BRANCH

Stemming from the Wolverhampton line was an important branch of $5\frac{1}{4}$ miles from Aldridge to Norton Canes, where it joined the Cannock Chase & Wolverhampton Railway and colliery lines. It was authorised in two stages—from Aldridge to Walsall Wood (the Brownhills branch) in 1876, and to Cannock 4 years later. Completion was more closely spaced, the branch being opened for goods from Aldridge to Brownhills in April 1882 and throughout in November. A passenger service between Aldridge and Brownhills (never extended) began in 1884, with an intermediate station at Walsall Wood. Brownhills subsequently had 'Watling Street' added to its title. Its position, $\frac{1}{2}$ mile from even the outskirts of the town, was isolated, and it was little used because there was a well situated station on the Walsall–Lichfield line.

But the branch was not built mainly for passengers; coal was to be its staple trade, for it served five big pits whose output was so great that the branch was double tracked. The Brownhills branch was closed to passengers 7 years after grouping, and 9 months later a similar economy was made on the Wolverhampton–Walsall route. The traffic on the northern section of the Brownhills branch declined as pits closed, and it was reported in the autumn of 1960 that the branch had been lifted north of Walsall Wood, through Brownhills, to Conduit Colliery.

Passenger trains were withdrawn between Birmingham and Walsall via Sutton Park on 18 January 1965, but the line survives for freight, retaining a double facing junction at Castle Bromwich. After the passenger economy was made, mail trains continued to call at Sutton Park.

West of Walsall the line was cut at Birchills on 28 September 1964 to make way for the M6 Motorway. The middle section of something less than 3 miles was lifted, but freight is still worked over two sections now singled: Ryecroft Junction–Birchills power station, and Heath Town Junction–Noose Lane, Willenhall.

The latter section was closed from 4 October 1965 until 1970, when it was reopened to serve a large works built by the Weldless Steel Tube Company at Wednesfield. It is used by block trains from Round Oak steelworks. At Wednesbury, the original embankment, 8ft high, was tapered to the works sidings at ground level.

WOLVERHAMPTON RAILWAYS TODAY

Modernisation had a profound effect on the railway system at Wolverhampton, for, while the BW & D was eventually severed, the town became more 'electrified' than Birmingham in the sense that three of its four routes were energised—to Birmingham; to Stafford and the north; and to Walsall, though this line does not carry a passenger service. Only the Shrewsbury line is diesel-operated. Electrification involved the conversion of the GJR south from Bushbury, and it is often used as a diversionary route by Inter-City expresses, which can reach Wolverhampton station over the 'loop' between Stour Valley and Portobello Junctions, via Heath Town. A second link between the GJR and the Stour

Valley in the short distance between Birmingham and Wolver-hampton is provided by the energised Soho line.

Since the completion of the original mainline scheme, two short stretches of line have been converted: the already noted extension to Oxley carriage sidings, and the branch of 50 chains from Monmore Green to Wolverhampton Steel Terminal (for-merly, Walsall Street Goods). The latter is also used by block trains to the British Oxygen Company depot opened on 24 September 1971, and there is access to both depots from the BW & D near Priestfield.

'A GREAT RAILWAY TOWN'

When Wolverhampton 'went electric', an exhibition about its railways, 1837–1966, was held at Bushbury Community Centre. While modest in scope, it sought to express the great pride the town felt in its connections with railways. As the steam era ended, it was marked by moments of sentiment. The GJR's arrival in 1837 was noted as a date of importance which disregarded the ill-feeling there had been in civic circles about the puny station at Wednesfield Heath.

The souvenir programme of the exhibition reflected that the works at Stafford Road and the motive power depot at Bushbury had gone, soon to be followed by Oxley power depot. 'Wolver-hampton will then return to being merely one more town passed through en route to London—a far cry from its days as one of the great railway towns of Britain.'

Wolverhampton was left with its electric railways, whose coaches were clean and airy, but many travellers looking out through the carriage window were disturbed by the sight of embankments strewn with rubbish. The chairman of Wolver-hampton Civic Society, Eric Robinson, called for 1972 to be a 'railway clean-up year'. He attacked railway slums throughout Britain, pointing out that they were the first impression a native or foreign traveller has of a place, and asked: 'Is it any wonder that a town like Wolverhampton has such a reputation when the railway area is so foul?'

CHAPTER VII

Black Country Routes

RAILWAYS OF STOURBRIDGE

Wolverhampton's direct link with Stourbridge via the ow & w never developed intensively for passengers. Besides tram and bus competition in later years, Stourbridge and the intermediate towns, including Dudley, were very much self-contained. Stourbridge was a flourishing centre of the glass industry long before railways and the growth of heavy industry made it one of the most prosperous towns on the Black Country fringe. The needs of different industries were met first by barges using the River Severn to Stourport, and by canals, for which rail feeders were developed. There were several private lines locally before the arrival of the ow & w main line, notably the Shut End Railway, and also the Dennis Railroad, built in 1829 with an inclined plane to run through the Dennis Valley to 'Coalbourn-brook depository'.

The Shut End Railway opened the same year 'amidst an immense concourse of spectators from the surrounding country'. The 3 miles between the Staffordshire & Worcestershire Canal at Ashwood Basin and Lord Dudley's colliery at Shut End remained unaltered, apart from additional sidings, for more than 20 years. The railway complex grew from the mid-1850s, with extensions crossing Pensnett Chase to Brierley Hill and other places. It handled a wealth of minerals mined and quarried locally—coal, iron and limestone, and sand.

The railway, owned by Lord Dudley, was known under several names, of which the most permanent became the Pensnett Railway. It had three connections with the GWR—at Round Oak (at the centre of the complex); at Cradley Heath (on the southern extremity); and at Askew Bridge (Baggeridge Junction), opened in 1875 on what was later extended to be the Kingswinford branch. In their detailed book, *A History of the Pensnett Railway* (1969), W. K. V. Gale and T. M. Hoskison stated that it had been intended to make the last junction many years earlier, but the branch was not completed that far north because of the uncertain fortunes of the ow & w and, later, the West Midland Railway.

In its heyday, the Pensnett Railway employed 150 men and boys. It declined steadily as road competition increased and $3\frac{1}{2}$ miles linking Round Oak steelworks with Baggeridge closed in September 1966—3 years after the railway switched from steam to diesel. A section remains as part of the internal system of Round Oak steelworks and Old Park Engineering at Holly Hall.

Through its inheritance of the Shut End Railway, the Pensnett may have been the most historic of local lines, but it was the GWR which took control of major lines in the district. Although the ow & w virtually put Stourbridge on its main line, other companies attempted to reach it. The original Stour Valley plans included an extension from Oldbury, and also one to Dudley and Halesowen. This was preferred by the Commons to plans by the Oxford company to reach Halesowen with a branch from Dudley, but the Lords rejected the Stour Valley proposals—a decision that led to Paddington gaining firm command of a wide area.

The LNWR revived in 1853 a plan by the Shrewsbury & Birmingham for a branch to Stourbridge and was prepared to pay the high price of £33,000 a mile for the $8\frac{1}{2}$ miles, confident of a 'very handsome profit'; but it would not meet Parliament's 'price', which specified that if the branch was built, the ow & w was to have running powers, not only over the line itself but into New Street via the Stour Valley.

The GWR *Guide* of 1860 regarded Stourbridge's belching chimneys as proud symbols of the industrial age. Plans to extend the local network were influenced by the formation of the West Midland Railway. Among six lines in which it held interests was the Stourbridge Railway, incorporated on 14 June 1860 to build from the ow & w at Stourbridge to Old Hill, $3\frac{1}{2}$ miles along a natural route towards Birmingham, with two short branches. Despite the local nature of its title, the Stourbridge Railway was conceived as an alternative link between Birmingham and Worcester, where it had its head office. Just over a year later it was given authority for a 5 mile extension from Old Hill to the Stour Valley line at Smethwick.

Construction was straightforward and the first $2\frac{1}{4}$ miles to Cradley were opened by the West Midland on 1 April 1863, together with a $\frac{1}{2}$ mile branch to Corngreaves Colliery. Two months later another short branch of $\frac{3}{4}$ mile was opened from Lye to a goods station at Hayes Lane and also to serve pits. The 'main' line section from Cradley to Old Hill was ready by 1866, and the Stour Valley was reached at Galton Junction in the following April; the line then continued west to the GWR at Handsworth to give Stourbridge a passenger link with Snow Hill as well as New Street. This connection replaced a tenuous link via Dudley and an indirect one used by through trains that reversed at Wolverhampton.

The direct line by-passed Dudley, but this situation had been remedied when the GWR built a $1\frac{1}{2}$ mile line from the BW & D at Swan Village to the LNWR South Staffordshire line at Horsley Fields Junction in 1866. The GWR used running powers from there to Dudley. An intermediate station was opened at Great Bridge between Swan Village and Dudley Port, and a short branch opened at the same time served Swan Village canal basin.

STOURBRIDGE TOWN BRANCH

Despite the new lines, the rail network at Stourbridge was not quite satisfactory, for the station was some distance from the town centre and in 1865, the Stourbridge Railway got powers for a branch of little more than a mile, but they lapsed before construction could begin. The GWR got a fresh Act in 1874, yet 5 years passed before completion, when the OW & W station was renamed Stourbridge Junction. The branch was altered and extended in 1901, when a new station with two island platforms was opened at the Junction about $\frac{1}{4}$ mile south of the original. This could not be improved because the branches to Town station and Birmingham turned away too close to the platform ends.

The Stourbridge Railway was never well known, but it achieved one piece of notoriety during its short life through W. T. Adcock, who became secretary and superintendent when the West Midland company merged. After he disappeared in 1870 it was found

that he had issued false stock worth £52,000, probably having
noted the example of Redpath of the Great Northern.

DUDLEY & OLDBURY JUNCTION

Besides by-passing Dudley, the Stourbridge direct line also passed
wide of another important town—Oldbury. Even though it was
served by the Stour Valley, there was agitation for a second line,
stretching 1½ miles from Langley Green and involving three canal
crossings. First initiative came from a private company, compre-
hensively called the Dudley & Oldbury Junction Railway. It was
incorporated in 1873 and 3 years later the GWR agreed to work it.
Five years later still the company became the Oldbury Railway,
opened to goods in 1884 and passengers in the following year. It
amalgamated with the GWR in 1894, and was closed to passengers
in 1915. In essence the Oldbury branch was a freight line and
so it has remained, about a third surviving to feed block trains
of 100 ton tank wagons in and out of a large tar distillery, where
new sidings and pipelines handle up to 50,000 tons of crude oil
a year imported through Immingham.

Cradley developed into a busy freight junction on the opening
in 1907 of the Spinner's End branch. Cradley goods yard also
gave access to the Pensnett Railway.

Railways around Stourbridge have been pruned as well as
uprooted. Two severe losses were the closures of Stourbridge
Junction locomotive shed (known locally as Amblecote) and the
marshalling yard at the junction; announced in 1965, the second
economy came only 5 weeks after, it was claimed locally,
improvements costing £45,000 had been completed. More than
200 men lost their jobs and others did so when the sheds were
closed and the site cleared for houses. The roundhouse of twenty-
eight pits had been opened in 1926 to replace a small straight
shed that was then used for railmotors. Reception roads in the
roundhouse were known as Newquay and Klondyke. Their
passing was well recorded by a former driver, Alderman Harry
Hardwick, a former mayor of the town:

> There were times when some of the men would describe the place
> in unprintable terms. There were times when something went wrong
> or when they were hauled before the boss for some misdemeanour,
> but at heart one can be sure that most former drivers and firemen

were proud to have worked at the Amblecote shed. Certainly whenever they got together, be it on the footplate or off-duty, the main point of conversation revolved round engines and trains, shed and timetable. Call it talking shop if you like, but the fact remains that both drivers and firemen took much pride in their jobs.

Stourbridge's importance as a freight centre dwindled when the goods branch, which ran into its heart for a short distance beyond Town station to a depot and the canal basin, was closed in 1965.

When cuts were proposed in 1968 in the local diesel service to Birmingham because of heavy financial losses, there were fears that thousands of workers might have to give up their jobs in Birmingham, and local MPs had hurried talks with management. When the Shrewsbury and Wolverhampton locals were threatened with withdrawal in 1971, the Stourbridge locals were left as the last of the original GWR services in the Region not under such a threat. But they were heavily subsidised; the 1971 total of £146,000 included the route through to Kidderminster. It was an average subsidy for such a service, for the smallest in the London Midland Region that year was £37,000, to maintain the one-coach connecting service on the Town branch.

Today the Stourbridge line bisects a newly created area—the County Borough of Warley, formed on 1 April 1966 from the towns of Smethwick, Oldbury and Rowley Regis, and taking in Langley, Cradley and Blackheath. In 1969 the population of Warley was 168,970.

RAILWAYS OF HALESOWEN

Halesowen, a small town sandwiched between Stourbridge, Dudley and Birmingham, grew dramatically during the Industrial Revolution, and the first major outlet for its heavy products was a canal from Netherton, near Dudley, to Selly Oak. The Stourbridge line missed Halesowen, quite naturally, passing $1\frac{1}{2}$ miles to the north at Old Hill, where it cut through high ground. A short branch was needed and the first scheme was quite ambitious: the Halesowen & Bromsgrove Branch Railway to join the Birmingham & Gloucester. It was authorised in 1865, with a branch to Longbridge providing a second connection with the Midland. It was to be worked jointly by the Midland and the GWR, the latter having inherited powers secured by the West Midland in 1862 for a branch to the H & BR from Old Hill, and another from there north to Netherton (later Blowers Green), just under 3 miles away. They opened together on 1 March 1878, and although there was no through running, for the junctions at Old Hill both faced east, they were referred to locally as one —the Dudley & Halesowen Railway.

The *Dudley Herald* reported :

> The line has been constructed amid great difficulties and at great expense, in consequence of so large a number of bridges having to be erected through the mining operations in the district . . . The new station at Old Hill is now completed, and is one of the best stations, as a junction, in the Midland Counties.

A reader signing himself *Veritas* wrote to say the line would be a great boon and that eventually, Halesowen would become the Wolverhampton of the Black Country.

Although the route was popular with passengers (2,000 went to Dudley on the first Saturday), it was mainly a goods line, and in the following year a branch was opened to Withymoor Basin (later Netherton) goods. A half-mile branch to Halesowen Basin was born in circumstances similar to those of the branch to Stourbridge Town, being conceived by one company and built by another. The line to the Basin was originally authorised by an Act of 1862, one of the few obtained by the West Midland Railway during its short existence. Nothing was done and it was left to the GWR to secure fresh powers in 1898. The branch was opened in 1902.

There was an appreciable time lag, too, between the authorisation of the Halesowen Branch Railway and its opening. The first move, made 5 years after incorporation, was the abandoning, in 1870, of the branch from Halesowen to Bromsgrove and the concentration of effort on reaching the Midland at Northfield. The MR and GWR agreed working arrangements but no start had been made on construction by the time the company changed its title to The Halesowen Railway in 1876. By the spring of 1882 the line between Halesowen and Northfield was approved by the Board of Trade, yet it did not open until the autumn of the following year. The single line had stations at Hunnington and Rubery. It was vested in its joint operators in 1906.

Traffic receipts were reaching £6,000 and after the deduction of half for operation, dividends of about 6 per cent were paid annually on about a quarter of the 250,000 issued shares.

Passenger traffic was dominated by a single factory: the Austin Motor works at Longbridge, $\frac{1}{4}$ mile from the main line at Northfield. The first siding for the works was opened sometime during 1915, and a platform on the Halesowen branch early in that year, probably February. Platforms on the up main line (the Bristol & Gloucester route) between the end of Cofton Tunnel and Halesowen Junction were brought into use in 1917. Workmen's specials used the branch platform for some 40 years after the regular locals were withdrawn. They ceased between Halesowen and Northfields in April 1919 and on the 'leg' between Halesowen and Old Hill 8 years later. The Old Hill workmen's service ran until 1958, and that between Halesowen and Northfield until 1964. The section included the steel trestle viaduct at Dowry Dell, demolished in 1965 (see page 170).

Old Hill lost its status as a junction when the motor trains were withdrawn in 1964 on the Dudley branch. There was little mourning, little ceremony. The guard of the 6.30 pm from Old Hill on the last day was quoted as saying: 'If we get one passenger on this particular train, that's as many as we'll ever get. We may get him twice a week and he usually gets off at Windmill End.'

SOUTH STAFFORDSHIRE RAILWAY

Nobody will agree on the boundaries of the Black Country, but broadly it is fringed by the four big towns of Wolverhampton, Walsall, Smethwick and Stourbridge. Casual travellers cannot be sure which town or village is which, for one flows into the other, but the area does include the southern half of the South Staffordshire Coalfield. The northern part is centred on Cannock Chase.

One line above all others pierced what is clearly identifiable as the heart of the Black Country: the South Staffordshire Railway. It was authorised by Parliament at the same time as the Stour Valley and other schemes, including the Birmingham, Wolverhampton & Dudley. But, unlike those, it met little opposition. It was conceived as a cross-country route through the region

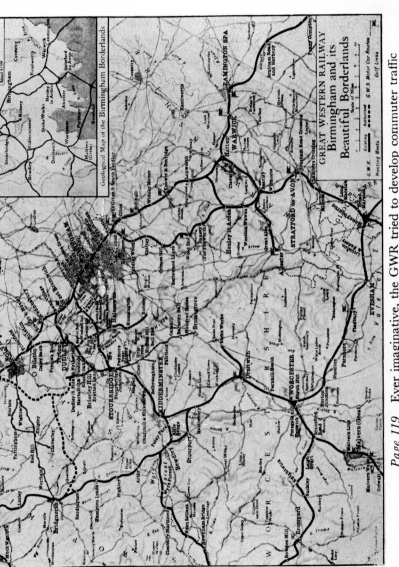

Page 119 Ever imaginative, the GWR tried to develop commuter traffic amid 'Birmingham and its Beautiful Borderlands'. A map of 1914 shows the authorised Kingswinford branch and that to Bridgnorth

Page 120 (*above*) Oxley yard was the regional goods hub of the GWR, for it had nothing comparable at Birmingham. An undated photograph of an outside frame 0–6–0 shunting at the Shrewsbury end of the yard. Coaches include four-wheelers; (*below*) Oxley in later years. The scene about grouping with saddle tanks in charge of shunting

as an alternative to the Derby–Birmingham–Gloucester route, and was advanced as the Midland Railway was struggling to get control of the area from Burton to Walsall and Dudley. The Midland's aspirations were closely watched by the LNWR, which was anxious to reach Walsall from Birmingham, and also serve the South Staffordshire coalfield and its busy towns of Wednesbury and Dudley.

The SSR was formed by an amalgamation of the SS Junction and the Trent Valley, Midlands & Grand Junction companies, both incorporated in 1846. They had powers to construct lines from the OW & W at Dudley to an end-on junction with the TVM & GJ at Walsall (Albert Street), and on to the Midland at Wichnor. There were to be spurs from Pleck to James Bridge (later Darlaston), to the Grand Junction at Bescot, and to the Trent Valley at Lichfield. Several other SSJ branches were planned but none was built.

As authorised by their Acts, the two companies amalgamated, and a new board adopted the title of South Staffordshire Railway Company on 6 October 1846. Originally the TVM & GJ had received stronger backing, having been promoted by a provisional committee of no less than forty-two directors, including four MPs, George Hudson among them.

The biggest clash of interests developed at the western end of the route because the BW & D (incorporated the same day) was given powers to reach Dudley from Swan Village if the SSJ failed to do so by 1 November 1849. In any event, the BW & D was to have running powers to Dudley, the SSJ getting in return access to Wolverhampton via the BW & D between Wednesbury and Priestfield.

Dudley had long been a source of dispute between the London & Birmingham and the GWR when they discussed common boundaries. The LNWR chairman, Glyn, related the L & B version to shareholders in February 1846 :

A line of demarcation was drawn by the negotiators [*sic*], as to the districts of the Companies; and though a proper line, I confess that when I first saw it we looked very *thin*—but we were willing to give up something, and accordingly we adopted the line of demarcation referred to. And what, think you, did they want? That we should give up to them the town of Dudley, that we should throw the traffic on to their line—and that Dudley should not have the advantage of a straight line to Birmingham and on to London, but go round by Worcester! They did not ask us to negotiate after *that*.

The Dudley clause inserted in the SSJ Act set the scene for a potential broad-gauge battle. The SSJ board consisted of three groups, representing the LNWR, the MR and independent shareholders, a trio of interests dedicated to defeating any broad-gauge incursions. And that possibility became stronger when the BW & D was vested in the GWR in 1848.

RACE TO DUDLEY

Completion to Dudley was a close-run thing, and on the day of the deadline in 1849 the SSR was forced to run a special from Pleck to Dudley, a section on which stations were far from complete. Regular goods services did not begin until the following March. Dudley station had not been finished by the time passenger trains began running 2 months later, and for a short time trains used a temporary station—a platform adjoining the goods shed.

A colourful picture of early days on the SSR was provided in his *Railway Reminiscences*, by G. P. Neele, who was appointed the company's first chief clerk after failing to get the post of general manager. That job went to J. D. Payne of the Birmingham & Gloucester, who had caused deliberate chaos when the Gauge Commissioners visited Gloucester to watch the transshipment of goods from broad to narrow wagons.

Neele recalled that the temporary platform at Dudley was followed by another—

> . . . of a sadly inefficient type nearer the town; and adjacent, nearly side by side but without any direct connecting line, was the equally shabby shedding that did duty for the Dudley station of the OW & W. Numerous suggestions were made for constructing a joint station, but to no avail. Years passed by, and the same unsightly and disjointed buildings remained as the passenger station. At length a fire broke out in the premises, and the inhabitants of Dudley may thank it for the existing structure.

The Dudley section was not the first part of the SSR to be completed, for 1¾ miles were opened in 1847 from Bescot to Walsall, where there was a temporary terminus in Bridgeman

SOUTH STAFFORDSHIRE RAILWAY,

BETWEEN BIRMINGHAM AND THE TOWN OF WALSALL.

For the CONVEYANCE of PASSENGERS and PARCELS.

TRAINS,

On and after the 1st of December next.

DEPARTURE FROM BIRMINGHAM TO WALSALL.	1st & 2nd Class. A. M.	1st & 2nd Class. A. M.	1st & 2nd Class. P. M.	1st & 2nd Class. P. M.
	9 0	11 0	4 0	7 15
DEPARTURE FROM WALSALL TO BIRMINGHAM.	1st & 2nd Class. A. M.	1st & 2nd Class. A. M.	1st & 2nd Class. P. M.	1st & 2nd Class. P. M.
	9 50	11 30	4 45	8 0

In connection with Trains to and from London.

SUNDAY TRAINS.

DEPARTURE FROM Birmingham TO Walsall.	1st & 2nd Class. A. M.	1st & 2nd Class. P. M.	DEPARTURE FROM Walsall TO Birmingham.	1st & 2nd Class. A. M.	1st & 2nd Class. P. M.
	8 40	7 15		9 40	8 0

FARES.

BIRMINGHAM to WALSALL, WALSALL to BIRMINGHAM, } First Class, 1s. 6d.; Second Class, 1s.

RETURN TICKETS.—First Class, 2s. 6d.; Second Class, 1s. 6d.

Children under 10 Years of Age Half-price.—Children in Arms unable to Walk, pass Free.

RETURN TICKETS issued on SATURDAY, will be available up to the MONDAY NIGHT following.

PARCELS, (under 15lbs. including Delivery, immediately on the arrival of each Train,) 4d. Exceeding 15lbs. ½d. per lb.

First & Second Class Passengers allowed to carry Luggage not exceeding 100lbs. weight.

South Staffordshire Railway Station, Bridgeman-Place, Walsall, 20th November, 1847.

J. R. ROBINSON, ALBION OFFICE, DIGBETH, WALSALL.

Train services three weeks after the opening of the first part of the South Staffordshire Railway, 1 November 1847. Half fares were restricted to children under ten

Place. Walsall's original station, 2 miles away on the Grand Junction, reverted to its original name of Bescot Bridge.

The bulk of the line—the $17\frac{1}{4}$ miles from Walsall to Wichnor —opened on 9 April 1849, the SSR having running powers to Burton. The temporary Walsall station was replaced, and others were opened at Rushall, Pelsall, Brownhills, Hammerwich and Lichfield. Another at Trent Valley Junction followed in August. In that railway age, there was little novel about the opening of such a line but it involved a lot of preparations forgotten today. For, as Neele wrote,

> The preparations and issue of announcements of the opening of the line—the posters, the time-tables, the calculation of fares, the supply of clothing and stores, the obtaining of the needful forms for accounts, the train marshalling, the trial trips, the placing of men at their various points of duty, all these kept us fully employed; but at length, the line having been inspected by Captain Wynne, the opening was an accomplished fact, and a dinner at Lichfield, with a ball at the Guildhall, distinguished our opening day.

There was not always harmony between the three groups of the SSR board, and by 1850 it was split over a proposal by the independent members to lease the line. The LNWR and MR interests opposed the move and it was twice rejected by shareholders. Their attitude changed when the LNWR and MR refused to guarantee dividends, and the company was leased by the engineer, John Robinson McClean, for an exceptionally lengthy period of 21 years to 1871. The Act giving authority was the first for a lease to an individual passed by Parliament. During McClean's lease the head office remained at Lichfield, and he worked from Walsall.

Neele described McClean as 'a man of restless enterprise : not only was he engineer of the broad gauge line between Wolverhampton and Birmingham, but he was also the active originator and engineer of the South Staffordshire Water Works Company'.

The terms of the SSR lease provided for a clear dividend (less income tax) of 2 per cent for the first year, and twice that afterwards, eventually increasing to 5 per cent after 14 years. McClean had to deposit £10,000 to guarantee that he would carry out the contract.

The South Staffordshire always realised that the completion of the Stour Valley route would greatly reduce its Dudley traffic, and in 1851 it obtained authority for a $\frac{1}{2}$ mile spur from Sedgeley Junction to Dudley Port. Opened in 1854, construction was coupled with running powers between Dudley Port (High Level) and Dudley. In contrast, there was no direct link with the BW & D, which crossed above it at Wednesbury, and Neele noted : 'The want of junctions and the difference of gauge then existing kept the Great Western aliens to us'.

EXTENSION TO CANNOCK COALFIELD

McClean was responsible for the next development of the SSR, for once he found coal under Cannock Chase, he personally obtained valuable mining concessions from the Marquis of Anglesea. As lessee of the railway, McClean found himself in an embarrassing position when the GWR went to Parliament in 1852 for powers to lay a third rail between Wednesbury and Dudley. It was rejected, as was a further attempt 2 years later. McClean opposed the GWR, even though at that time he was building the BW & D.

The GWR was no more successful when it tried to carry the broad gauge into the Cannock coalfield, Parliament preferring the SSR alternative of a 7 mile branch from Walsall to Cannock and one of 3 miles to Norton, approved together in 1854.

At this time relations between the shareholders and the LNWR grew closer because of the fear of a Midland take-over. The branches opened in 1858, having stations at Bloxwich, Wyrley & Church Bridge and Cannock. LNWR interest in the district increased and the chairman, Moon, toured the new lines in an engine.

The fate of the SSR for many years to come was sealed when McClean relinquished his lease in 1861, when it had 10 years to run, and it was transferred to the LNWR. Soon Euston clashed with its erstwhile friend, the Midland, when it attempted to use the SSR's original freight running powers to reach Burton. This action led to one of those personal battles, delicious and bloodless, which are the interesting punctuations of railway history. This time the LNWR found itself in the unusual role of challenger rather than defender. Neele relates the battle at Wichnor :

> I came down from Birmingham in charge of the first train. Arrived at Wichnor Junction I was surprised to see a large number of plate-

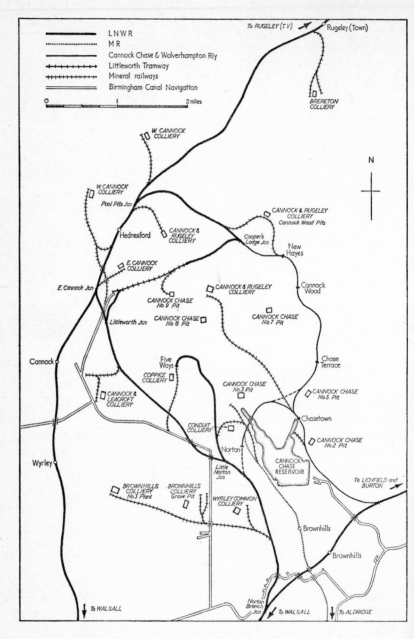

The extensive Cannock Coalfield became a magnet for railway promoters. The LNWR and Midland were successful, but the GWR was left in the cold

layers about, two or three engines in steam. One of the engines had attached to its tender the V crossing of the junction. I drew forward on our engine as far as safety allowed, claiming to proceed. This was again refused; there was nothing to be done but to retire.

In the same afternoon, the Midland relented and the LNWR made 'a triumphal journey towards Burton, the engine driver taking the opportunity of sounding noisy and repeated cock crows on his steam whistle'.

Having established the most valuable rights, Euston soon exploited them. Goods trains began running to Burton in December 1861 and less than a month later to Derby, clearly the more important traffic centre in Euston's eyes, for it had opened its own goods depot there in July 1861 with a stationmaster, passenger department—and shunting engine.

Not many towns got two replacement stations at once, but it happened at Lichfield in 1871 when the original Trent Valley Junction station was replaced by one about $\frac{1}{4}$ mile further south, and the original SSR station was closed and a new one opened a little further west.

LNWR BRANCHES

Wolverhampton–Walsall trains ran over the GJR via Darlaston, once the junction of a branch, almost half moon in shape, to the SSR at Wednesbury. It was one of two legacies of that company which the LNWR built between 1861, when it leased the SSR, and 1867, when it absorbed it. The line from Darlaston (James Bridge in those days) was authorised on 23 July 1855 and sustained by a 2 year extension of construction time from 1859. The line joined the SSR just north of Wednesbury station. The second line —the Princes End branch—left the system a similar distance to the south and ran $2\frac{3}{4}$ miles through Ocker Hill and Princes End to the Stour Valley at Bloomfield Junction, Tipton—just south of the OW & W spur.

The SSR Act contained powers for goods branches of just over 2 miles to Walsall Wood and of half that distance to Wyrley. One of just over a mile was built from north of Pelsall to Walsall Wood Colliery, and another from south of Pelsall to Aldridge Colliery. Both collieries were served by the Midland's Brownhills branch.

The other branches were opened at the same time in 1863 and

were complemented by a new station at Wednesbury. Freight traffic was heavy and the Darlaston branch was also notable for the intensity of its original passenger services, which declined quickly once tramway systems were built. The branch had fifty-six trains running daily between Darlaston and Wednesbury. In 1877 fifteen trains a day ran between Darlaston and James Bridge, while almost as many ran the opposite half from Darlaston to Wednesbury. Ten years later they were withdrawn after a progressive decline, and 5 years later still the Darlaston Local Board reacted strongly against the withdrawals and embarked on what became two classic cases of railway law. The Board applied to the Railway Commissioners to have the service restored. They agreed, but as their decision meant the LNWR would have to rebuild a station which had been demolished, an appeal was made to the High Court, which ruled that the Commissioners had no power to make the order.

The LNWR was taken to the High Court by the Darlaston Local Board in December 1893 and it again successfully defended itself against a claim for a service to meet every train each way at either end of the branch. The Court ruled that while it was impossible to say that the LNWR had not violated the Act by withdrawing passenger trains, people could not expect to have them unless the railway company chose for their own purpose to provide them.

The Princes End line was used by through Walsall–Wolverhampton trains that used the Stour Valley until the opening of the direct line after the construction of the Pleck and Portobello curves in 1881. The original branch service of some seven trains each way was more than halved soon afterwards, and they were withdrawn in 1890. They were restored 5 years later after a successful pressure campaign by local authorities, and the two intermediate stations, still *in situ*, were reopened.

The three trains each way on weekdays between Wednesbury and Dudley Port (High Level) were withdrawn as a wartime economy in 1916, the only LNWR passenger closure regionally between the turn of the century and grouping. The line survived for goods until 1958.

Walsall was something of a 'grand junction' of the South Staffordshire system, for of eight passenger services, seven survived until the mid-1960s, using some part of the SSR to reach the station. Apart from those over the whole of the route to

Dudley and Lichfield, there were others to Wolverhampton via the GJR; to Rugeley; to Birmingham, via Sutton Park; and to Birmingham via Aston and Bescot. Former SSR services were withdrawn within a few months—between Walsall and Dudley in May 1964; between Dudley Port (High Level) and Dudley, a steam pull-and-push service, 2 months later; and between Wolverhampton (High Level)–Walsall–Burton the following January.

Walsall station, now used by the Birmingham electrics, is of late LNWR vintage. With its round high-ceilinged hall, it is a building of distinctive character, far more striking than many of the concrete stations of electrification; but in the early 1970s it forfeited any claim to charm by its shoddy run-down state.

Although almost shorn of its passenger services, the SSR remains a busy freight artery piercing (as a through route) and feeding (through spurs to the GJR and BW & D) heavily industrialised areas.

CANNOCK MINERAL RAILWAY

The Cannock coalfield was also served by the Cannock Mineral Railway, which the LNWR snatched from under the nose of the North Staffordshire Railway. The CMR could trace its ancestry back to the Derbyshire, Staffordshire & Worcestershire Junction Railway, which was the third in the field (with the SSJ and the Trent Valley, Midlands & Grand Junction), in attempting to promote a link between Dudley and Walsall, although it was more ambitious, aiming to drive north to Cannock Chase and the NSR at Uttoxeter. It had visions of forming an important part of a through route between the Black Country and Manchester, via the Churnet Valley line, but the NSR was not interested.

The route was engineered by Sir John Rennie and also George Remington, who admitted to a Select Committee in 1846 that he had never laid a line through such a thinly populated district, although he expected that there would be great passenger traffic between Wednesbury and other towns. He confessed that he did not know if there was a great connection between the people of the Potteries and Wednesbury and other towns, even though passenger traffic between the two areas was being relied upon as one of the main sources of profit. Cannock Chase, he pointed out, was 'by no means more unpopulated' than Chat Moss on the Liverpool & Manchester. The DSWJ would be a source of great profit to shareholders and an advantage to the public.

The Bill was rejected by the Lords but the company applied in the next session for a modified route of 18¼ miles between Cannock and the Trent Valley at Rugeley. It was authorised in 1847, utilising a glacial valley running diagonally across the Chase from Hednesford to Rugeley, close to developing collieries. Construction was not begun, but in 1855 the company changed its name to the Cannock Mineral Railway. It was to run from Cannock, where the company was to reduce expenditure by sharing the SSR station, to Rugeley; the section to Uttoxeter was abandoned. Capital of £160,000 was backed by loan power of £40,000.

NSR TAKE-OVER ATTEMPT

Although the Act included powers to lease to the LNWR, the engineer, John Addison, secretly approached the NSR, which received him cordially. Addison proposed on 9 February 1856 that the North Staffordshire should maintain and work the CMR for 50 per cent of gross receipts, claiming it would give the NSR new local traffic and an independent outlet from the Potteries to southern England. He estimated surplus annual profits, which the companies would share, at a minimum of £2,660. The NSR would get an extension to its system without any guarantee or charge on fixed resources, and clearly with prospects of gain.

Despite NSR support, the Commons rejected the Cannock Bill. Not easily defeated, both companies agreed in October of that year to seek powers in the next session for a double line from Flaxley Green to Cannock. The original route was to be altered to join the NSR instead of the Trent Valley at Rugeley. There were also plans for an extension to Wolverhampton. The NSR was to have a 5–4 majority on the Cannock board under the agreement, proposed by the Cannock's chairman, William Malins of London.

When it was reported to the NSR on 10 March 1857 that the Cannock was unable either to carry out the agreement or prosecute its Bills in Parliament, the NSR offered to do so, providing the undertaking was transferred. The NSR immediately planned an extension from Colwich to Wolverhampton, but 2 months later the directors were shocked to hear that the CMR had signed an agreement with the LNWR. The Commons refused even to hear the NSR evidence against the Cannock Bill.

The NSR directors then decided there was no merit in spending money fighting a lost cause and in July agreed to the deputy chairman and other directors resigning from the CMR board, as its new chairman had requested. Euston had snatched victory by offering a slightly better guarantee of 5 per cent.

The line was built by Thomas Brassey, who completed it 5 months ahead of the original forecast. The LNWR lease, effective from the opening in 1859, was one which Euston had negotiated very much on its own terms. It absolved the company from any extraordinary expenses of maintenance arising from mining operations where the company had failed to purchase the minerals. The LNWR appointed five of the nine directors. The rent would be reduced to £5,000 a year if another line was opened between Colwich and anywhere near Cannock. The CMR was not vested in the LNWR until 1869, but it was in command long before. Neele noted that the solitude of the Chase was welcomed by railwaymen :

> The heathery banks and undulating slopes had been an attractive sight for travellers by the railway. Their deserted solitude had, however, proved attractive to some of the company's servants for a different purpose. Mysterious robberies of goods were constantly taking place, and all the police talent failed to detect the thieves until they, as usual, fell out among themselves, and then mysteriously disappeared. The guard, fireman, and driver of the night goods train systematically stopped opposite the wildest part of the chase, rifled the most promising truck, and hid the spoils in a regular smuggler's cave that they had constructed: the absence of any system of signalling from section to section removed any means of recording undue delays that might have taken place while this 'little game' was being played; a lengthened term of imprisonment was the sequel to this performance.

A station was opened at Rugeley Town on 1 June 1870. The date is memorable for it marked the start of hopeless confusion, of which only railways seemed capable, between station names. For Rugeley (Trent Valley) then became known under that title in branch timetables, but simply as Rugeley in those for the main line. The confusion was sorted out during World War I—a period during which, one imagines, staff were working harder than ever —when it was laid down that Rugeley (Trent Valley) was the only title for that on the main line, the ruling being effective from 15 April 1917.

CANNOCK CHASE RAILWAY

Euston influence was paramount on a line authorised to carry the system deeper into the coalfield—the Cannock Chase Railway, for which the Marquis of Anglesea got powers on 15 May 1860. The first section was planned from the CMR at Hednesford to Coopers Lodge, whence a section was to strike almost at right-angles to Heathy Leasons (delicious name!) to join the Little-worth Tramway, which belonged to and served the Birmingham Canal. It had been projected under the Cannock Extension Canal Act of 1854. It was constructed by the LNWR and probably opened about 1863—the year the company took over powers from Lord Anglesea for the CCR. No opening date for this line is known; the minutes of LNWR Officers' Meetings for May 1867 refer to the opening of 'the Anglesea Railway', and this is probably the best clue. Lord Anglesea's name was spelt in several ways. The CCR ran almost to the North Western's Norton branch and in 1880 the company obtained powers for the Littleworth Extension Railway to link up with the opposite end of the tramway, which was more than a mile long.

CANNOCK CHASE & WOLVERHAMPTON RAILWAY

Other lines in the Cannock complex were promoted by an independent company, the Cannock Chase & Wolverhampton Railway, incorporated in 1864 to link the GWR at Cannock Road to the private Cannock Chase Railway at Burntwood, a hamlet $3\frac{1}{2}$ miles west of Lichfield. A branch was to join the Cannock Chase Extension Railway and the company was empowered in 1866 to build a 5 mile extension to the South Staffordshire at Hednesford. Neither was built.

The CC Extension (a nominally independent concern) was authorised in 1862 from the Norton branch to the CCR at Coopers Bridge. This was not built either, but eventually 11 miles on the cc & w concept were constructed as single lines and opened about 1867. They joined the ccr at Coopers Lodge Junction, the ssr at Anglesea Sidings and the Walsall Wood line of the Midland. Further mining developments led to the opening in 1894 of a link between Norton Green Colliery and Five Ways.

Economies in recent years have taken much out of the heart of the ccr (nationalised into the National Coal Board on 1 January 1947), and of associated lines of the North Western and Midland. The economies have been due to the closure of many pits, although several survive. The Rawnsley branch remains open between Hednesford and Cannock Wood pit, more than a mile to the east. Mid-Cannock sidings were reopened after open-cast mining increased with the aim of digging 200,000 tons a year from the Poplar site. A fragment of the system survives in steam—that operated by the Chasewater Light Railway, which maintains a 2 mile line made up of part of the cc & w and the Brownhills branch (see page 109).

CHAPTER VIII

Through Valleys and across Plains

TRENT VALLEY RAILWAY

The north-south trunk route provided by the London & Birmingham and the Grand Junction was quickly extended by the Manchester & Birmingham and Chester & Crewe, and the most important development of the trunk itself was to come with the opening of the Trent Valley. There was to be no more strategically vital line built in the West Midlands than this route between Rugby and Stafford.

The extent to which traffic was poured on to railways in the region from the moment they opened was emphasised in 1845 in a report by the 'Five Kings'—the body set up to investigate schemes launched during the Railway Mania, when the gauge war was at its height. They felt that if there were to be unavoidable breaks of gauge they should be at Bristol and Oxford, towns where through traffic would be lightest, rather than at Rugby, Wolverhampton, Birmingham or Gloucester, which they regarded as busy traffic centres.

Paradoxically, the moment railways got to Birmingham, moves were made to take traffic away by exploiting the shorter north-south route that could be built through the Trent Valley. The first scheme, promoted in 1839 while the Grand Junction was at war with the Manchester & Birmingham, was for an extension of the M & B from its projected route at Stone to Rugby, to reach a line to London independent of the Grand Junction. There was to be a branch from Lichfield to the Midland at Alrewas. The scheme failed to get Parliament's approval, but the concept of a more direct route between the North West and the Potteries and London was kept alive by promoters in the Potteries, whose schemes will be examined later.

Promoters keen on exploiting the Trent Valley found plenty of local allies, like influential men who met at Nuneaton and agreed that the Trent Valley Railway

> . . . will be of the greatest advantage to the Town and Neighbourhood, in affording the Inhabitants thereof the readiest communication with the Metropolis, and also, with the great Commercial Towns of Manchester and Liverpool and other places on the Line, and by that means facilitating the sale of extensive manufactured Silk, Cotton, and Worsted Goods, as well as the numerous mineral productions of this and the adjoining Parishes.

The word 'Parishes' is perhaps misleading, for a report of the meeting noted fourteen with a population of upwards of 30,000. Besides Nuneaton, they included Hinckley, Bedworth and Bulkington.

An independent company formed in 1843 to further the Trent Valley aspirations appointed a young man called Edward Watkin as secretary, the position in which he made his debut in railway politics. Two years later it arranged that the L & B should lease the route between Rugby and Stafford, although it had originally suggested the lease should reach only as far as Tamworth. The agreement was made in haste:

> With regard to the suggestion of giving further time for the consideration of these arrangements, I should not, gentlemen, have hesitated to do so had it been practicable. But, gentlemen, let me tell you this: that matters of this kind must be settled as soon as possible after they have been propounded. It will not do to let reports go out so as to raise the price of stock for a particular object. The thing must be concluded at once.

The Trent Valley schemes caused a major rift in the friendly relations between the Grand Junction and the London & Birmingham, which regarded such a line as a useful by-pass to Birmingham, where rail congestion was growing already, and as a good way of getting to Manchester. The GJR was on the defensive because it knew such an independent route would rob it of the Manchester traffic, and that from the Potteries, once railways were built there.

When the original promoters revived their scheme in 1845, two branches were proposed—Armitage-Wichnor, and from Stafford to Stoke, a line for which the Grand Junction was also pressing. Both branches were quickly dropped from the Trent Valley project, but the L & B cast its net wider by provisionally agreeing to absorb the Manchester & Birmingham and the Trent Valley, as well as the Churnet Valley line in North Staffordshire, if it became established.

Victory went to the Grand Junction for, with the ruthless ever-scheming Huish at its helm, it played its opponent at its own game, and won. It did so by seeking a route south from Wolverhampton independent of the L & B. As noted already, this meant the Grand Junction not only supported the Oxford, Worcester & Wolverhampton, but inspired the Birmingham & Oxford. The Grand Junction further strengthened its position by getting authority to subscribe a large amount of the capital of the Trent Valley and to have full running powers, under the Trent Valley authorisation Act of 1845.

Manchester & Birmingham shareholders revolted against their board and formed a committee to negotiate better terms with the L & B, being sick of disputes, as were their colleagues of that company. Many held stakes in both companies and felt friendly relations would be financially beneficial to everyone. This was the prelude to the formation of the LNWR, but already the damage had been done because the OW & W and Oxford companies were by then firmly rooted.

'CONDUCIVE TO THE PUBLIC BENEFIT'

The first sod of the Trent Valley was cut in November 1845 by the Prime Minister, Sir Robert Peel, who was MP for Tamworth from 1830 until his death 20 years later. He thanked landowners for their co-operation:

> I assure them that there are many persons in this neighbourhood who have not scrupled to sacrifice private feeling and comfort, by consenting to their land being appropriated to the Trent Valley Railway. They have given that consent from a conviction that this undertaking was one conducive to the public benefit, and that considerations of private interest should not obstruct the great one of the public good.

Construction was well under way by the time the LNWR was formed and when the Trent Valley was bought outright by the London and Birmingham, GJR and Manchester & Birmingham in April 1846. The engineers were Robert Stephenson and George Bidder, with T. L. Gooch in charge. Brassey was contractor, and among his assistants was George Findlay, whom Pendleton described in *Our Railways* as a man who 'combined a genial disposition with an inflexible will. He was methodical, believed in doing one thing at once and in doing it well; and from the day in 1845 when he began work with Thomas Brassey on the Trent Valley Railway, to the end of his railway career, he disciplined himself and his staff, and set an example of indomitable perseverence.'

The biggest engineering work was Shugborough Tunnel of 774yd, with its flamboyant portals that gave it the nickname of 'the Gates of Jerusalem'. Bridges were the main feature of the line and because of the relative narrowness of the floor of the valley, the river had to be spanned several times. The line was opened in spectacular style, and guests at a banquet at Tamworth included the emerging figure of George Hudson, who was said to have behaved rather badly.

Peel compared the railway to the opening out, nearly 2,000 years earlier, of the great north-western communication from London to Chester under the superintendence of Julius Agricola. Despite the brave words, the line was not quite ready for opening out, for there was concern about the bridges, which were made of cast iron like that of the Chester & Holyhead across the Dee at Chester, which had collapsed in spectacular fashion a short time before. The line was inspected by Captain Joshua Codding-ton, who was to become secretary of the Caledonian Railway later in the year.

Glyn stated on 13 August 1847 that the line

> . . . would have been opened for general traffic before this date, if the Directors had not considered it proper, in deference to Public feeling, and with a view to the utmost security of the Passenger Trains, to direct the several Iron Bridges on the Line to be carefully inspected, and so strengthened and improved where any ground for improvement presented itself, as to place their stability beyond question or cavil.

The Government appointed a commission to study cast-iron bridges, and although Coddington's report was favourable, the Railway Commissioners called for a further inspection. He stuck to his guns, and goods and two locals ran from 15 September, but the route was not fully used until the beginning of December. The final delay was not of the LNWR's making but was due to the Post Office, which disputed both the diversion and timings of mail trains.

Glyn told the half-year meeting in February 1848:

> Owing to the imperfect consolidation of the new line of Way, and to the unfavourable weather, for some time after the opening, the journeys were performed with less regularity than along the old route by Birmingham. The opening, and the new Post Office arrangements required for the conveyance of the Mails by that line, afforded a favourable opportunity for introducing uniformity between Railway and Post Office time; and for regulating the expression of all local time, as far as practicable, in conformity with the longitude of Greenwich.

The standard time arrangements had been introduced from 1 December 1847. Until then, Birmingham local timetable was 7 minutes ahead of Greenwich.

There was a string of eleven intermediate stations, the same total as the much longer Grand Junction had on opening—Colwich, Rugeley, Armitage, Lichfield, Tamworth, Polesworth, Atherstone, Nuneaton, Bulkington, Shilton, and Stretton. Tamworth was at once established as a mail-exchange point, perpetuating its role of coaching days.

PROBLEMS AND PROGRESS

The Trent Valley traffic placed heavy pressure on the comparatively small and badly laid out station at Stafford, and the chairman, Admiral Moorsom, confessed in 1861 when improvements became a necessity: 'Stafford has been a difficulty with us for many years. We have staved off the alterations as long as we could.' Nineteen years later a shareholder protested about £45 being spent on station improvements at Stafford and Crewe. He said they should be postponed until dividends—then 5¼ per cent on ordinary shares—were 'satisfactory'.

More stations were soon needed in the Trent Valley. Milford & Brocton was opened in 1877 and a goods station was added at Armitage a few weeks later.

Of the five junctions established in the valley, Colwich, the most northerly, was the only one centred on a village. It is among the most attractively situated mainline junctions in the region, sited where the main line crosses the river and the North Staffordshire line from Stone sweeps in beside the Trent & Mersey Canal. The station was LNWR, but the NSR had full access.

The Trent Valley was widened in several places between 1871 and 1909, and there was a memorable legal battle in 1898–9 when Warwickshire County Council got an injunction forbidding the LNWR from running trains across the A5—the Holyhead road —at Atherstone at more than 4 mph. It led to bridges being opened in 1903. The main line was not the only railway to cross the A5 on the level locally; another was a branch to the Trent Valley from Baddesley Colliery, which had one of only four Garratt locomotives built for British industrial systems. Years later the LMS was faced with litigation, though non-contentious, because of serious mining subsidence at Polesworth. It bought the mineral rights beneath the track so that the line could be permanently restored for high-speed running.

THE TRENT VALLEY TODAY

One of the most disconcerting sights I know as a casual footplate traveller is threading the reverse curves at maximum speeds on electric locomotives and flashing past small occupation crossings with their rows of bells strung out parallel to the track to prevent high loads touching the overhead wires. No such crossings exist on motorways, where traffic regulation is less disciplined and speeds are lower.

Railway guidebooks have often pointed out that it is possible to get a good view of the Three Spires of Lichfield Cathedral from the train, but in recent years that has become more difficult as the city has expanded towards the main line. Lichfield's growth in recent years has been significant, partly because of overspill development, which is also continuing to take place at Tamworth and Stafford. Like Rugby, Stafford has increased in industrial importance, partly due to heavy electrical industry in both places, where large works stand beside the main line.

Despite rising populations, there has been no marked increase in the demand for local passenger services. An EMU stopping service introduced on electrification proved over-optimistic in frequency, and there is now one stopping train at roughly two-hourly intervals between Stafford and Rugby. A further economy came in the autumn of 1972 when Atherstone, Polesworth and Rugeley were reduced to unstaffed stations. The local service suffers from a characteristic of the route—and an unusual one for a main line—by which it only skirts the intermediate towns rather than running through them.

Modernisation included the rebuilding of Tamworth Station, which is one of Britain's busiest mail-exchange points, used by several TPOS, whose crews are changed there.

RAILWAYS OF RUGBY

Rugby's fame has rested more on the reputation of its school than on railways, even though they did much to transform it from a busy and important market town into a large town on a broader base with industrial development prominent. Once the railway age was born, promoters could hardly have missed Rugby, for it lay in too strategic a position to be ignored, although it was excluded from Rennie's original plan for the London & Birmingham. The Stephensons corrected that error. A pleasant description of the L & B's arrival was presented by Robert Stephenson during the harsh winter of 1838. He noted of Rugby station :

> The works at this point are at present in rather a backward state, owing to the severe and continuous frost, which has almost entirely put a stop to the brickwork and permanent road. The booking office walls are built, the timbering of the roof put on, the engine and tank house in a forward state, as also the huts for the enginemen. The turn-plates will be fixed in a few days.

Only 2 years after the L & B opened, Rugby became a junction with the completion of the Midland Counties Railway, opened from Nottingham and Derby to Leicester on 5 May 1840 and extended to Rugby on 30 June. The opening of lines further north on the following day gave Rugby (and Euston) direct routes to Leeds, York and Hull. A bigger station at Rugby became essential and it was resited because of the MCR line of approach. Further improvements were necessary as three more lines converged on the junction within four years up to 1851. First was the Trent Valley, followed by that from Market Harborough in

1850, and a more local one from Leamington in the following year. Station improvements at Rugby were authorised by an Act of 1848, which also provided for a new approach road to that at Tamworth.

As Britain's main line network developed, Rugby's fortunes as a junction ebbed as well as flowed. It lost a good deal of traffic when the Midland opened its direct route to St Pancras in 1868, but its traffic increased when the Northampton loop was finished in 1881. This necessitated Rugby having station no 3—the barn-type structure that stands today. Professor Jack Simmons pointed out in his admirable booklet *Rugby Junction* (Dugdale Society Occasional Papers) that the new station followed a pattern then becoming fashionable, as exampled by Darlington, of a huge island platform with bays at either end, the outer faces long enough to handle two mainline trains at the same time, with scissors providing independent paths of approach and departure.

When the third station was ready in 1886, the LNWR had a virtual monopoly at Rugby, but this was soon to be broken by the Manchester, Sheffield & Lincolnshire drive for London—a move supported by some commercial interests at Rugby for the usual reason that competition would give them better service. They were to be disappointed because the station, completed after the creation of the Great Central, was nearly $\frac{1}{2}$ mile further away from the centre and on the town boundary. But the GCR did give Rugby useful outlets to the West Riding, Newcastle, Hull, South Wales, the South West and the South, notably Southampton.

The GCR began tapping Rugby traffic from its opening, and that traffic was further threatened, although to a much lesser extent, by the opening by the LNWR in 1895 of a branch from Weedon to Leamington. Guidebooks hailed it as offering 'An alternative and more direct line between Leamington Spa and London', omitting to mention poor connections. Research by C. R. Clinker has shown that Euston never contemplated it as a through route, for which it would have been quite useless because of sharpish curves and stiff gradients (it was a switchback of 1 in 72–80, up and down). Until 1918 the Leamington line ran into a bay at Weedon and had no direct link with the main line. Auto trains between Northampton and Warwick had to shunt three times to get to and from the branch.

Rugby has never rivalled, or attempted to rival, Crewe as a

railway centre, but a 1909 guidebook noted it as having 'the advantage of almost unequalled railway facilities'. As an after-thought, the guide stated : 'The GCR also has a station at Rugby'.

Today Rugby is more important a town than ever it was, and much less of a railway junction, having, within seven years, lost lines to Peterborough, Leamington, and Leicester as well as the Great Central. The mainline electrification has robbed Rugby of Inter City status, for few expresses stop there, local people having a semi-fast service to and from Euston and Birmingham.

Such economies and changes have altered the appearance of the railways of Rugby. The famous double-decked signal gantry just south of the station has been demolished. In the early 1970s the bridge that carried the GCR across the main line lay derelict, boarded off at both ends, and under its shadow lay the defunct locomotive-testing station.

Rugby, however, has gained two imposing structures—a power signal box alongside the station and a concrete flyover nearly a mile long that carries the up Birmingham line clear of the Trent Valley and has greatly increased track capacity.

LINES TO COVENTRY

> I waited for the train at Coventry
> I hung with grooms and porters on the bridge,
> To watch the three tall spires.

The train for which Tennyson waited must have been North Western, for no other passenger trains were ever allowed to run regularly to Coventry. The LNWR's almost total stranglehold on the city is perhaps one reason why it has never been considered an important railway centre, except by those who know the area; and in relation to its neighbours, Birmingham and Rugby, it never was. Besides the L & B main line, only two routes radiated from Coventry—a useful link to Nuneaton, which helped to draw Coventry more tightly into the West Midlands as the region grew, and a relatively unimportant line to Leamington.

The earliest railway significance of Coventry was during the building of the L & B, when Robert Stephenson used it as his headquarters for the Birmingham–Rugby section. Despite this, the directors made the same grievous mistake as they had at

Rugby by providing a station totally inadequate for the obvious needs of such a centre of population. By 1840 a second station had been built, and that did not have inconvenient steps between platform and road level. The replacement station was enlarged several times before electrification, including an extension for which the LMS received powers in 1935.

During the Railway Mania, the L & B fought hard to keep Coventry to itself. Its southern approach was protected by the branch to Warwick, described later in the chapter. Next came the authorisation of a line to Nuneaton in 1846—a move that outmatched the plans of the Oxford, Coventry & Burton-on-Trent and the Coventry, Banbury & Oxford Junction, which was to join the Birmingham & Oxford.

Projected at the same time from another direction was the Coventry, Nuneaton, Birmingham & Leicester, which quickly failed and left the LNWR to inherit the L & B powers. Euston had to get sanction to raise capital for the Coventry and Nuneaton construction. This was achieved uneventfully and the line opened in 1850, with immediate stations at Counden Road, Foleshill, Longford & Exhall, Hawkesbury Lane, Bedworth and Chilvers Coton. The section between Coventry and Counden Road was closed for nearly 3 years from 1857 after the collapse of the twenty-three arch Spon End viaduct—one of the minor sensations of the 1850s. It was replaced partly by an embankment.

The line ran through a rich mining area, and the LNWR built feeder lines. In the summer of 1848 it obtained powers to reach Craven Colliery, lying some distance from the main line at Exhall, and to build the Mount Pleasant branches from Bedworth. Another branch served Griff Colliery on the western outskirts of Nuneaton. The coalfield further developed in the 1880s as the richest areas of the South Staffordshire field became worked out. Pits sunk around Nuneaton were sited to give easy rail outlets.

The Nuneaton line provided access to Coventry for the Midland Railway—the only one to have running powers to the city. They were granted in 1865 after the completion of a line between Nuneaton and Leicester via the South Leicestershire Railway. That company's Act of Incorporation in 1860 gave the LNWR running powers between Rugby and Leicester in return for those for all traffic between Leicester and Coventry. The LNWR had to build a direct Leicester–Coventry loop at Nuneaton. It turned out to be another of railway history's white elephants, for C. R. Clinker states in his *West Midlands Chronology* that it was seldom, if ever, used.

The Midland built a shed at the north end of Coventry station for a shunting engine, the companies having agreed not to station train engines 'on foreign ground' at Coventry.

Passenger trains ran between Coventry and Nuneaton for almost a century, mainly continuing to Leamington Spa. They called at a halt with the name of Daimler, familiar enough today but unheard of in the heyday of railways. It was used mainly by car workers. The line closed to passengers in 1965 but its future is assured by the industries along it. A large oil depot opened near Bedworth in 1967 handles block trains from major refineries, including Thames Haven and Ellesmere Port. Although well used by freight trains, the double track portions between Coventry and Leamington were singled from 7 December 1972. Two lines were retained at both ends, and a crossing loop at Kenilworth. Late in 1972 Labour Party transport experts were seeking talks with British Rail to consider the reintroduction of passenger services between Coventry and Nuneaton.

The area is growing—not by chance, but by design—and there is a prospect that passenger services may be revived. The 'Coventry Corridor', as it has come to be known to the planners, stretches nearly 15 miles from Nuneaton through Coventry to Leamington, and is faced with a massive growth in population. A 1971 report forecast a rise from 340,000 to 1,410,000. While several new roads will be opened by 1976, the report stated that transport prospects were otherwise poor.

COVENTRY LOOP LINE

There is no evidence to suggest that the LNWR used its monopoly continually to resist major improvements at Coventry, for which need was proved. The most notable improvements were made early in this century: the station was extended in 1904 and 3 years later came powers for the Coventry Loop Line.

The double-track freight-only route of $3\frac{1}{2}$ miles between Humber Road Junction on the main line and Three Spires Junction on the Nuneaton route was to serve large new factories on the western outskirts. It was not finished for 7 years—until a week after the outbreak of World War I. It had public goods depots at Gosford Green and Bell Green and a connection to the Royal Naval stores depot from which heavy guns were sent to the Grand Fleet.

Access to the Ordnance Works was over the Foleshill Railway, a distinctive industrial system, opened in 1901 originally to serve a brickworks, and extended to what became the Ordnance Works in the following year. It also served a big factory owned by Courtaulds, which bought the line in 1922. It was operated with steam until it was closed officially on 8 April 1972. By then the only access to the branch was from Three Spires Junction, that at Humber Road having been severed before electrification.

There was talk as the line had gradually fallen into disuse of it being converted into Britain's first urban motorway, but in 1970 a car delivery firm opened a rail depot at Gosford Green similar to King's Norton. Double-decker trains deliver 200 cars to Johnstone in Renfrew and return south with Scottish-built vehicles. Only a short time later the Bell Green yard, which once had a capacity of 174 wagons, was redeveloped in a similar way by another delivery firm. Work involved the removal of thousands of tons of soil dumped there during the rebuilding of New Street station at Birmingham.

The best known symbol of modern Coventry is the Cathedral, rebuilt from the ruins of that destroyed during World War II. It was consecrated in 1962. About the same time the city got a new glass and concrete station. The former one was only slightly damaged in the blitz, but it was too old, too dirty and too cramped for electrification. Many improvements were made in the new station. A road bridge across its centre, which had restricted the layout of twin tracks, was demolished and replaced by one spanning four lines. Platforms were doubled to four and the junctions of the Leamington and Nuneaton branches were realigned, and a large parcels depot was built at the London end. A light and airy structure greets passengers arriving at Coventry, who find it in pleasant harmony with the modern architecture of the new city.

COVENTRY & GREAT WESTERN JUNCTION

Only one company with the name of Coventry in its title was ever authorised, and its line was never built. The Coventry & Great Western Junction was formed in 1865 to provide a mixed gauge link of $8\frac{1}{2}$ miles to join the locally projected railway at Southam. This, too, was not built. The GWR never showed much enthusiasm for either line, particularly as the six original directors of the C & GWJ were local men. The GWR believed, no doubt, that the door to Coventry, if it ever wanted to go there, would remain open via Leamington. It was not anxious to support a separate company, especially one in which the LNWR was to have facilities laid down in the Act of Incorporation.

RAILWAYS OF LEAMINGTON

There is a danger that the term 'railways of Leamington' may give them an importance they never enjoyed. Leamington, despite its genteel tourist industry, had far more lines than its modest size could hope to support successfully. The company that had supremacy as owner of the town's only main line was the GWR. Leamington was only at the end of LNWR branches. But it was a town of some importance from the earliest railway days; a map prepared by the L & B promoters showed it as having a population of 6,209 in 1833—about one-fifth that of Coventry. It became 'Royal' Leamington Spa 5 years later and has since grown gradually until it now has some 45,000 inhabitants.

The L & B was the first company to show interest, projecting a branch from Coventry, but when the line was surveyed early in 1836, it ran into strong opposition, the L & B directors lamenting on 3 February 1837

> . . . that notwithstanding the pains that have been taken to select a line which should be unobjectionable to the Landowners through whose property it was to pass, the great majority of them are at present opposed to any practicable line, and the project has therefore been abandoned for the present, but the Directors will be glad at any future time, when, as they hope, the objections to the Landowners may be removed, to give all the support they can to this desirable undertaking.

WARWICK & LEAMINGTON UNION

The directors of the L & B were able to fulfil their promise after the formation of the Warwick & Leamington Union Railway in 1842, the L & B agreeing to buy the concern. The chairman, Glyn, soon made it clear that the L & B would do things its own way, telling shareholders a month after the take-over:

> It is our duty, gentlemen, to carry out the scheme with the strictest economy. We are prepared to go into an investigation of the accounts that have been rendered to us, and of the sections and estimates. We do not feel ourselves bound implicitly to follow out the plans which have been handed over to us by the other Company, for if we can still further promote economy it shall be done, without reference to anything that is past.

The line opened in December 1844 despite doubts by the chairman as to whether it would be wise to do so in winter. It ran from Coventry to a station at Milverton called Leamington, the company preferring to advertise the Spa rather than the historic merits of Warwick. No such confusion reigned over the one intermediate station. It was simply called Kenilworth.

Leamington was regarded by the LNWR as a frontier town, a place where a line or lines were needed in attempts to keep out other companies, in this case the GWR. Glyn claimed in 1846 that traffic between Warwick and Leamington and London 'naturally comes to the L & B'. While its route via Coventry was circuitous, it would still be shorter than one the GWR proposed via Oxford and Rugby. The LNWR prepared to meet the threat by extending the branch from Milverton to Leamington and building a branch from there to Rugby.

RUGBY & LEAMINGTON RAILWAY

The LNWR regarded a link between Rugby and Leamington as rather unimportant, Glyn telling shareholders that it was 'merely a local improvement, called for by the inhabitants, and almost too small an affair to occupy you with'.

The Milverton–Leamington extension was authorised in 1846 with Royal Assent to a Bill originally promoted by the L & B. Six other schemes were put forward and from them crystallised the

Rugby & Leamington Railway from Rugby to Leamington Priors (Avenue station in its final years). The R & L quickly lost its identity when the LNWR was formed, and it was bought out 3 months later.

Doubts were soon raised whether the line would ever pay. When the point was put to the chairman 2 years later by Lord Lifford, a shareholder, Glyn replied that the Board agreed with the noble Lord that this was unlikely. The Board considered in September 1848 whether to abandon the line, temporarily or permanently, but work resumed early in 1850 after Warwick sent deputations to the company and to MPs. The single line was completed in 1851.

Some 18 months later, Leamington got mainline status through the opening of the Birmingham & Oxford. Besides giving the Spa a direct link to London, it also gave it a much better connection to Birmingham. This also became the only one (except via Rugby) for a short time in 1861 when the Coventry line was closed because of the collapse of a bridge at Leek Wootton, near Kenilworth. Neele remembered that he got news by telegram early on the morning after the opening of the Coalport branch in Shropshire. The collapse killed the crew of a goods engine. The cause was the failure of iron plating, which had cracked and been strengthened with fishplates.

Speculation that the GWR might get running powers to Coventry was rife after the completion of a spur at Leamington with the LNWR in 1864. Such powers were not asked for and it was thought that Euston deliberately kept the GWR out of Coventry by refusing to double the whole line. The section between Kenilworth Junction and Milverton was doubled some 20 years later, but this was done to cope with extra traffic expected following the opening of a cut-off between Kenilworth Junction and Berkswell on the L & B mainline in 1884.

WEEDON, DAVENTRY & LEAMINGTON SPA BRANCH

Euston was adept in giving importance to small lines that never had any. On company maps, for instance, the Weedon branch looked just as important as the West Coast main line. It opened in 1895, and besides being the last to reach Leamington, it was to be the first closed to passengers. The Rugby–Leamington line became sufficiently busy to warrant doubling over the short eastern leg between Rugby and Dunchurch in 1882, and the Weedon branch gave the opposite end of the branch extra traffic, for it shared the section between Leamington and Marton Junction, created deep in the rolling Warwickshire countryside, and one of the most remote sections in the West Midlands.

Both routes carried through coaches between Euston and Leamington. That via Weedon—a slip coach—was very short-lived, but the service via Rugby ran until 1932. Between July 1909 and December 1912 it was maintained by a slip coach. To the end, trains between Warwick and Weedon ran to and from Northampton Castle, reversing at Blisworth.

Despite Leamington's slow growth, it managed until the late 1950s to have railway luxury—for how else could four services to so small a town be termed?

The Weedon branch closed to passengers in 1958 and freight closures followed in stages—between Southam & Long Itchington and Napton & Stockton in 1962, and from there, via Daventry to Weedon, a year later. The short section from Marton Junction to Southam carries coal to a large cement works.

Block trains from Rugby reverse at Marton, which ceased to be a junction when the stretch to Leamington closed in 1966. Marton Junction signal box was used until 4 June 1967. Double-line working between there and Rugby (Bilton Siding) continued, and a ground frame controls the junction at Marton to the single line.

Nine months after the Weedon closure, the Rugby passenger services were withdrawn in the summer of 1959. Severing the Marton–Leamington section robbed Rugby and Coventry of a by-pass route more in theory than in fact.

The Leamington lines were involved in several boundary changes, those of 1958 giving the Western Region complete control of the short section between Leamington Spa Avenue and Milverton stations.

The Leamington–Coventry–Nuneaton passenger link was withdrawn in 1965, as was the associated Birmingham service via Berkswell, where the junction was removed to eliminate a 95 mph limit on the up line. The rest of the Kenilworth branch was lifted later in the year, a short siding, sometimes used for stabling the Royal train, being retained at Berkswell. Then came embarrassment as increased freight began delaying Inter City electrics, and in the winter of 1971 there was talk of relaying the Berkswell Loop as a single line to carry freight clear of Coventry by running direct to Leamington, where freight exchange sidings were replaced in 1966 by a new junction north of the GWR station. It was put in for freight diverted from the Great Central and to allow that using the Leamington–Wolverhampton route via Snow Hill to reach Bescot via Berkswell.

What's in a name? That was a question that the LNWR never resolved at Leamington—or was it Warwick? For the company's stations were to have fifteen different names—Leamington or Warwick or variations—a Gilbertian situation in a Shakespearian setting.

JUNCTIONS AT NUNEATON

Nuneaton, though small, had an important mineral industry hundreds of years before railways. It is known that in the thirteenth century mining was flourishing in the belt to Coventry through which that branch was built in 1850. Stone quarrying, which equally disfigured the landscape locally, also developed ahead of railways, although only by a few years.

Nuneaton was only a second-class station when the Trent Valley opened, the promoters putting greater emphasis on the status of Atherstone, Tamworth and Lichfield, all first-class stations. Yet Nuneaton was to grow into the largest of the five junctions that were developed in the valley, receiving its second line from Coventry in 1850, and lines from Hinckley in 1862, Leicester in 1864, and Moira in 1873. The prime reason for Nuneaton's later importance was that it was the only intermediate town, and the only one with junctions, lying on the direct route projected by the Midland Railway between Birmingham and Leicester. It was partially provided by an independent company, the Nuneaton & Hinckley Railway, which received powers for a $4\frac{1}{2}$ mile line in 1859. When it became the South Leicestershire Railway in the following year, it set about reaching the Midland at Wigston Magna, $11\frac{1}{2}$ miles east of Hinckley, the route being completed in 1864. The Birmingham–Leicester link lacked one section, provided later in the year, between Whitacre and Nuneaton. There were three local stations: Shustoke, Arley and Stockingford.

The original Birmingham & Derby Junction station at Whitacre was replaced by one ¾ mile south of the new junction. The Midland's first Nuneaton station had a short life, being replaced after only 9 years by one built 150yd further west to make way for the last line, the Ashby & Nuneaton Joint, a LNWR-MR venture opened in 1873 to what became Abbey Street station at grouping. Nuneaton's network was completed by a spur between LNWR and MR in 1880.

The South Leicestershire was vested in the LNWR in 1867 with the Stour Valley and South Staffordshire companies. It was a profitable little concern, having worked dividends up to 4½ per cent.

Although many Midland pits have closed in recent years, some have been opened, and rail facilities were developed for the Daw Mill Colliery beside the Nuneaton line near Coleshill, opened in the mid-1960s. Block trains were loaded by a travelling gantry across the sidings, and handled up to 200 tons of coal an hour.

Nuneaton has not suffered too severely under the economies of recent years. Birmingham–Leicester services are maintained by DMUs, recommended by Beeching for modification and now heavily subsidised—by £132,000 in 1971.

The Ashby & Nuneaton Joint line closed between Abbey Junction and Market Bosworth in 1971, a short head-shunt and connection being retained to private quarry sidings near Abbey Station. The section from Weddington Junction (which served the now-lifted spur to Trent Valley) was kept for a time as a wagon store. Shortly before these economies Nuneaton's mainline marshalling yard was lifted.

GNR IN THE WEST MIDLANDS

When the Trent Valley line opened, it quickly became Stafford's most important route, traffic on the Grand Junction to Birmingham dropping in volume. Stafford also had a junction with the route to Wellington and one, often forgotten now, with the Great Northern line from Uttoxeter, made possible by running powers over the North Staffordshire.

Even when its relations with Euston were cordial, the NSR did not regard the North Western as the only route to London. For years it gave pride of place in its public timetables to the GNR service from Derby to Uttoxeter and Stafford. Why? As a tilt at Euston? The mystery deepens when it is realised that the service was one of the least used of all in Staffordshire. As the Great Northern trains used running powers for only 12 miles between Bromshall Junction and Egginton, the NSR could never have received much revenue, even if the trains were jammed to capacity.

Stafford was the most westerly outpost of King's Cross, but it was never intended to be, for the GNR aspired to reach Wales after its successful advance into the Nottinghamshire coalfield. The Stafford & Uttoxeter, its instrument of conquest, was in trouble from the earliest days, troubles both legal and financial. There was little opposition to the original scheme, but after the S & U Bill passed committee, a clause was inserted to reduce its value by preventing the GNR using the running powers over the NSR 'to divert Traffic by any circuitous routes from the lines of the LNW or Staffordshire Companies'.

The quote is taken from the minutes of the Euston directors. The S & U was incorporated in 1862 to build a line of $13\frac{1}{4}$ miles with a branch of almost 2 miles to Weston on the NSR between Stone and Colwich. The S & U, which had its registered office miles away at Wellington, was given 5 years for completion. The need for customers other than the occasional farmer in the country through which it passed was satisfied once King's Cross took an interest. This arose out of the GNR's desire to expand into the Nottingham–Derbyshire coalfield. A line was opened from Colwick to Pinxton in 1875 and from Amsworth Junction (Kimberley) to Egginton 3 years later, mainly to serve Burton. A service to Stafford began in 1881 after the GNR bought the S & U (which had opened in 1867) for £100,000.

For years there was talk of building a spur between the S & U and the NSR at the point where, in the middle of the countryside, the lines crossed. The first published Ordnance Survey map showed a north to east spur, but there is nothing to suggest it was built.

Despite its isolation from the main system, the S & U was full of distinctive GNR characteristics, and it had its own goods station at Stafford, Doxey Road, reached by a branch $\frac{1}{4}$ mile long.

Stafford was one of the places that fascinated T. R. Perkins who explored every one of Britain's passenger lines. He was a great exploiter of Stafford because of the peculiarities that existed under competitive fare arrangements standard until grouping. He once took a tourist ticket from Stafford to Ilfracombe via King's Cross and Waterloo—at the same fare as that from Surbiton. C. R. Clinker recalls they had considerable potential since they were valid for three months and allowed breaks of journey at any station. In 1922 he noted that at Stafford GNR fare tables quoted to no fewer than 280 destinations. They included a large proportion to competitive towns at standard fare, including London, although the mileage to King's Cross was 179, compared with 133 to Euston.

The GNR maintained a stationmaster and a staff of eleven at Stafford LNWR until 1915, when the LNWR took over all duties. Stafford Common had a separate stationmaster.

For so little used a line, the S & U had a long life. It lost its passenger service on 4 December 1939, but RAF specials continued to a camp near Stafford Common, which helped to postpone complete closure until 12 years later. The track remained in place until shortly after the running of a special of the Stephenson Locomotive Society in 1957.

Nobody ever took much notice of the S & U and a footnote in the NSR timetables was insulting : 'The times of these Trains are given for information only'.

CHAPTER IX

Shropshire Networks

GWR IN COALBROOKDALE

Railways were built in Shropshire to go places rather than serve places. The Shrewsbury & Birmingham, whose goals were so much beyond the county, fell within that definition, but its branches were the one exception, for they were purely local lines that pierced the rich heart of the district that cradled the Industrial Revolution. Today the area has twin symbols of identification: the historic Iron Bridge across the Severn, and the trendy architecture of a New Town, named Telford after the engineer who drove the Holyhead road through the rolling countryside.

Ironworks and mines established around Coalbrookdale in the early 1700s had grown into large concerns by the time the Shrewsbury & Birmingham was created. Among them was the Coalbrookdale Company, where the Industrial Revolution really started in 1709, when Abraham Darby (1677–1717) fired a blast furnace with coke and cast his iron in sand.

Cast-iron cylinders for steam engines were first made at Coalbrookdale and it is probable that it achieved another 'first'— the laying of cast-iron rails in 1767–8. They replaced some early wooden ones running $2\frac{1}{2}$ miles to ironworks at Horsehay. This system developed to such an extent that in 1847 the s & b got authority to link it with its own line 4 miles away at Shifnal. It provided access to ironworks at Madeley, and the mainline connection was at Madeley Junction.

The Coalbrookdale branch had a short life as part of the s & b, being transferred to the GWR only 3 months after opening in 1854. It was extended $1\frac{1}{2}$ miles from Lightmoor to Coalbrookdale 10 years later, when Coalbrookdale was reached from the

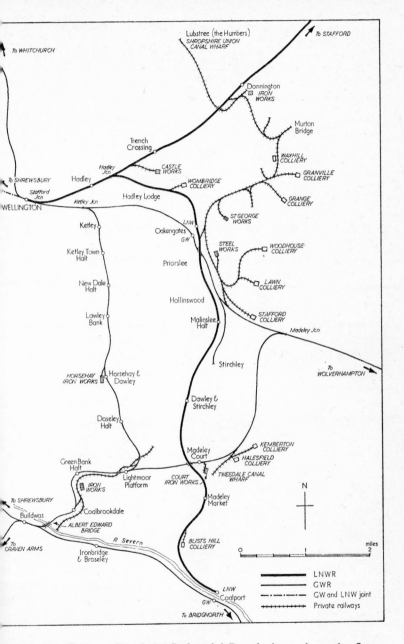

Severn Valley—cradle of the Industrial Revolution, where the first cast iron rails in the world were laid. GWR dominated, but the LNWR had a foothold

opposite direction by the Wenlock Railway, which the GWR worked from the start and absorbed in 1896.

The Coalbrookdale branch was never a successful passenger line, although a service was maintained until 1915. A 2 month experimental revival in the summer of 1925, after local pressure, failed also.

The GWR regarded the intermediate Madeley area as one where traffic was highly competitive with the LNWR and later the LMS. There was competition, too, after World War I from buses. Parcels traffic to villages like Madeley was concentrated—yes, the GWR used the term more than half a century ago—at Shifnal. It was worked forward in the van of the local goods between Oxley and Buildwas. More than parcels were needed to sustain the line, and besides the products of local ironworks, there was coal from pits like Kemberton Colliery near Madeley, which, in the mid-1920s, produced about forty wagonloads a day. As the four pit sidings held only ninety wagons, extra trains had to be worked over the single line to maintain the fine balance between wagon supply and demand.

The branch was modernised in the autumn of 1969 to handle merry-go-round trains to a second power station at Ironbridge, which is capable of generating the peak hour capacity of a city the size of Birmingham. It burns coal from Staffordshire and Granville Colliery at Donnington. A new signal box and a loop, more than $\frac{1}{4}$ mile long, was put in on the main line at Madeley Junction to stable loaded trains waiting for those of empty wagons to clear the single line.

WELLINGTON & SEVERN JUNCTION

Lightmoor—and so Coalbrookdale—was connected to the S & B from another direction by the Wellington & Severn Junction, a local company formed in 1853 to reach Coalbrookdale with a $\frac{3}{4}$ mile extension to Broseley. The short line of $4\frac{1}{2}$ miles, engineered by Henry Robertson, opened from Ketley to Horsehay in 1857, and south to Lightmoor some time after March of the following year; the actual date is not known. It was worked for the first 4 years by the Coalbrookdale Iron Company, which held about three-quarters of the shares and used its own engines, including some built at the works. After negotiations lasting several years, the line was leased to the GWR and the West Midland Railway in 1861. It was vested in the GWR in 1892.

There was traffic to and from a number of pits and works, especially around Horsehay, where there were ten sidings and a spur for 200 wagons. Horsehay also handled milk and pigeons. Despite the traffic volume the line remained purely a branch in character, with small manned crossings. Typical was that on a by-road at Dawley Parva, where, in 1924, the keeper received £2 6s 0d a week and paid half-a-crown rent for his cottage. The equipment he worked was a keyless disc and bell and telephone.

The GWR always regarded the Severn Junction line as more than a local branch, classing it as part of an integral route of 24 miles between Ketley Junction, Wellington, and Marsh Farm, north of Craven Arms on the Shrewsbury & Hereford. To meet growing bus competition in the mid-1930s, halts were opened at New Dale, near Ketley; Green Bank, near Coalbrookdale; and at Ketley Town.

Through passenger services were withdrawn in two widely separated stages—between Much Wenlock and Craven Arms in 1951, and north from Much Wenlock to Wellington 11 years later. The northern tip from Ketley to the S & B Junction was closed completely. The $1\frac{1}{2}$ mile section between Lightmoor Junction and Horsehay was closed for a time, but it reopened in 1965 experimentally after talks with local industrialists.

The Severn Junction line was paralleled less than $\frac{1}{4}$ mile to the east by the last railway developed locally. It was a goods branch of $1\frac{1}{4}$ miles opened by the GWR in 1908 from the main line at Hollinswood to Stirchley to serve a concentration of industry comprising a brickworks, chemical plant and two road slag works. Originally called the Old Park Line, access was through Hollingswood down sidings. Soon after grouping, plans were considered for converting it into a light railway to save working time, which was lengthy because of a 5 mph restriction. Night working was prohibited. The line closed in 1959.

LNWR COMPETITION

Once established at Wellington, the LNWR attempted to break the local GWR traffic monopoly. While that company had direct access to ironworks and pits, the LNWR had to work what traffic it could obtain over an independent canal, the Shropshire, which ran from the Shropshire Union, near Trench, to Coalport, beside the Severn. There was a branch through Horsehay to Coalbrookdale. The canal served the Lilleshall Company pits and ironworks. established in 1760, at Priorslee; the Court ironworks at Madeley; furnaces near Coalport; the Horsehay ironworks; and the Coalbrookdale company—all the industry that mattered.

The canal suffered badly from subsidence and water shortage, and the manager, Robert Skey, fearing that traders might send traffic via the GWR, early in 1855 recommended its conversion into a railway. That was 2 years after the rejection of plans by the LNWR for lines from Wellington to Coalport and Ironbridge, and to Hadley on the Wellington–Stafford line. The LNWR chairman, Major General George Anson, claimed in 1853 that, instead these powers had been given in mutilated form, to the Severn Valley and the S & B : 'I believe this decision is one for which neither company will be very grateful. We have, however, nothing further to do with the matter : as far as we are concerned the project is dead.'

His words were drowned, so to speak, by the continual deterioration of the Shropshire canal, and in 1856 it was agreed to let Euston spend £80,000 on a less ambitious railway of 8 miles to Coalport rather than £30,000 on repairs. In 1857 the LNWR got powers to buy the canal and convert a section, and also the Shropshire Union Railways branch canal from Hadley Junction to Wombridge, near Oakengates, opened in 1849. The line was built along the canal to a point near Dawley and then followed an independent route to Coalport, reached in 1861. It was single, with loops at Oakengates and Dawley.

Parts of the Coalport branch have been used by the Telford planners as an attractive pathway through parts of the New Town. It passes a new museum of industrial archaeology at Blists Hill.

The creation of Telford as one of Britain's largest New Towns is not likely to provide a lot of fresh rail traffic. Although the town is expected to have a population of 220,000 in about 10 years time, it is being projected as a 'Motorway Town of the Seventies'. It was not until 1972, after years of negotiations, that British Rail recommended the construction by 1975, with Government financial backing, of a two-platform station on the site of

Hollinswood yard. Telford's heart remains pierced by the Buildwas and Horsehay lines.

SHROPSHIRE UNION RAILWAYS & CANAL COMPANY

The SUR's fortunes were inexorably tied up with the S & B, for
the SUR & CC was the instrument that the LNWR used in its
attempts to prevent the GWR reaching the Mersey. Wellington was
always well-to-do in the eyes of neighbours and the reason for its
prosperity was that it had quite a railway history, becoming a
junction in 1849 with the opening of the first part of the S & B
and of the SUR line to Stafford.

The resistance of canal owners to railway schemes was gradually overcome as the railways showed their obvious supremacy,
and one of the most enterprising ways in which the canal owners
met their competition was by the creation of the SUR & CC. Its
story was told succinctly in Bradshaw's *Manual* in 1859 :

> This company was formerly an amalgamation of railways and canals,
> with a view to converting the latter into the former. This object it
> was found impracticable to carry out, especially after an arrangement
> had been entered into with the L & NW, which was itself invalid until
> sanctioned by parliament.

The Shropshire Union owned 29 miles of railway comprising
the Stafford–Wellington route and a half share in the joint line
west to Shrewsbury. The Stafford line was engineered by George
Lee and no major works were needed. Newport, the only intermediate place of any size, was historic, but no more than a village.

While the S & B battles raged, the LNWR quietly developed the
Stafford line, especially at the approach to Wellington, where
industry and mining were growing fast. There was little traffic to
be found in the countryside east of Donnington, and even during
the busier days of the Kaiser's war it was not considered necessary to stop locals at all six intermediate stations. The line's
primary function as a through route to Shrewsbury kept it alive
until the 1960s.

Rerouting of trunk freight services led to the withdrawal of
Stafford–Wellington workings in 1966. The section between
Stafford and Donnington was closed in the same year, but the
remainder was retained to serve a colliery and engineering works.

PROJECTED ROUTES

The original SUR plan included a branch of 11 miles from Stafford into the Potteries at Stone. That was soon forgotten, as were schemes for the rest of the 155 miles the company intended to build, mainly by converting the beds of its bankrupt canals. The aim, the company proclaimed, was not only to help itself but the public as well. The discarded projects were much more ambitious than the Stafford–Wellington scheme. They included a link between Crewe and Newtown in mid-Wales, and a rather more interesting and important line of 45 miles between Chester and Wolverhampton. The Chester line poised a powerful threat to the Grand Junction, for it was to be only $1\frac{1}{2}$ miles longer. It was planned from the Chester & Crewe at Calveley, near Tarporley, via Nantwich, Market Drayton and Brewood. After crossing the Stafford–Wellington line, it was to join the S & B near Oxley. Robert Stephenson engineered the route, assisted by W. A. Provis, and all but 4 miles were to be built through canal conversion. The estimates of cost were modest, being put at £730,000. The Earl of Powis headed the provisional committee.

The case was put to a Select Committee in May 1845, when it was claimed that most iron masters favoured it. Skey, who was then the Shropshire Union canal carrying agent, said the main traffic was up to 2,000 tons of heavy iron castings, carried north; the building of the Grand Junction had deprived it of most other traffic. If a line was made direct to Birkenhead, the cost and trouble of transhipping canal goods destined for the Liverpool area would be obviated.

The scheme raised fears about the future of the shipping trade at Stourport, for a lot of money had been spent improving the River Severn to make it easier for boats to reach the town. Other towns, notably Newport and Market Drayton, welcomed the prospect of a railway.

Robert Stephenson said the importance of the heavy mineral traffic that would flow on the line could not be overrated. It would be decidedly superior to the Grand Junction, which was 'better calculated' for passenger traffic. It would carry the heavy traffic while the GJR would handle the light. The SUR was not mixed up with competing systems and it would form part of the best direct route between Birmingham and Ireland.

Stephenson stated that the line was to be taken into Wolverhampton on the same level as the s & b, not by the lower level approach of the Oxford, Worcester & Wolverhampton. A high level would be best for the public because it could be carried into the heart of the town. If a low level were selected, canals would prevent it reaching the centre. Stephenson said he was so convinced of the desirability of railways having elevated stations that he was at present going to some expense in devising plans so that every railway might enter towns at high levels, which would have the effect of accelerating trains on starting.

The main opponents of the sur plan were other canal owners, who felt that the public was vitally interested in preserving canals to keep alive rivalry with railways. A more unusual protest came from people at Acton who said the Bill did not guarantee their rights and privileges 'respecting the obtaining and carrying of manure'.

All hopes died from the moment the lnwr leased the su in 1847; for it wanted no rival to the gj route.

ROUTES TO MARKET DRAYTON

Wellington's last junction was that of a line to Nantwich, part of what became a system centred on Market Drayton, which was conceived in the wake of several rather wilder schemes that failed at the planning stage. They included the provisionally registered Sheffield, Shrewsbury & South Wales Direct Railway, from Sheffield via Leek, Whitmore (crossing of gjr), Market Drayton and Hodnet. Its London-based promoters boasted that it would form

> one of the most important railways in the kingdom, connecting as it does, all the principal Manufacturing Towns in the country with Shrewsbury and North & South Wales. The Surveyor has made a most favourable Report, and on no portion of the projected Line does any Engineering difficulty present itself.

It was left to difficulties bigger than those of engineering to destroy the scheme, but North Staffordshire remained ripe for conquest, and the lnwr and the gwr both saw Wellington as a base from which to launch forays into the territory of the North Staffordshire Railway. In the early 1860s the NSR was consolidated behind its western lines on a ridge of rising ground on which Silverdale and Audley were prominent mining areas.

Plans for a line from Wellington to Crewe, through Madeley, with a branch to Silverdale, were advanced by the Shrewsbury & Potteries Junction Railway (merged to form the more famous Potteries, Shrewsbury & North Wales Railway in 1866). The plan was well timed, being announced when the LNWR and NSR were at loggerheads. The proposal received enthusiastic support from Euston, but the two companies soon patched up their quarrel and the LNWR dropped its support of the Crewe plan.

The early 1860s brought ideas, equally abortive, for the Wellington, Drayton and Newcastle Railway, quickly followed in 1862 by a potentially more promising scheme, brought about by a determined GWR bid for an independent route from North Shropshire to Manchester. The GWR's plan was to exploit a scheme of the Wellington & Cheshire Junction Railway from Wellington to Market Drayton, Nantwich and Northwich in the salt-mining area.

The combined opposition of the LNWR and the NSR scotched the plan, but it was revived and managed to reach the Lords before being thrown out. The way was now paved for the NSR to march into Shropshire, albeit rather reluctantly because of Euston's refusal to mount a joint venture.

Eventually Market Drayton—a small market town; no more —gave its name to three companies. Besides the Silverdale & Market Drayton, to be discussed in Chapter XI, there were two which met head-on to provide a north-south link between Wellington and Nantwich, and gave the ever-lusting GWR a foothold in the North West at Crewe.

First came the Nantwich & Market Drayton Railway, incorporated in 1861, which completed its route of almost 11 miles in 1863. Although it was isolated from the GWR, its close affinities remained and it was absorbed in 1897. The Wellington & Drayton Railway, incorporated in 1862, had to build a line of $16\frac{1}{4}$ miles. There were few problems of construction and its completion in 1867 freed the N & MD of isolation from Paddington.

The Wellington–Nantwich route, classed as a secondary main line, had little local value for the GWR, especially when the North

Sundays, Dec. 1st & 29th

EXPRESS EXCURSIONS

TO

| | RETURN FARES THIRD CLASS |
| | From Man'r &c. &c. From STOCKPORT |

MARKET DRAYTON	- 3/6	3/6
WELLINGTON (For the WREKIN and the SEVERN VALLEY district. See Note A below)	- 4/6	4/-
OAKENGATES	- 4/9	4/3
WOLVERHAMPTON (LOW LEVEL)	} 5/-	5/-
BIRMINGHAM (SNOW HILL)		

Leaving <u>MANCHESTER (London Road)</u> 9-55 a.m. STOCKPORT (Edgeley) 10-5 a.m.

Arrival Times				Return Times same day
12 35 p	BIRMINGHAM (Snow Hill)	...	...	7 30 p.m.
12 12	WOLVERHAMPTON (Low Level)	...	...	7 45 „
11 48 a	OAKENGATES	...	...	8 5 „
11 40	WELLINGTON	...	...	8 15 „
11 16	MARKET DRAYTON	..	...	8 40 „

Return Train due STOCKPORT 9-45 p.m., MANCHESTER 10-0 p.m.

A—PASSENGERS FOR THE SEVERN VALLEY DISTRICT.
Rail to Wellington—thence Road Motor Omnibus. (For Particulars see Handbills).

TICKETS IN ADVANCE—Tickets can be obtained in advance at the Railways Enquiry Offices: 47, Piccadilly; 16, Corporation Street; 16, Peter Street; 15, John Dalton Street; at London Road Station; or from the usual Agencies.

Paddington Station, November, 1935
th. 73

JAMES MILNE, General Manager

Sunday excursions from Manchester by the GWR, rather than the LMS, in the winter of 1935. Motor omnibus connections to the Severn Valley—not trains

Staffordshire reached Market Drayton, the only intermediate town. The 'very flat and purely agricultural' nature of the area was acknowledged by officials who reported to the GWR Chester Division in 1924. Hard-pressed to write much of interest about the line itself, they resorted to some countryside notes: 'The Shropshire and Cheshire Foxhounds hunt in the district. The Hawkstone Otter Hounds also hunt the Rivers Weaver and Tern.'

Passenger trains were few. Stations were far apart and little used, yet there was agitation for more; the company was pressed in 1924 to provide a 'station or siding' between Crudgington and Peplow, the case being presented through 'an influential MP'. Talks broke down when Paddington asked for a guarantee of 2,000 tons of extra traffic each year. Unexpected traffic had come a few years earlier through the establishment of a large aerodrome at Tern Hill, for which another siding was laid.

The report on the line digressed to reveal that at Moss Hall—about 5 *miles* from Audlem station—there were three subterranean passages entered through secret doors. Not until several pages later was their significance revealed: they were hiding places used by the owner of the Hall when Cromwell marched against the family.

Another kind of march, that of progress, never troubled the railway. GWR locals were so few that the NSR was allowed to run to Hodnet on market days.

The local service was threatened before Beeching, but it continued until September 1963, being withdrawn on the same day as the trains through the Severn Valley via Bridgnorth. This was 7 years after the severing of the Stoke passenger link.

The line was used extensively during electrification and its future looked secure when plans were announced in the mid-1960s for a major marshalling yard at Walcot, between Shrewsbury and Wellington, to take over marshalling in the northern area of the Western Region from smaller yards at Oxley, Shrewsbury, Wrexham and Chester, all incapable of handling traffic from such a wide area. A west to north spur was to be put in to gave the Market Drayton line a double-facing junction at Wellington and provide a useful secondary route between Shrewsbury and Crewe. Walcot never got beyond the planning stage, once the concept of block trains was favoured, and the Market Drayton line was doomed when freight between the West Midlands and Crewe was diverted via Stafford on electrification. It closed completely in 1967.

The route always remained a frontier—first between the GWR and the LMS and later between regions. Nantwich–Crudgington passed from Western to London Midland control in 1950, and the rest of the line 8 years later.

Two personal journeys of contrast linger in the memory—on a stopper from Crewe to Market Drayton (GWR 2–6–2T) in the early 1950s, when the rich dairy-farming country through which we gently chugged lay empty, ravaged by foot and mouth disease. The train was empty, too. In the dying days of steam, a happier experience—through Market Drayton behind a *Royal Scot* on a special to Swindon that went on to pass through Snow Hill, middle road, non-stop.

SHREWSBURY & CREWE

Another of the lines that went through Shropshire rather than served it was the Shrewsbury & Crewe, which the LNWR developed as local interests in Mid-Wales began promoting a line between Shrewsbury and the coast. Euston 'heartily approved' and the directors collected among themselves to give the Welsh financial backing. The LNWR felt the Shrewsbury & Crewe would be a through route linking South Wales with Lancashire, as opposed to Cheshire, for a reason clarified by the chairman, Anson : 'We have no intention whatever of interfering with the Chester & Birkenhead line, or of losing any ties of friendship which now bind the two companies together'.

The S & C was authorised in 1853, but its title was slightly misleading, for there was a ludicrous gap in the line : the Lords refused to let the LNWR enter Shrewsbury and develop a joint station with the GWR; instead, it was to terminate in a field more than a mile from the station. The reason was later revealed by the LNWR chairman, Lord Chandos, who said in 1856 that the line had been cut short by the Lords with the 'avowed intention' of compelling the company to seek better access to the town. They had not sought powers for completion for 3 years because they had had to make a considerable deviation and have talks to see if the line could be completed more economically than first proposed. These delays were authorised by an Act of 1856 which also extended time by a year.

Little construction work was done until the revised route had been approved. Brassey was contractor, and J. E. Errington engineer. Errington reported in August 1857 that while earthworks and some track were finished between Crewe and Nantwich, only half the excavations on the remaining 26 miles had been finished. The contractor had possession of land 'except some Gardens close to Shrewsbury, where negotiations are still pending with the Great Western and other Companies interested in the General Station, to obtain an entrance more convenient to all parties'.

Construction was estimated at £350,000, or £10,600 a mile, and the route opened in 1858. Its success was immediate and 18 months later it was considered expedient to lay a second track. One reason for the traffic build-up was the increasing volume over the Shrewsbury & Hereford, which had been worked since its opening in 1852 by Brassey as contractor. From 1854 there had been access to South Wales via Hereford, and as widening the Crewe line was planned, the first section of the Central Wales from Craven Arms was being completed.

Chandos explained to LNWR shareholders that although the doubling and station improvements had been considered 5 years earlier, they had been deferred until it was necessary to keep out any competitors.

Widening, finished in 1862, brought about a big rise in the LNWR's own traffic, and gave fresh impetus to the promoters of independent Welsh lines. They included the Oswestry, Ellesmere & Whitchurch, whose story I told in volume one of the history of the Cambrian Railways. It opened throughout from Whitchurch in 1864 as the last stage of the Aberystwyth main line of the Cambrian Railways, formed two days earlier.

The Cambrian inherited the OE & W turntable and access to Whitchurch from a junction just south of the station. Whitchurch got a second junction in 1872 with the opening of a rural branch, examined in the next chapter, to Tattenhall, near Chester.

MOTOR BUS SERVICES

Railways in Shropshire faced competition they were never able to stem once the motor bus became reliable in the early 1920s. One reason why trains suffered badly was the sparsely populated countryside, which buses could serve so much better. The GWR reported the situation at Ketley in 1924:

> The Midland Motor Bus [*sic*] Company run a local service between Wellington and Oakengates in addition to through services, and are keen competitors. There is also competition with the owners of small cars who ply between Wellington and Ketley.

But the railways did not give up:

> The district served by the Severn Junction Line has recently been covered by the Midland Motor Omnibus Company and schemes have been submitted shewing how the Great Western Company could inaugurate services to meet the competition . . . There is considerable road motor competition in the (Horsehay) district, the Midland Motor Bus Company serve practically the whole neighbourhood. Owners of small cars also ply between Horsehay and Wellington and do a fair business.

The report was made a year after Horsehay had handled traffic producing receipts of £25,222. They were made up of

Passengers	£2,481
Parcels	£635
Goods	£22,106

The goods receipts, so high a proportion of the total, came mainly from milk, castings, pigeons, roadstone, ironwork, sanitary pipes and general traffic.

Much the same sort of competition, though not traffic, was met on the Wellington–Nantwich branch. From Hodnet it was reported: 'Both the Midland Red Motor and Crosville Buses run through the district to Market Drayton on Wednesdays and are keen competitors'.

CHAPTER X

Cheshire

GRAND JUNCTION : THE LATTER DAYS

Undisputedly, the Grand Junction was the most important line ever built in Cheshire. Running north-south, it sliced the county roughly in the middle, serving nowhere until it created Crewe. Later the system became quite busy round the salt town of Winsford, a few miles to the north.

Crewe's place on the railway map was assured by the first two Acts incorporating new railway companies to which Queen Victoria gave Royal Assent—the Chester & Crewe and the Manchester & Birmingham, authorised on 30 June 1837—4 days before the Grand Junction opening.

Nature helped to develop Crewe, for once the Grand Junction found that the heavy clay soil of the area—then known as Monks Coppenhall—was good for the foundations of large buildings and heavy machinery, it prepared to move its workshops from Edge Hill, Liverpool. Houses had to be built in the empty countryside before workers could be attracted, but once they were ready, the carriage and wagon works were able to move, in March 1843. Even though the LNWR later concentrated those sections at Wolverton and Earlestown, Crewe was kept prosperous by locomotive building, begun with *Columbine* in 1845. When fears of a French invasion of Britain were rife in 1859, there were enough men living locally to form a voluntary railway corps.

Cholera broke out in the 1860s and 1870s, and the outbreaks led the LNWR to tap a better water supply from sandstone around Whitmore. Until a hospital was built, people seriously injured in accidents were sent by brake van to Chester. The railway kept law and order, appointing its own men as policemen. They took over from Richard Stockley, the first parish constable, who car-

Page 169 (above) Stourbridge—Stourbridge Town as it is now—a charming station, more rural than urban in atmosphere, though in the town centre. The line beyond, since removed, ran to a goods depot beside the canal. Trains on the short branch to Stourbridge Junction were replaced by GWR buses during World War I; (below) the original Oxford, Worcester & Wolverhampton viaduct at Stourbridge, replaced by the present one in 1882. The river below was channelled to pass between two piers

Page 170 (*above*) The lattice viaduct at Halesowen. Local with GWR clerestory stock headed by Pannier no 2718, 12 July 1939; (*below*) LMS local at Wednesbury, headed by 2–4–2 tank no 6661. An air of dereliction pervaded many small stations before closure

ried a stout whip 'which struck terror into many lawless citizens'.

Works and station grew apace. Further station improvements were necessary when the main line to Stafford was quadrupled in 1876. That, in turn, caused more congestion and a major remodelling of Crewe and the approaches around the turn of the century, including the construction of goods lines under the station to carry freight from the Manchester and Liverpool lines clear of the platforms.

One man was responsible for the creation of Crewe: Francis Webb, whose power stretched far beyond his post of Locomotive Superintendent of the LNWR for 32 years. As Lord Stalbridge said as Webb retired in 1903:

> His name will always be joined to that of Crewe, as he has, almost from its very beginning, been the main-spring of the greatest of our manufacturing departments, and its growth, during the years that he has been with us, can be measured by the following facts: When he entered the service on the 11th August 1851, there were only 840 houses in Crewe, with a population of 4,491, while we employed in our works and steam shed only 649 workmen. At the present time there are over 8,771 houses in Crewe, with a population of 43,237, and we now employ 10,146 persons.

The statement brought cheers from shareholders. They were proud of the works, as was the company, which stated in the *Railway Year Book, 1908*:

> The locomotive works, covering 116 acres, 36 of which are covered in, and employing about 10,000 men, are situate at Crewe, where a town of 43,000 inhabitants has in consequence arisen, which is wholly dependent upon the railways for its prosperity. It is hardly necessary to state that Crewe works form the largest and most celebrated railway establishment in the world.

The Railroad runs through the middle of the house was a song of the 1960s, but the concept of a railway running through the middle of a works was a reality long ago at Crewe. It happened when the works were expanded on both sides of the Chester line, and lasted until a diversion was built along the new southern boundary of the works in 1878. The original route runs into the works past the office block.

Crewe's claims to fame were not restricted to railways. In the vicarage beside the Potteries line at Crewe Green, John Ellerton wrote a hymn that is loved all over the world: *The Day Thou*

L

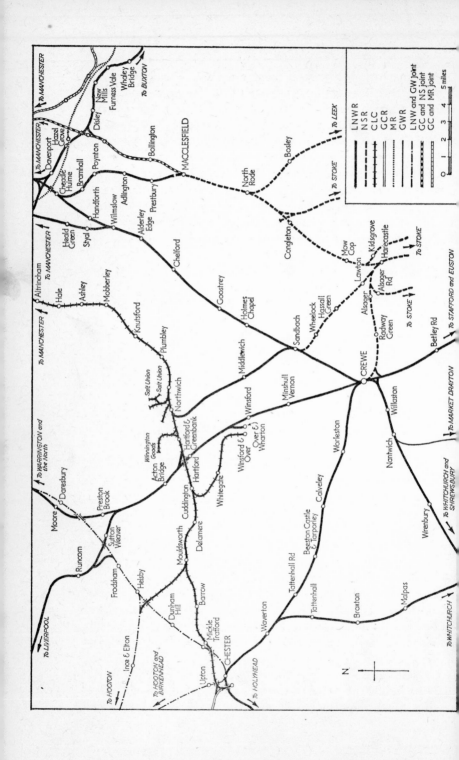

Gavest. Church and railway had close connections, for Euston built Crewe Parish Church, and one of its first vicars was Canon Webb, brother of Francis.

Crewe is remembered as a 'one company' town, but there were intruders: the North Staffordshire, which had exchange sidings within sight of the station and a goods depot (Thomas Street from 1910) on the main line north, and the GWR. No obvious traces of Paddington's influence remain, but once it was respectable enough. Besides Gresty Lane Marshalling Yard, as the GWR called the five sidings holding 206 wagons, there was a small shed for locomotives that turned at Basford Hall; and the company used the Shrewsbury bays at the south end of the station, where it had its own booking office, passenger agent's office, and lamp and porters' room. After grouping, fixtures were allocated to the LMS, moveable furniture to the GWR. The latter's staff of 27—almost half goods guards—was headed by a station-master until 1915, but afterwards by a yardmaster, class 2.

Most Great Western freight trains received at Crewe were sent from Oxley, but there was difficulty for years about engines turning. It was reported to Paddington in 1924:

> Considerable time is occupied by the GW engine in getting to and from Basford Hall, and strong representations have been made to the LM & S Company and the London Authorities.

When the first section of mainline electrification was completed between Manchester and Crewe in 1961, the occasion was celebrated by a glossy, highly futuristic book called *All Change at Crewe*. The title is true in another sense, for the town is no longer a purely 'railway' one. It now has a broader based economy, notably as the home of Rolls Royce cars. Rolls Royce is Crewe's other major employer and together they cause problems when it comes to summer holidays. When it was decided to close schools from mid-July until the end of August 1972, locomotive workers protested that the children would be breaking up just as they were ending their holidays; and Rolls Royce stated it could not allow holidays at the same time as the railways because its holidays had to coincide with those taken by firms that supplied components.

Production changed at the locomotive works after they passed to the control of British Rail Engineering Ltd. Ships' anchors and bridges were made for private customers, besides locomotives for BR. Some locomotives belonging to private companies were also repaired. Crewe, together with several other works, was hit by redundancy during a 1971 recession in freight, which meant that fewer locomotives needed repair.

Crewe is a town where the country is never far away, a fact mentioned by a reader of *Rail News* when recalling his days in Basford Marshalling Yards. While he found shunting in blizzards a drawback, good shifts outnumbered the bad. One compensation he enjoyed was the chance to observe wild life, which abounded in and around the yards, and showed no fear of men or locomotives.

Basford Hall yards, which were fully electrified, suffered serious decline in May 1972 when the marshalling of long distance freight trains was transferred to Warrington, and Crewe was left to deal with only local ones.

The first section of the Grand Junction to be electrified formed part of the Liverpool–Crewe route, switched over on 1 January 1962. The work was not vastly different from that completed 16 months earlier between Crewe and Manchester, but it did include more track modifications. Work on the 18 miles between Crewe and Weaver Junction was complicated by the density of traffic. One of the local stations rebuilt was that at Winsford, the only intermediate town of any size. It was first put on the railway map by the Grand Junction, but the line passed about a mile to the east. Winsford grew rapidly in Victorian days until almost all its working population was in the salt industry.

OVER & WHARTON BRANCH

By then, the town had a second railway, a tenuous link from the Cheshire Lines, near Hartford, which will be discussed later in the chapter. That line opened in 1870. When the LNWR found it would be profitable to get into the heart of the town, it did so much more economically, opening a line of no more than a mile in 1882. Its junction with the main line was north of the station and its terminus was called Over & Wharton—alias Winsford. It served half a dozen sidings to salt and other works, and three-quarters of the line remains busy handling salt and sand quarry traffic.

Although Winsford was served so well by railways, there was still competition from coasting ships of up to 350 tons using the River Weaver.

It was hoped that the expansion of Winsford to provide homes and jobs for Merseyside's overspill would increase commuter traffic, but the town remains small, with a population of about 25,000.

CHESTER & CREWE

One line that helped Crewe to become the only 'railway town' in the region was the Chester & Crewe, about which it was said during construction that 'it began in a field and ended in the rotten old city of Chester'. Certainly, it ran almost entirely through fields, serving only tiny, widely spaced villages on its 21 mile crossing of the Cheshire Plain. Yet it had an abundance of gentle curves and largely followed the Shropshire Union Canal. There was no major engineering feature—the main one being an eight-arch viaduct over the Weaver, one of the county's more important rivers, near Crewe.

In concept, the c & c was much more than a local line, its promoters aiming to take a railway through Wales to carry the growing traffic to and from Ireland. Soon after its creation, the c & c authorised George Stephenson to survey a line forward from Chester to Holyhead and an alternative to Porth Dinlleyn. Stephenson favoured the 84 mile route along the coast to Holyhead, even though it meant a major bridge across the Menai Strait. The Government supported him because Holyhead had a much better harbour than its rival.

Just over half the c & c was built by Brassey, working for the first time under Robert Stephenson as engineer. Brassey's two earlier contracts had been for Locke.

The rural nature of the line was reflected in some of the quaint names given to stations before opening: Crow's Nest, which became Tattenhall in the first timetable, and Black Dog (Waverton). Worleston was known as Nantwich until the title was more accurately taken over by a station built for the Shrewsbury & Crewe.

The Chester & Crewe was absorbed into the Grand Junction on 1 July 1840, 3 months ahead of opening.

The character of the Cheshire countryside has changed little through the centuries: there has been little industrial or residential development in the rich farming area. To estate agents, Waverton remains a 'Delightful village 4 miles south of Chester with easy access to industrial Merseyside'.

Beeching recommended the Chester–Crewe local service for modification and it was given a grant of £40,000 a year; but this was withdrawn from 1971 and the service adjusted. The line's value as a through route remains, for the 19.20 from Chester regularly carries up to 250 passengers to join the last Euston express of the evening from Crewe.

MANCHESTER & BIRMINGHAM RAILWAY

The Grand Junction absorbed the Chester & Crewe to prevent it falling into the hands of its arch enemy of the time, the M & B. The animosity dated back several years to when the first route was projected between Manchester and Birmingham by a group of influential Manchester men, dedicated to reaching London independently of the Grand Junction, even suggesting a line running beside it for miles. This plan never materialised because a rival group promoted the Manchester South Union via Stockport, Congleton, and the Trent Valley to Tamworth. Parliament forced an amalgamation of the ideas and the next line projected was via Stockport and Congleton through the Potteries to the Grand Junction at Chebsey, near Norton Bridge. It proved too costly and the Grand Junction suggested that the M & B should be curtailed to a line between Manchester and Crewe, on the understanding that it could run its own trains south of the junction. But the moment the M & B was authorised in this restricted form, the GJR withdrew that concession.

The row became so bitter that when the M & B was opened in May 1842, trains ran only to Sandbach. It took another 3 months of talks to give Crewe the fourth of its six junctions. Details of the first interchange arrangements are sketchy, but it seems that the M & B was allocated a bay at the north end of the station. Through vehicles were transferred to and from the Grand Junction by a double-end siding—a procedure also followed by the LNWR and GWR at Oxford for many years.

The M & B fairly sprinkled rural Cheshire with stations between

Stockport and Sandbach, then the only intermediate towns. There were stations more or less on the pattern of today : Cheadle (later replaced by Cheadle Hulme), Handforth, Wilmslow, and Alderley, to which the present title of Alderley Edge was given in 1876. All now serve a highly populated commuter belt, between which and Sandbach lie the original stations of Chelford and Holmes Chapel.

TELESCOPES AND GOALPOSTS

The M & B changed little until electrification, although the Styal Loop was added in 1909. The Loop and the mainline formed the first section to be converted, one of 42 route miles. Power boxes were built at Wilmslow and Sandbach, a district electric depot at Crewe, opposite the works on the south side of the Chester line, and a supply control room to feed the Liverpool and Manchester routes.

A cellular embankment was built at Elton, near Sandbach, with adjustable Rugby-style goalposts to prevent the overhead wires sagging in an area where subsidence is constantly occurring. Near Goostrey the line passes the giant radio telescope at Jodrell Bank, and although the railway is in a cutting, passengers get a grandstand view of it. Hopes, never strong, that Manchester's postwar expansion would extend the commuter belt to Crewe came to naught, the suburbs being contained around Alderley Edge.

Intensive Manchester–Crewe local services introduced on electrification in 1961 were detailed in a leaflet opening out to a width of more than 3ft, but they were soon modified. The locals are heavily subsidised, a 2 year grant of £355,000 being necessary from 1971.

MID-CHESHIRE BATTLEGROUND

The rail network that developed in the area bounded by Crewe, Warrington and Stockport was shaped largely by tactical battles fought by several companies. Schemes for a line between Stockport and Warrington were put forward in 1864–5. The Macclesfield & Knutsford was to be worked and managed by the Cheshire Midland and the North Staffordshire, or both. The Cheshire Midland was to exercise a similar function over the proposed

Knutsford–Warrington, sharing responsibility with the Warrington & Stockport.

Both schemes were largely local in scope, but they had the support of the Manchester, Sheffield & Lincolnshire—a situation which the LNWR saw as a threat to its territory. It gained the upper hand by offering to withdraw opposition to the Macclesfield, Bollington & Marple provided that the Sheffield company stopped backing the Knutsford schemes. The Marple line was far more valuable because it would complete an alternative route between Manchester and the Potteries to that via Stockport.

The MB & M was incorporated in 1864 as an independent company with two representatives of the North Staffordshire and the MS & L on the board. It was dissolved in 1871, when its property was vested in the 'Macclesfield Committee'.

Macclesfield businessmen were given authority for the Macclesfield, Knutsford & Warrington Railway in June 1866. It was to be no more than single. The MS & L was given running powers over the 26 miles and seemed set to achieve the route from which it had withdrawn two years earlier; but before construction could start a major slump set in and killed, for all time, a direct link between the Cheshire Lines and the NSR.

When the economic climate improved in the early 1870s, the Macclesfield directors hoped for assistance from the Cheshire Lines; but it was not interested in building the entire line, suggesting it should be reduced to 11 miles between Macclesfield and Knutsford. The MK & W got powers in 1871 for an extension of time for construction and the Sheffield company was given acquisition powers; but nothing was done and the company was dissolved just over 3 years later. Powers were transferred to the NSR, but it never sought to use them.

Only one Cheshire line promoted in the mid-1860s became a reality: the Northwich–Sandbach, for which the LNWR received sanction in 1863. Although mainly single, it served a developing salt and industrial area. It was completed in two stages, goods running from November 1867, and a passenger service starting 8 months later.

It remains a busy freight artery because its value increased when a west to south facing spur was put in at Northwich in 1957 for oil trains from the refineries at Ellesmere Port, among the biggest in Britain, to reach several areas without reversal.

One such area, initially, was the Potteries, the trains continuing via Sandbach and Harecastle.

Local passenger trains were withdrawn in 1960. They were never intensive and Cledford Bridge Halt, between Middlewich and Sandbach, had closed in 1942.

The line and two of the Northwich salt branches were among those designated for exploitation under the BRB *Network for Development* plan of 1967. The Sandbach branch was to be complementary to the Sandbach–Harecastle line as a route avoiding Crewe. This concept collapsed with the closure of the Harecastle line, as will be noted, in 1971.

CHESHIRE LINES COMMITTEE

Northwich was served primarily by the Cheshire Lines Committee. Outside its area the company was, and remains, comparatively little known, and so its status as probably the most important of Britain's joint lines has never been properly recognised.

Contrary to its title, its busiest lines were in industrial South Lancashire, as the company itself was forced to admit:

> The title of the Railway is somewhat misleading, because to the uninitiated it conveys the impression that the lines of railway which are controlled by the Committee are solely confined to the district of Cheshire, whereas the most important part of the system is actually in Lancashire.

Despite heavy mineral traffic to Northwich, the character of the system in Cheshire was different, for it was mainly rural.

The Midland's stake in the route was as the youngest of the three partners in the Cheshire Lines. With the Great Northern and the Manchester, Sheffield & Lincolnshire, the Committee inherited the Chester route, which had been conceived by three small companies. The Cheshire Midland was incorporated in 1860, when a big revival of the salt industry was forecast, to complete almost 13 miles from the Manchester, South Junction & Altrincham to Northwich. The terrain was conquered in respectable time, Altrincham and Knutsford being linked in 1862 and Northwich reached at the beginning of the following year.

NORTHWICH AND WINSFORD

Northwich was the centre of one of the world's richest salt areas, and to capture traffic being carried on local rivers and canals, a

CHESHIRE LINES.

Easter Holiday Excursions

On GOOD FRIDAY, SATURDAY, SUNDAY and EASTER MONDAY,

APRIL 14th, 15th, 16th and 17th, 1922,

DAY EXCURSION TICKETS will be issued to

CHESTER

(NORTHGATE STATION), as under:—

STATIONS.	GOOD FRIDAY and EASTER SUNDAY	SATURDAY		EASTER MONDAY		Fare to Chester and Back. ONE DAY. Third Class.
	A.M.	A.M.	P.M.	A.M.	P.M.	**5/-**
MANCHESTER (Central) .... dep.	10 0	10 0	1 30	9 30	1 15	
CHESTER (Northgate) ...... arr.	11 45	11 40	3 15	11 15	3 0	

Children under Three years of age, Free ; Three and under Twelve, Half-Fares.

The Day Tickets will be available for returning from CHESTER (Northgate Station) on Good Friday and Easter Sunday at 7 45 p.m., on Saturday and Easter Monday at 6 40 and 8 0 p.m.

SATURDAY TO MONDAY TICKETS—

CHEAP WEEK-END TICKETS are issued between any Two Stations, available on the Outward Journey on Saturdays by any Train, and to return on Sundays by any Train after 6 0 a.m. (where Train Services permit), and on Mondays by any Train, at a **SINGLE FARE AND A THIRD** (plus fractions of 3d.) **FOR THE DOUBLE JOURNEY.**

MINIMUM :—FIRST CLASS, 10/- ; THIRD CLASS 5/-.

For full particulars apply at the Company's Stations, Agents, and Town Offices.

Excursion Tickets.—Excursion tickets are not transferable, and are available only to and from the stations named upon them, and by the trains named in the Company's Bills, etc., announcing the excursion, and if used to or from any station beyond, or short of, the stations named on the tickets, or by any trains not advertised in the bills, &c., they will be forfeited, and the holders thereof will be charged the full ordinary fare for the whole distance travelled. **NO LUGGAGE ALLOWED.**

IMPORTANT NOTICE.—Tickets may be had at the Stations any time in advance, and in Manchester and District at the Agents' Offices shewn below :—**Messrs. T. Cook & Son,** 77, Market Street, Victoria Bridge, and Midland Hotel ; **Messrs. Dean & Dawson,** 53, Piccadilly ; **Messrs. Swan & Leach,** 27, Princess Street, and 212, Stretford Road ; **Mr. Frank Short,** Tower Entrance, Royal Exchange ; **Mr. A. Carter,** 152, Alexandra Road and 6, Oldham Road, New Cross ; **Great Central Railway Co.,** 3, Oldgate ; **Midland Railway Co.,** 47, Piccadilly ; **Mr. J. Gibson,** 337, Regent Road, Salford.

Central Station, Liverpool, March, 1922.   **JOHN E. CHARNLEY, Manager.**

C. TINLING & CO., LTD., Printing Contractors, 53, Victoria Street, Liverpool.   No. 47

The Cheshire Lines worked hard to boost Chester excursion traffic soon after World War I

network of branches was built, extending to nearly 5 miles. They were opened in 1867 and 3 years later another was added between Hartford and Winnington, the descent to the terminus at 1 in 53 giving the CLC its steepest gradient. A special run by the Railway Correspondence & Travel Society on 29 March 1960 to the intermediate sidings at Oakleigh was believed to be the first passenger train to use the branch. A north to east spur at Hartford was built by the LNWR in 1870.

The route west from Northwich was continued by the West Cheshire Railway, incorporated in 1861 to join the Birkenhead Railway at Helsby 14½ miles away. It was fully opened in 1869, construction having been protracted. It veered away northwards from the direct approach to Chester (the obvious target for a link from Northwich) at Mouldsworth, leaving Chester to be reached eventually by the CLC as inheritors from 1866 of the powers of the Chester & West Cheshire Junction Railway. It had been formed a year earlier to link the West Cheshire at Mouldsworth with the Birkenhead Railway at Mickle Trafford, and build a terminus at Chester (Northgate).

Chester was reached late in 1874, but the junction at Mickle Trafford, one of the two intermediate stations, remained uncompleted because of a 'who-does-what' dispute. The row, with the Birkenhead company, was never settled, and the spur was lifted in 1903. It was restored for wartime use in 1942.

The Cheshire Lines claimed that Winsford—with Northwich and Knutsford—was one of the principal towns that it served, even though it lay at the end of a 6 mile branch from Cuddington. The line meandered through wooded country and was bedevilled with crossings before reaching its modest terminus of a single platform and a few sidings. There was only one intermediate stop at Whitegate. The branch was not built primarily for passengers, but for salt, and the company's claim about Winsford gains credibility when it is realised that the line served eight busy salt works and two sidings. Authorised in 1862 with that to Winnington, it opened on the same day 8 years later.

CLASSIC LEGAL BATTLE

Passenger trains did not run to Winsford until a month later and they were withdrawn after only 4 years. They were restored *twice*, before being withdrawn for good after one of the first legal battles that took place in Britain over competition between road and rail. It began after the CLC announced the withdrawal of the passenger trains from 1 January 1931, after the LMS had stated that buses would provide an alternative link. They were introduced by the Stockport-based North Western Road Car Company. A few months later Winsford Council went to court, taking advantage of a ruling, peculiar to the line, made after its original closure to passengers in 1874. Services had been resumed in 1886, but following an accident soon afterwards, the Board of Trade banned them until £7,500 had been spent interlocking points and signals. Unwilling to pay, the Cheshire Lines stopped the passenger service. The local board, as it then was, protested to the Railway & Canal Commissioners, who ordered the company to provide 'all due and reasonable facilities for receiving and forwarding and delivering passenger traffic upon and from the Winsford branch'.

The ruling sustained a passenger service from 1892 until 1930. When the Winsford Council claimed closure was a breach of the 40-year-old order, the CLC—for such it had remained despite grouping—presented evidence of decline. It stated that between 1924 and 1930 passengers had fallen by nearly a third—from 99,000 to 68,000. Ticket receipts had slumped even more—from £1,700 to just over £800—and season ticket sales had fallen from £117 to £37. Running expenses of more than £5,000 in 1924 had been reduced by £1,300 in 1930, mainly by using a steam railcar.

The Commissioners rejected the Council's case, agreeing unanimously that it was within the discretion of the CLC to decide whether it would resume passenger traffic. It never did.

Today the line is again open to 'passengers', for after closure in 1968 the County Council bought the trackbed. The southern section, the least attractive, was suggested as part of the route of a Winsford–Middlewich by-pass, while the rest became the evocatively named 'Whitegate Way'—what the planners termed a greenway through pleasant woods and heath, linking the town with the extensive Delamere Forest—pierced by the Altrincham–Chester line.

The Winsford branch defeated the aspirations of individuals as well as councils—as Sir Edward Watkin learned to his cost. He saw it as the means by which the CLC could join the North

Staffordshire and proposed an extension of about 7 miles to join the branch from Harecastle. When his Cheshire Line partners refused to have anything to do with the idea, Watkin got a 'do-it-yourself' Act for the Sandbach & Winsford Junction Railway in 1872. It contained a clause—probably unique—forbidding the laying alongside the railway of any pipes through which brine could be pumped out of the district. It allowed adjoining landowners to enter the company's property to remove any pipes if laid, without being deemed trespassers. In the event the powers were never needed for the s & wj had a short paper life of 3 years, being abandoned because no other support could be found.

Little change took place on the lines of Cheshire until recent years. The Altrincham–Chester line carries a tremendous volume of limestone to the ICI works at Northwich and Middlewich. One of the plants, Wallerscote, produces soda ash, extensively used in glassmaking, and in 1965 block workings began to a new railhead at Larbert in Central Scotland to serve four glass factories.

The Cheshire Lines system south of the Mersey lost its passenger hub through the closure of Chester Northgate in 1969, after the reinstallation of the 1874 crossover at Mickle Trafford, to switch Manchester trains to the Birkenhead & Lancashire Junction route into Chester General.

Despite the loss of Northgate, much of the Cheshire Lines flavour lingers. Tall, quite handsome, signal boxes, matched by equally elegant signals, and a handful of stations remain mostly intact. Gaslighting at Knutsford caused problems when natural gas reached the area in 1970. Because of an impending switch to electricity, it was not thought economic to modify seven of the twenty-five lights to the new gas pressure, and the old ones were left burning day and night for about a year. How long *electric* lights will be necessary is in some doubt, for the Manchester–Chester locals are heavily subsidised, the 1971 figure being £316,000—substantial for a line that does not provide the only link between the two cities.

THE WHITCHURCH BRANCH

The branch, double-tracked, that ran 15 miles from Whitchurch through rural Cheshire to the Chester & Crewe at Tattenhall

Junction was planned as a through route to meet competition (or provide it), the promoters giving little thought to serving the intermediate area. It was of no great vintage, not being opened until 1872. The flat countryside placed no major barriers in the way of Euston's ambitions to break the GWR monopoly between Shrewsbury and Chester. Its aim was well summarised by Neele, who noted that it provided

> a direct line of our own from Ireland to Hereford and South Wales, and a competing route between Shrewsbury & Chester, unsatisfactory, probably, to the Great Western Company, who had hitherto possessed a monopoly of the traffic.

In fact, it made little impact on the GWR and could sustain no more than a sparse local passenger service. It was one of Cheshire's least known, and least used, lines, and few people stayed up late to watch the last regular train run in 1957. Two of the four stations—Malpas and Broxton—were retained for goods for 6 years. During that period the line was used for test runs by the experimental gas turbine locomotive GT 3.

FUTURE OF DISUSED LINES

Cheshire has a County Council keen to persuade people to enjoy life out of doors and the Whitchurch branch was among four disused lines once planned for conversion into Country Parks. They included part of the Nantwich–Market Drayton route, soon dropped because it was felt that the flat, rather monotonous, countryside would not attract walkers. The Wirral Country Park has become a reality through the adaptation of the Hooton–West Kirby branch, which ran mainly beside the Dee estuary. Nothing has been done with the Whitchurch branch, apart from the establishment of a picnic site at Broxton, on its most attractive stretch. Flanked by a ridge of hills to the east, and with the Welsh hills as a distant backcloth to the west, the line ran through an intensely farmed part of Cheshire. The plan for conversion to a Country Park was soon dropped, and in the autumn of 1972 a report of the Countryside Committee of Cheshire County Council stated that investigations had shown that it had 'very little potential for recreation'.

The same was stated about the former North Staffordshire Railway branch (see p. 208) between Sandbach and Harecastle.

The Committee stated that one of the former salt branches at Northwich (Marston–Wincham), and the Macclesfield, Bollington & Marple trackbed were, like the Nantwich & Market Drayton, under discussions with local councils and organisations. Experience had shown that old railways were expensive to redevelop and unlikely to give an economic return on expenditure unless other countryside facilities could be linked to them, as had been possible on the West Kirby line, at Broxton, with the former CLC branch to Winsford & Over, and on the NSR at Malkins Bank at Congleton.

The Committee lamented that there is, as yet, no satisfactory means of assessing in advance which lines are likely to become redundant in the foreseeable future. When one did become available, local authorities were normally only given a year in which to decide whether to buy or not—not an over-generous period. While problems associated with disused lines are not new, the scale of recent closures had made them more pressing.

LANCASHIRE, DERBYSHIRE & EAST COAST RAILWAY

An abortive scheme that would have done much to alter the railway map of north-east Cheshire deserves mention in detail, if only because it was authorised by Parliament. It was that of the Lancashire, Derbyshire & East Coast Railway of 1891, which was to have run 130 miles from Warrington to Mumby (Great Northern) and the Lincolnshire coast at Sutton-on-Sea. The western end between Macclesfield and Warrington was called the Lancashire Section, although almost the whole of it was in Cheshire! In the words of an exhaustive Descriptive Statement, issued shortly after incorporation, 'the outlet westwards will for the first time make the excellent Derbyshire steam coal practically available to the vast commercial marine of Liverpool'.

The line was to reach Cheshire after a mountainous crossing of the High Peak via Buxton :

> There is in this district every prospect of a considerable local traffic. The number of tourists, both to Buxton, which is only served by branch lines, and to Chatsworth, which is hardly accessible by rail at all, is, even under existing circumstances very large.

I wonder who told them about the busy local traffic of tourists. Certainly not Euston (although it was still waiting to build the

Buxton–Ashbourne line), or Derby. The Descriptive Statement continued :

> At Macclesfield, which is a town of 40,000 people and the centre of the silk industry, connection will be afforded with the system of the North Staffordshire Railway, so giving an outlet both to Stoke and the Potteries, and also to Birmingham and the Black Country. Northwards connection to Stockport and Manchester will be obtained by a branch traversing a new district very suitable for residential purposes . . .

The branch was to join the North Western at Cheadle Hulme and the CLC at Heaton Mersey. The LD & EC mainline was to continue west, passing between the small villages (now towns) of Alderley Edge and Wilmslow, to Knutsford.

> Here a junction is made with the Cheshire Lines, over which the great alkali manufacturers and salt miners of the Cheshire district, who heartily support this line, expect to be able to draw a large portion of their lime and coal from Derbyshire. In the district between Northwich and Winsford something like 1,500,000 tons of small coal are annually consumed by the salt and chemical trades. The Knutsford Junction also affords access to Chester and so to Wales and Ireland, and likewise, *via* Helsby, to Birkenhead and the Mersey. From Knutsford to Warrington there is no direct Railway connection at all, though the district is a rich dairy country and eminently suitable for residential purposes for the people not only of Warrington, but of the district beyond it to the west, which has been rendered almost uninhabitable by the fumes of the great chemical works with which it abounds.

There was never any chance of the LD & EC reaching Warrington. The company was forced to concentrate its slender financial resources on building the lucrative middle section through the coalfield east of Chesterfield. Money soon ran short and the company was forced to approach the Great Eastern, which had been sympathetic from the start. In 1894 it offered to provide capital of £250,000 on condition that all work was abandoned west of Chesterfield. Such capital would have seemed small to the LD & EC promoters, for the original Act provided for the raising of £5,000,000, the largest amount of railway capital ever authorised in a single Act.

Page 187 (*above*) Dudley. Crab no 42897 eases a special from Burton & Walsall round the South Staffordshire curve into the station, 16 August 1953. Oxford, Worcester & Wolverhampton route to Wolverhampton and goods yards in left background; LNWR yard, right: (*below*) Church Road Junction, Five Ways. The right and centre lines led to the now closed Suffolk Street (Midland) goods depot. On the left at a lower level, the Birmingham West Suburban Railway. Water column with heating stove, centre

Page 188 (*above*) Shropshire and Cheshire byways. The end of the line
at Coalport, beside the Severn. The little station viewed from the buffers,
9 August 1932; (*below*) South Cheshire wayside station: Broxton, near
Malpas. Chester—Whitchurch local, the 2.14 pm on 1 October 1955

CHAPTER XI

North Staffordshire Railway

LITTLE KNOWN LINE

The boundary of the Black Country is among the vaguest in Britain, but there is little doubt about that of the Potteries. It is an area, loosely within the West Midlands, where railways were conceived independently by men of vision, and developed in the same spirit. Today the old NSR remains identifiable within the nationalised whole. Half a century ago the Potteries mourned the death of a company known far beyond its bounds. As one of its champions, J. W. Walker wrote in 1910 :

> Next to the North Western 'diamonds', it is probable that no British railway company's trademark is so generally recognised as that of the North Staffordshire: engines, coaches, wagons, sheets and uniforms all display the familiar Staffordshire Knot.

The company thought differently, stating in 1908 :

> There is probably not another British railway of the size and importance of the N.S. Ry. that is so little known in London. This is accounted for by the fact that the N.S. Ry. is purely a local line, although through N.S. Ry. coaches work to and from St. Pancras, and its milk vans can be seen on the trains of the G.N. and other railways. Jointly with the L. and N.-W. Ry., the N.S. Ry. works through traffic between Euston and Manchester. The N.S. Ry. is also interested jointly with the Midland, the G.N., the G.W., and other railways in various lines.

A local line—yes. It approached its peak of success in the Edwardian years and was congratulated in *Bradshaw's Manual* review of 1906 for being among a handful of companies (all much bigger) which depended on suburban traffic for a great part of their revenue, and which had managed to distribute

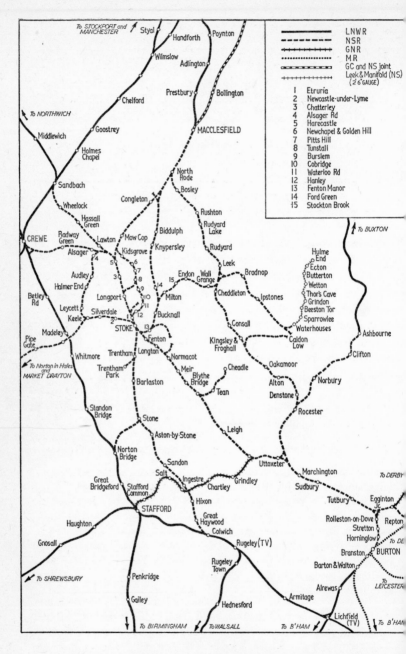

The North Staffordshire Railway, once described by a chairman as a 'small octopus'

improved dividends as a result of 'economies in various directions'. The dividend had risen to 4⅜ per cent, which was satisfactory, but the proud, independent Knotty was to be known in its final 4 years up to grouping by a title it liked—'A 5 per cent line'.

CANAL AND TRAM ROADS

It was also a very historic line. Long before railways were born in the area, there were short tramroads on Caldon Low, near Leek, a 1,000ft mountain of almost solid limestone.

The first great transport vein through the Potteries—a tremendous achievement in its age—was the Trent & Mersey Canal, from which a branch canal was built to Froghall in the Churnet Valley, at the foot of the hill. In 1776 the T & M was authorised to build a tramroad on inclined planes from the basin to a terminus 649ft above. The Act gave the NSR a birthright dating to the reign of George III. Although North Staffordshire was, and is, renowned for its pottery, heavy industry developed once it was found to be one of the richest coal areas in the world, and one where there was also ironstone. Once the Industrial Revolution led to a complex of mines, blast furnaces and ironworks, tramroads were quickly developed as feeders to the canals, one of the earliest being that to the Earl of Granville's ironworks at Hanley. At the extreme west of the industrialised area the owner of a large coalmine at Madeley ran a tramroad and later a railway to the Grand Junction mainline at Madeley station.

The tramroads were no more than curtain raisers, and it was early railway promoters lusting to get through the Potteries to open up the most direct route between London and the North West that eventually shaped the mainline system. Local people saw trains depicted on the mugs and teasets they made long before they ever saw one. Despite the early growth of the Potteries, it was still barren of lines when the Railway Mania arrived. At once it became the target for several schemes—good and bad. The Railway Department of the Board of Trade called for a year's breather while detailed, and detached, consideration was given to the best. The pause was put to good use by a group of local men who had kept alive for 10 years a plan with no suspicion of mania. The group, led by the MP for Stoke, John

Lewis Ricardo, revealed their plan in 1846 as the North Stafford-shire, or Churnet Valley & Trent Junction Railway.

Parliament passed a scheme without opposition and what was to be the backbone of the NSR was authorised on 26 June 1846. The company was to have four connections to the LNWR, and another to the Midland. In embryo the system resembled a pair of scissors, one arm being the route between Crewe and Derby, the other that from Macclesfield to Colwich. Branches included those to Newcastle, Silverdale and Sandbach, and there was an important line through the Churnet Valley from Macclesfield to Uttoxeter. Most of the main lines were completed in the short space of 3 years. The main problem was financial, for most share-holders did not want branches started until the main lines were finished and they were getting returns on their investments.

FIRST LINES

Stoke was on the railway map from 17 April 1848, the temporary terminus of a short branch from Norton Bridge. The lines were built first south from Crewe through mainly flat country, because north of Stoke the railway builders had to conquer the same barrier as the earlier canal pioneers—the high watershed ridge at Harecastle, between the Trent and the Mersey. The line from Stoke reached Uttoxeter on 7 August 1848, and Burton-on-Trent a month later. Stoke and Crewe were linked on 9 October, and the section between Harecastle and Congleton was finished the same day; but Harecastle tunnel was not ready until the follow-ing summer, when a train service began to run through it to Macclesfield. In the interim the Stone–Colwich route had opened in May 1849.

The Churnet Valley between North Rode and Uttoxeter had opened in July 1849. It included a section where the trackbed was laid over part of the Uttoxeter branch canal. A short line from Marston Junction to Willington, opened at the same time, followed a route authorised after a landowner objected to the original one, and completed a triangular junction between the NSR and the Midland main line.

Looking ahead, Uttoxeter was developed into a triangular junction in 1881 by a north-west curve for trains from Stoke to reach Ashbourne and the southern Churnet without reversal.

The Churnet was one of the Knotty's scenic routes—lines which surprised people who in their mind knew only the smoky industrial heart of the Potteries. The Churnet's virtues were appreciated by the author of a 1900 *Guide to the High Peak*:

> We change carriages at Rocester Junction in order to enjoy a run up the Churnet Valley. We use the word 'enjoy' advisedly, for there are few more charming valleys in the kingdom . . . The line passes through a most picturesque and beautiful district, every few yards traversed revealing new charms.

The shareholders' calls for quick completion of main lines led to some scrimping, with stations being opened before completion. Sometimes there were no fixed stop-blocks on back points on their sidings, scotches or sprags being used to prevent vehicles running loose and fouling running lines. But the stations were designed handsomely—as can still be noted at several places, including Leek and Stoke. The charm of NSR architecture remains, too, at Keele, where the station house, which dwarfed the station itself, is well preserved, with the company knot in the wall.

RAILWAYS OF THE VALLEYS

The company was under tremendous pressure for years to complete lines as iron and coal masters scrambled to get rail connections to move their heavy materials, raw and finished. Some took railway connection into their own hands when they doubted the NSR's intentions or ability to build what they wanted. One of the earliest examples of independent enterprise was a line from Etruria to the Granville Ironworks at Shelton. It ran almost to the site of what became Waterloo Road station, and the terminus became Hanley's first goods depot. An influential iron master, Ralph Sneyd, built the Silverdale & Newcastle Railway without powers, using it from 1850. He had feared, rightly as it turned out, that his extensive works would not be connected for some time, because the directors would not want to take the Newcastle branch west of the village while shareholders were critical of branch expansion.

Despite Sneyd's independent action, relations with the NSR remained friendly, and in 1859 the S & N became a public railway. It was leased to the NSR the following March, together with a short related line—the Newcastle-under-Lyme Canal Extension Railway, opened by Sneyd about 1854. The outlet for both Sneyd's railways was provided by the Newcastle branch of 1852. An associated line was a branch to Apedale ironworks of the following year.

Such was the power of the coal and iron masters that they were able to force a small company like the NSR to build lines where they wanted them, as with the Potteries, Biddulph & Congleton Railway, authorised in 1854 to serve extensive ironworks and rich coalmines in the Biddulph Valley east of Stoke. The industrialists said that if the NSR did not build the line, they would. When agreement was reached, they made the NSR pay their expenses! The line opened to goods and minerals in 1859, but it was another five years before a passenger service began.

Another purely goods line built without powers was the quaintly named Talk o' th' Hill branch, opened by Sneyd's North Staffordshire Coal & Iron Company in 1860. Authority for conversion to a public railway was given a year later.

The last NSR line of 1850s' vintage was a short branch to Hanley from the main line at Shelton, which, though authorised in 1859, was not ready for traffic until the end of 1861. It was a success from the moment it penetrated an area ablaze day and night with the flames of furnaces. The success was an embarrassment because local people clamoured for an extension to areas that were rapidly growing a little to the north, with row upon row of terraced houses straggling over the steep hillsides.

BATTLES WITH THE LNWR

It is now time to go back in history and recall a very distinctive phase of the company's existence: the first 13 years from its creation in 1846, when it was constantly at war with Euston. Only once have I noted the NSR described as wondrous—in a late Victorian travel guide. While it might sound a little boastful, it *was* wondrous how it managed to keep out of the clutches of so domineering a neighbour.

The LNWR was often arrogant towards the NSR. The chairman, General Anson, told his shareholders in 1853:

> That line is part and parcel of our own system; it is like a hand—a
> Line in the middle of our country with a quantity of branches, and its

traffic cannot be carried on so efficiently under separate management. Therefore I have no doubt that the amalgamation with the
North Staffordshire Company will be granted.

Amalgamation was attempted several times, but it never came
about, largely because of the independent spirit of the NSR directors, led by Ricardo. He resented some of the methods by which
Euston tried to force them to submit, and went to Parliament
to try and get Euston-type tactics outlawed nationally by
promoting a Traffic Regulation Bill in 1850. It was to be com-
pulsory for companies to stop passenger trains at all junctions,
and to run through coaches from other systems if there was enough
demand. It was not a popular bill but, although it failed, it
provided the embryo for a similar one introduced by the government only four years later.

The NSR's own problems were reflected in low dividends, only
1 per cent in 1850, although they had risen to 3 per cent in 1853.
In its battles the NSR was never short of the advice of shareholders. One contended in a lengthy pamphlet:

> No one can travel on the LNWR without being satisfied that some
> change must take place before long, and it is scarcely possible to
> conceive that the company will be able to do without us eventually.
> Their main line is even now very inconveniently encumbered with
> trains and the evil will continue to increase day by day until it becomes
> intolerable to the public.

It was felt that the best way of achieving sensible relations
with Euston would be to develop an independent route between
London and Manchester, and late in 1851 the NSR sought to
exploit the situation potentially dangerous to Euston, that was
created by the gauge war as the GWR drove north to Wolverhampton. NSR shareholders were told in 1852 about the line,
already noted, that had been surveyed from Colwich across
Cannock Chase to the GWR and the Oxford, Worcester & Wolverhampton at Wednesbury and Wolverhampton. To complement
this and provide a threat to Liverpool, the NSR sought to revive
the line planned from Sandbach to the Birkenhead, Lancashire
& Cheshire Junction Railway near Warrington.

The gauge was to be mixed so that the GWR could extend
through the Potteries and have a route to Merseyside not greatly
longer than its rivals. The NSR was to have running rights over

the BL & CJ to Birkenhead, over the Warrington & Altrincham Junction, and over the asociated Manchester South Junction & Altrincham. The NSR was prepared to welcome the GWR into the Potteries because of the outlets it would provide into South Staffordshire. The deputy chairman stated that it was impossible to overrate the importance of such a move.

During the squabbles between Stoke and Euston, three attempts were made at amalgamation. The first bill was withdrawn after a Select Committee advised Parliament against amalgamations generally. The Cardwell Act, which followed the Report, led to a second bill being barred, and the third attempt failed because of the opposition of the GWR, Manchester, Sheffield & Lincolnshire and the Midland, which did not want to see the now-thriving NSR fall into Euston's hands.

When relations with the LNWR again deteriorated in 1855, Stoke revived interest in a number of schemes, notably the link with the OW & W at Wolverhampton, and, for a third time, a line to Liverpool, the NSR engineer surveying a route from Sandbach to the St Helens Railway. A survey was also to be made on behalf of the NSR for an extension of that line from Garston to central Liverpool.

Plans described as 'Liverpool Extensions' were completed on 1 November 1855. A 19¼ mile line from the Sandbach branch was to cross the Manchester–Birmingham route south of Sandbach station and, after passing east of Middlewich and Northwich, follow the Trent & Mersey Canal to join the BL & CJ at Daresbury (birthplace of Lewis Carroll). North of the Mersey, access to Liverpool was to be over the Warrington & Stockport Railway (which had a branch running south from Warrington) and the St Helens Railway.

Such plans were quickly forgotten and the NSR's next territorial hopes centred on the take-over of the Cannock Mineral Railway. The NSR's already noted defeat by Euston did not please the directors but they accepted it with good grace. While there was little else they could do, their action enabled the company to avoid further bitterness and open the way to a lasting peace by an agreement, under an NSR Act of 13 August 1859, which consolidated traffic arrangements with the LNWR. NSR shareholders were alarmed that the company had accepted £8,000 from the LNWR to settle a claim of £62,000 for through traffic revenue, but the agreement gave Stoke its proper share of Manchester traffic and formed the basis of the eventual relations between the companies, with each using extensive running powers over the lines of the other.

STRIKING WEST FROM STOKE

The NSR pleaded poverty at times because it was having to strengthen its system around Apedale to keep away companies trying to penetrate the Potteries with independent lines from the west. Friendly relations with the LNWR and the leasing of the Silverdale & Newcastle Railway from Sneyd influenced battles that developed around 1860 against the GWR and its satellites. Paddington was not so much interested in the Potteries themselves but rather in establishing an independent route to Manchester by exploiting a scheme promoted by the Wellington & Cheshire Junction via Market Drayton, Nantwich and Northwich, with a branch from Madeley to Newcastle. Combined opposition by Euston and Stoke brought about the rejection of the vital sections between Nantwich and Northwich, and of the Newcastle branch.

Circumstances forced the NSR to go further west in its counter-attack by projecting a line from Silverdale to Market Drayton. Euston was implored to become a joint party, but it was not interested. Left to 'go-it-alone', the North Staffordshire was the third line to reach Market Drayton, its authorisation in 1864 falling between the completion of the Nantwich & Market Drayton 9 months earlier and the completion of the Wellington & Drayton Railway in 1867. The NSR Act included a spur to the LNWR and running powers to the station at Madeley nearby. In return the LNWR was to have running powers to Market Drayton. All three lines to Market Drayton were destined to cost far more than their promoters intended. The N & MD had to double its capital to £120,000, the W & D found construction costly, and the NSR complained that landowners had demanded excessive compensation. They were paid, however, and the line opened in 1870.

The NSR further developed its western fringe with branches authorised on the same day as the Market Drayton line, the Audley lines, as they became known, between Silverdale and

Alsager, with branches to pits at Jamage (a corruption of Gem Edge), and Bignall Hill. They were opened in 1870, just a week inside the time limit. Passenger services were introduced via Audley 10 years later, about the time powers were obtained to divert the southern end of the line to provide an east rather than west facing junction with the Market Drayton line. Mining subsidence had made the originally planned line between Silverdale and Leycett troublesome.

The 'Audley' Act also provided for a branch to Chesterton, a busy mining area just across the hill from Audley. Access was through the sidings at Chatterley, though plans were prepared from time to time for a direct connection to the main line.

THE IMMORTAL LOOP

Much as the NSR is loved by many, only one part can claim immortality—the Potteries Loop. It was built with great reluctance; indeed, it is doubtful if ever a line was driven into such a densely populated area with such little heart.

Its concept was that of an 'inner circle' to serve six tightly packed towns, which merged into one. Despite the clamourings caused by the opening of the line to Hanley, 4 years elapsed before the NSR received authorisation, in 1865, for the Loop, a mere $7\frac{3}{4}$ miles in length, to unite Hanley with Kidsgrove, the northern extremity of residential areas. Almost immediately there was a national trade slump, which the company saw as an opportunity to abandon the Loop and branches to Burslem and Tunstall. Shareholders readily agreed. Local authority protests to Parliament were so strong that the Commons threw out the company's request to abandon the line, the Board of Trade making an Order confirming the members' decision on 6 May 1870. The NSR hated being forced to complete the Loop and a deputation inspected the Ffestiniog to see if the Loop might be finished more economically in narrow gauge. The Board rejected the idea.

The Loop was eventually completed on 15 November 1875 and was an immediate success. Of a different character were a number of branches built to serve new or expanding pits. The company had sought to abandon some of them at the same time as the Loop. There was one from the main line at Longport to the Loop at Tunstall Junction called the Tunstall Lower Branch, and another from Pinnox to Newfields called the Tunstall Upper Branch. The Lower Branch was known locally as the Pinnox Branch, after exchange sidings serving large pits of the Chatterley–Whitfield Colliery company, whose private system continued east into the Biddulph Valley to its own pits and ironworks.

The Biddulph Valley line was originally to have been extended to several pits lying south of the route finally adopted, and it was left to an independent company to reach the mines. The Longton, Adderley Green & Bucknall Railway was sanctioned in 1866 to run 4½ miles from the Biddulph line to Longton with two pit branches. Later it was extended to Park Hall on the Derby line and became a circular route. This made coal hauls too short for the liking of the NSR, and after it bought the LAG & B for £22,500 in 1895, it promptly cut the line in two.

One of the largest towns lying on the frontiers of the North Staffordshire was Burton, to which it gained access progressively, beginning with a passenger service in September 1848. Exactly a year later it began running goods trains for private sidings connected to the Midland company's lines—an arrangement consolidated by an agreement between the companies of 1 January 1851 which gave the NSR running powers over all the Midland's branches in Burton. The NSR introduced a local collection and delivery service with horse drays on 4 February 1862, and appointed a Burton goods agent. The following year it received powers for a line which, although little more than a mile in length, took it into the heart of the beer town. It ran from Stretton Junction to Hawkins Lane Junction, and gave access to the LNWR goods depot at Horninglow Street, ¼ mile beyond. The same Act provided for a branch from the Biddulph Valley at Milton Junction to the Churnet at Leek Brook Junction to give Leek, an important market and silk town, a direct link with Stoke.

'A railway within a railway' that was built late and survives is that to Cheadle, a market town at the centre of a small coalfield. The branch was the outcome of several schemes, the 4 mile route from the Derby line at Cresswell being constructed by a private company, Cheadle Railway Mineral & Land Limited, which had the very necessary financial support of the NSR. Although authorised in 1888, the line was not completed for 12 years. The stumbling block was a tunnel under a 700ft high

NORTH STAFFORDSHIRE RAILWAY.

There are many places of great interest to Tourists and others on this Company's line which are easy of access from

Manchester, Oldham, Stalybridge, Ashton, Liverpool, Leeds, Huddersfield, Sheffield, Nottingham, Birmingham, and all other Lancashire, Yorkshire, Nottinghamshire, and Derbyshire Towns,

And to which Tourist and Excursion Tickets are issued each season ; such as

RUSHTON, for Danebridge, Ludchurch, Gun Hill, and the Hanging Stone

RUDYARD, with its Lake 180 acres in extent. Boats and Fishing can be obtained on application to the Proprietress of the Rudyard Hotel.

LEEK, for Rock Hall, the Roaches and Morredge Hills, and Thor's Cave.

ALTON, for the Towers, Gardens, and Castle. The Gardens and Grounds of Alton Towers are, by kind permission of the Earl of Shrewsbury, open to the public during the Summer Season on each week day. Admission, 6d.

ASHBOURNE, for its splendid Church, and

DOVE-DALE, Beresford Dale, Mill Dale, Ilam, Tissington Spires and Wells, Thorpe, &c. First-rate fishing can be obtained on application to the Hotel Proprietors in the Dove-dale district.

FROGHALL, for the great Limestone Quarries at Caldon Low. Geologists, Field Naturalists, &c , should not fail to visit here.

DENSTONE, for the College and the ancient ruins of Croxden Abbey, and Weaver Hills.

CONGLETON, for the beautiful Old Church at Astbury, and Moreton Old Hall.

STOKE, for the celebrated China Works of Messrs Mintons, Wedgwood, Copeland, Brown, Westhead Moore, and others, through which visitors are readily conducted.

TRENTHAM, for the Park and Grounds ; which are open to the public, by the kind permission of the Duke of Sutherland.

SANDON, for its beautiful Park (which is, by kind permission of the Earl of Harrowby, open to the public) and Gardens.

TUTBURY, for its Ancient and Historical Castle, and fine Church.

Also the magnificent Rock, Water, Wood, and Dale Scenery of the Churnet and Dove Valleys, through which Tourists travel over this Line.

All information as to train service, cheap tickets, etc., from and to this Company's System, can be obtained on application to any of the Company's Agents, or to

Railway Offices,

Stoke-on-Trent, April, 1898

W. D. PHILLIPPS,
General Manager.

From everywhere to everywhere—typical broad thinking by the Knotty. Even Stoke had its tourist attractions

ridge with tricky earth conditions. It proved continually trouble-some until the LMS diverted the line round the ridge in 1933. The Cheadle Railway was worked from opening by the NSR, which absorbed it 6 years later.

One joint line lying outside the scope of this work has its southern terminal at Macclesfield. That was the Macclesfield, Bollington & Marple, mentioned in the last chapter; it was authorised in 1864 and completed in 1870, but its concept was much older, for the NSR had often threatened to get an independent outlet to Manchester and Yorkshire during squabbles with Euston. The MB & M gained a little importance when it was linked with the Stockport–Buxton line by a spur at Middlewood in 1885. The NSR chairman hoped that the workers of the Potteries would make Buxton a recreation centre, but, working 6 days a week for small wages, they had little opportunity.

The NSR's reputation for independence was built solidly on fact. One of the factors that made it possible were locomotive and carriage works, established at Stoke in the early days. They reached their zenith in the early 1900s, employing nearly 900 men. In later years the company only placed orders with outside firms when the works were busy and more locomotives were needed quickly.

LEEK & MANIFOLD VALLEY LIGHT RAILWAY

A quotation from a 1900 travel guide will give an idea of the nature of this line, so different from all others of the company. It served the 'other Eden' of the Potteries.

THE LEEK, CALDON LOW, AND HARTINGTON LIGHT RAILWAY

This is the age of light railways. On the 3rd October, 1899, the Duke of Devonshire cut the first sod of a line of two feet six inches gauge running from Waterhouses in North Staffordshire to Hulme End, near the Hartington station of the Ashbourne and Buxton Railway in North-West Derbyshire. The distance is over nine miles, and the country traversed is one of many 'ups and downs,' necessitating sharp curves and severe gradients. The promoters of the undertaking are sanguine of developing tourist as well as mineral and agricultural traffic. The capital required is £35,000, £10,000 of which is given by the Treasury, an equal sum being advanced on easy terms by the

County Council, while the remaining £15,000 has been subscribed by the public, the landowners in most instances having taken up in shares the price of the land required for the line, confident of deriving substantial advantages from it.

If only it had turned out that way! The line's birthright was the Light Railway Act of 1896, and like so many others conceived by the Act, the L & M was always an ailing child. The NSR was lukewarm from the start, but work went ahead, and when the line opened in June 1904, it attracted attention because of its locomotives with flamboyant cabs (the inspiration of the engineer, E. R. Calthrop, who had recently built lines in India), and its unusual style of coaches.

One reason for the NSR's coolness was that it had to build two feeder lines of standard gauge, also authorised by a Light Railway Order of 6 March 1899. The first was of $4\frac{1}{2}$ miles from the Churnet at Cheddleton (later Leek Brook) Junction, to Ipstones, and the second was an extension to Waterhouses of almost equal length. This second section was to bring about the closure, many years later, of the Caldon tramway, since it gave direct access to the quarries. When the L & M was finished ahead of the Waterhouses branch, the NSR bought two steam buses to provide a feeder service until the branch was opened throughout on 1 July 1905.

There was a further complication on the L & MV route in feeling aroused in Leek at the prospect of Waterhouses getting a direct link with Stoke, and not with Leek, the local market town. Relations between Leek and the NSR had been touchy for years; it was stated openly that W. D. Phillipps, general manager for almost 40 years (1882–1919), hated Leek and everything about it. The station buildings were imposing, but its platforms were far too narrow for farmers and their wives taking produce to market. To pacify its critics, the NSR built a spur at Leek Brook Junction for direct running between Leek and Waterhouses.

Trains never faced much opposition in the Leek area until buses became reliable, but in the heart of the Potteries there was an earlier and successful competitor in the tram. To try and meet the threat, railmotors were introduced in 1905 and special halts were built, and a branch was also opened to Trentham Gardens, a great recreational centre. Authorised in 1907, this was the last NSR line. After it opened 3 years later, a light railway extension was sanctioned to Silverdale to form a western outer circle, but it was hardly started because of the Kaiser's War, and because of the scheme (passed in 1921 but killed by grouping) to widen the Stoke bottleneck. In 1920 the Caldon cable inclines had been closed, access to the large quarry continuing over the Waterhouses branch.

The NSR's pioneering spirit never flagged, and after early experiments with electricity, using batteries to light coaches, it switched carriage lighting from oil to electricity without having to use gas, so troublesome to many companies. Although the NSR never had an electrified line, there was one in the area—opened in 1899 to serve a large mental hospital just built at Cheddleton. The steeply graded ½ mile line ran from the Churnet Valley, and although it was used mainly for supplies, visitors' trains ran until about 1920.

The North Staffordshire line became the sixth largest LMS constituent on grouping in relation to the number of locomotives, but seventh in mileage. Nationally, it was the seventeenth grouped company in locomotive numbers; nineteenth in mileage.

YEARS OF DECLINE

The system shrank a little under LMS management, but not too severely. Far greater economies have been made since nationalisation, yet since 1923 no fewer than five new stretches of line—characteristically, all short—have been constructed. First was the Cheadle deviation of 1933, followed in 1940 by the Cold Meece branch to serve a large munitions factory. Electrification led to the opening of a chord at Madeley; the diversion of the Chesterton branch, and a major deviation at Harecastle.

The Cheadle deviation and Cold Meece branch were the major changes of LMS days, together with the closure of Stoke locomotive and carriage works in 1926. This closure caused deep shock locally, though little work was done after grouping : only four tanks were built, Hookham's 0-6-0 four-cylinder tank was rebuilt as a tender locomotive, and several LNWR engines were repaired.

Two railmotor halts were closed in 1923, four more in 1927—a year that saw the withdrawal of passenger trains through the Biddulph Valley from Stoke to Congleton. There was little

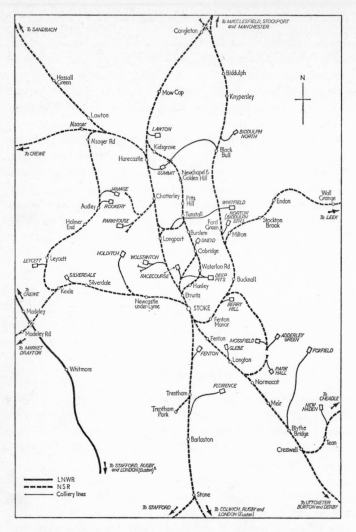

North Staffordshire Coalfield in decline. Collieries remaining in the Stoke-on-Trent District Goods Manager's Area in July 1937 after a number of pit closures. Some colliery names are confusing: Summit pit was Birchenwood; Biddulph North was Victoria. The map (copied from the official LMS List of Collieries) shows the Grange branch serving Hanley Deep pits as a through line, although it never joined the loop line at Cobridge. There was never a triangular junction with the Pinnox branch near Longport, and the colliery line from Black Bull turned north to Kidsgrove. Rail access to New Haden pit was from the direction opposite to that shown

surprise at this withdrawal, for the rail journey was roundabout for people shopping at Hanley The Biddulph was a line on which mineral trains run by iron and coal owners abounded—much to the NSR's pleasure, and, as it turned out, to LMS displeasure, for after grouping they were no longer welcome as a source of revenue and they ceased in June 1931. The workings, which consisted of local shunting and mineral trains run over NSR main lines, have been detailed by Dr J. R. Hollick in a privately produced booklet that deserves wider fame.

By 1930 there was industrial depression in the region. One of the major pits—Talke—had closed in 1928, throwing 1,000 miners out of work, and 2 years later five more pits around Apedale closed. When the pits closed, passenger services stopped —on the Sandbach branch in 1930, and on the Audley lines in the following year, when the tip of the Talke mineral branch was also closed. In 1934 much of the Market Drayton branch was singled, and on 12 March of that year the Leek & Manifold closed. There were fears that it would be converted into a road, but ramblers fought for a footpath, and in an age when the motor car was not so universally worshipped, the lovers of the open spaces had their way, and a small, but beautiful part of Britain was saved from the ravages of progress. Pressure remained for a road and in 1953 the section from Reahurst to Butterton, through the only tunnel, was converted into one.

Trams, which had long eaten into the potential revenue of local trains, especially those of the Loop, were themselves withdrawn and replaced by buses, which provided even stiffer competition. The LMS leased Caldon quarries in 1934 to a Sheffield firm, and 2 years later the three narrow-gauge quarry locomotives were cut up on site.

A wartime halt that has found a permanent place in the timetable (as a station since 1965), is Wedgwood, near Stone, opened in 1940 to serve the famous works.

The branch to Trentham, closed to regular passengers in 1927, though retaining excursion traffic from Birmingham and other places, gained fresh importance when the Bank of England Clearing House moved to the Hall during World War II. Trentham Hall, once the home of the Duke of Sutherland, was quite close to a wartime railway project—the Cold Meece branch of just under 1½ miles, stemming from the Stone–Norton Bridge line to serve the Royal Ordnance Factory at Swynnerton in the wooded country between the West Coast main line and the Potteries. The original access for goods and passengers was a connection at Badnall Wharf on the main line north of Norton Bridge, installed during the weekend war was declared in September 1939. An island platform and more sidings were added some months later, and a workers' service begun to and from Stafford on 4 March 1940; but the bulk of the munition workers used the Cold Meece branch.

It had a terminus of four platforms—one more than Stoke. The branch had a short life—officially 5 August 1941 to 3 August 1959—but it was busy. In 1943–4 it handled more than 200 trains a day, carrying 3 million passengers a year. Wartime secrecy meant Cold Meece never appeared in a public timetable, but the Germans knew about the factory, and it was the target for cynical comments by the propagandist Lord Haw Haw.

A Government testing station for goods vehicles has been built on the site of the terminus. Among final LMS economies was the withdrawal in 1947 of local passenger trains between Stone and Colwich, just before a major coal crisis that doomed branches all over Britain.

NATIONALISATION

Ashbourne lost its passenger trains when those between Buxton and Uttoxeter were withdrawn in November 1954 after a spirited fight by ramblers and local people had failed to beat the economists. Stoke–Leek locals came to an end in May 1956. They ran over a line still used by limestone trains from Caldon. At the same time as the Leek economy, passenger trains were withdrawn between Silverdale and Market Drayton, the Stoke–Silverdale stub retaining them until 1964, 2 years before complete closure. This left only a short section, served by the Madeley spur, which opened in 1962 on a trackbed that had been laid but never completed during construction of the Market Drayton line 90 years earlier. During electrification it carried Crewe traffic diverted from Stoke and places south. After the Market Drayton branch was severed at Newcastle, the Chord continued to be used by trains serving pits near Silverdale. The Market Drayton line west of·the Chord was closed in 1966, following the abandonment of plans for the Walcot marshalling yard at Shrewsbury, for which it was to have been a feeder route.

The Jamage mineral branch closed in the summer of 1954; the Newfields branch in 1959. After the Grange branch was abandoned 2 years later, it was redeveloped among a complex of sidings laid during extensions to Shelton steelworks. Passenger economies took place at intervals: Burton–Tutbury in 1960, and regular services through the Churnet from Macclesfield to Uttoxeter in the same year, though Leek–Uttoxeter workmen's ran until 1965. The Cheadle branch closed to passengers in 1963, though it retains a healthy mineral traffic, and the Loop locals stopped in the following year. The Audley freight branch closed in 1963, having been little used for some time.

Some of the economies were foreshadowed in the Beeching Report, which recommended reductions in local passenger services on all the NSR routes.

Towards the end of 1963 economies began affecting the Biddulph Valley and its asociated lines. The branch ceased to be a through route from 1 December 1963 because of the pre-electrification closure of a spur to the main line at Congleton. New access was provided to Whitfield Colliery to allow the closure of the Pinnox mineral branch from 1964. In 1968 the Biddulph branch was cut back from Congleton to its present terminus at Victoria Colliery, Biddulph.

In 1971 a Scottish schoolmaster suggested the preservation of the 4 mile section from Biddulph to Brunswick Wharf, and its reinstatement for commercial use. The move was welcomed locally, and the *Staffordshire Weekly Sentinel* commented: 'There are all sorts of excellent reasons for resurrecting these old lines and locos, not the least of which is the pride that people take in their work'.

In 1972 a short stretch of the trackbed at Malkins Bank, Congleton, was used by Cheshire County Council in a scheme for converting a chemical tip into a municipal golf course.

The Longton, Adderley Green & Bucknall Railway has gone. The southern section between Millfield Junction and Park Hall closed in 1963, and the remainder from the Biddulph branch to Adderley Green a few months later.

In recent years the Potteries have been making tremendous, and successful, efforts to remove the scars of old, of which the most unsightly were pit heaps. It has also made sure that new eyesores have not been created by railway lines left to become derelict after closure. After the LAG & B fell into disuse, the City of Stoke bought the northern trackbed and turned part of it into an attractive park. Another big reclamation scheme involved the Loop, which is progressively being converted into a recreation complex : once the Loop had been totally closed between Etruria and Birchenwood, BR handed over the land to Stoke, and the first part of the complex, Tunstall Greenway, was officially opened in 1972, with the unveiling of a plaque on a large plinth of concrete supporting a pair of driving wheels from a steam locomotive.

Not even Whitehall was able to keep pace with closures, and the Ministry of Technology was caught out in March 1970 when it advertised New Intermediate Areas of Britain, where industrial development was being encouraged. A map in its advertising showed the Churnet Valley as part of a through route of rail communication for the area.

The evacuation of Burton was done in stages. The southern tip of the Tutbury branch between Horninglow and North Stafford Junction closed in 1966, leaving the NSR fly-over across the Derby main line as the only access to Stretton sidings. The section between Stretton and the GNR Egginton curve closed 2 years later.

The Beeching Report was followed by one outlining the *National Network for Development*, which stressed the importance of the surviving section of the Biddulph Valley, the line from Stoke to Caldon and to the British Industrial Sand factory in the Churnet, the Cheadle branch, and the Madeley Chord.

The Harecastle–Sandbach branch closed completely on 1 January 1971, part being retained for a short time as an engineers' siding. For a year before closure the branch had been used only by trains from the Potteries, the junction at Sandbach having been damaged and clipped to prevent running in the opposite direction. Schemes to multi-signal platform 1 at Crewe to allow freight between the Potteries and North Cheshire to pass through the station without interfering with passenger movements were considered, but the expense was thought prohibitive.

From September 1971 the Madeley Chord and the single line through to Silverdale were worked from Madeley LNWR box as a siding, shunting of merry-go-round coal trains taking place in Silverdale Colliery Yard. This form of working allowed the closure of a modern box built to control the Chord.

The northern end of the Potteries Loop, retained to Birchenwood after closure, remains busy, and in 1971 the single track up the bank from Kidsgrove to Birchenwood Colliery was slewed into the bed of the old passenger line and extended to Golden Hill, where open-cast mining was begun and a big storage area established.

BENEFITS OF ELECTRIFICATION

The Potteries electrification was completed on 6 March 1967 and, with lines around Birmingham, formed the last section of the original programme. The Stone–Colwich section was closed for 3 years for conversion.

The work has given extra benefit to the Potteries, for it has placed Stoke on the shortest main line between London and Manchester and given the area a far better service than was possible in steam days, when the heaviest locomotives were barred from Stoke and, consequently, the fastest Manchester expresses ran via Crewe. One of the obstacles to electrification were the three Harecastle tunnels—two short and one long. They were abandoned after the building of a deviation $2\frac{1}{2}$ miles long through a shallow valley, a new tunnel of only 220yd being needed to pierce the ridge. Stiffer gradients proved no trouble to even the heaviest of electric trains. The deviation, and the associated diversion of the junction of the Chesterton branch, were opened before full conversion. The branch deviation seemed unnecessary, for the line closed shortly afterwards, when the local pit was worked out.

Doubts about the future of the Stone–Colwich section were aroused when financial experts examined the cost of maintaining the 11 miles as a duplicate to the route via Norton Bridge. There was a sense of occasion when the section was reprieved for the news was given first to NSR veterans at their annual lunch.

After grouping, Stoke lost its status as the headquarters of a railway, but later it became increasingly important as a divisional headquarters of the London Midland Region. It was enlarged in 1966 to include North and Mid-Wales from Holyhead to Aberystwyth. Since then there has been criticism in Wales at the

Cambrian and other lines being controlled from what is considered to be a remote centre. No one ever suggested a pre-grouping merger between the Cambrian and the NSR. Perhaps it might have been a good one!

Cheshire Countryside Committee's 1972 report on disused lines, already mentioned, listed seven old branches. Four of these are former NSR. Besides the Sandbach branch and the Macclesfield, Bollington & Marple, there are those of the Biddulph and Churnet Valleys. While mainly inside Staffordshire, they were noted as possible centres for a railway preservation society. The reference was presumably to the Cheshire & Staffordshire Railway Society, formed in October 1971, to try to revive a steam-operated branch. The society looked first at the north end of the Biddulph branch between the town and Congleton. When it was frustrated by Staffordshire County Council plans to use a mile of the trackbed for a by-pass, it was offered the 450yd tunnel at Leek, and plans were prepared for relaying track somewhere between Rudyard Lake and Oakamoor.

CHAPTER XII

In Derbyshire Hills

CROMFORD & HIGH PEAK RAILWAY

Few lines in Britain were better known than the Cromford & High Peak. Its spectacular methods of operation amid rugged scenery assured it of constant attention from enthusiasts. A stronger claim to fame, one often overlooked, was that it was one of the oldest railways in Britain, being incorporated on 2 May 1825 as a railway or 'Tram Road' from the Cromford Canal to a branch of the Peak Forest Canal at Whaley Bridge on the opposite side of the Pennine backbone.

The c & hp was mostly regarded as purely a Derbyshire line, but its birth lay in two counties, for at incorporation Whaley Bridge lay just within Cheshire. The 33 miles projected included eight steep inclines, graded up to 1 in 7, worked by stationary engines. Promoters saw it as something far more important than a local mineral line; their vision of it was as the route between eastern England and Manchester and Liverpool, one that could not be achieved by canals because of the hills.

While they did not quite achieve their hopes they managed to accomplish their ambitious aims in the construction of such a route. They took it to over 1,000ft above sea level, and completed it in 6 years.

The first section from Cromford to Hurdlow was opened in May 1830, and the remaining 17½ miles in July of the following year. The second stretch included curves so sharp that they alarmed contemporary writers. 'Strephon' wrote in *Pictures of the Peak* about 'The sky scraping High Peak Railway, with its corkscrew curves that seem to have been laid out by a mad Archimedes endeavouring to square the circle'; and a later writer felt that the line ran 'a course unequalled in Britain for abrupt curves and breakneck gradients'.

The c & HP remained isolated for more than two decades, until a short extension from Cromford Wharf to High Peak Junction connected it with the Manchester, Buxton, Matlock & Midlands Junction Railway in 1853. The next major improvement did not come until 1869 when the Hurdlow deviation was opened to avoid the 1 in 16 incline and allow locomotives to steam between Hopton Top and Bunsall Top. They were able to work through from Middleton Top to Bunsall Top when the gradient of Hopton Incline was eased in 1877.

The company was not authorised to act as carriers and a private firm—Wheatcroft—was licensed to convey passengers. It began a passenger carriage working from Cromford (actually Middleton Top) to Whaley Bridge and return, including passage of the inclines. The firm also operated a connecting coach between Whaley Bridge and Manchester. The c & HP took over the rail service in 1855, and in the following year restricted it to between Cromford and Ladmanlow, passengers having to walk the inclines. It ceased in 1877.

STOCKPORT, DISLEY & WHALEY BRIDGE RAILWAY

The LNWR successfully penetrated the Derbyshire Peak because of its control of the Stockport, Disley & Whaley Bridge Railway, which gave it access to Buxton from the north. Nominally independent, the company was heavily subsidised by the North Western, empowered to subscribe £85,000 of the original capital of £200,000. When that was doubled to finance an extension from Whaley Bridge to Buxton, the LNWR had authority to make a majority contribution of £105,000.

The original 10 mile line from Stockport to Whaley Bridge was authorised in 1854, and a Bill, promoted jointly with the Cromford & High Peak, provided for a short junction line at Whaley Bridge, to which the Manchester, Sheffield & Lincolnshire (an objector to the project), also had access, though only via the Peak Forest Canal. Construction was completed in 1857, just before authorisation of the Buxton extension.

Whaley Bridge was something of an industrial and geographical frontier, a travel writer noting that the line there 'quitting the region of toil and smoke, conducts us through the beautiful valley in which are the charmingly-seated town of Chapel-en-le-Frith and many other interesting spots, during the greater part of the journey presenting a succession of attractive views from the windows of the carriages'.

A lot happened before rail travellers could enjoy those views. Construction started so slowly beyond Whaley Bridge that in June 1860 the engineer, Joseph Locke, who was to die 3 months later, pressed the contractor to speed up work. The latter found an unusual obstacle—the supernatural world of 'Dickie's skull', kept in the room where he was murdered on a farm through which the line had to pass. Dickie was traditionally averse to any improvements in that area : it was claimed that he caused the foundations of a railway bridge on the farm to give way, and this led to the diversion of the line.

Llewellynn Jewitt, who published *The Ballads and Songs of Derbyshire* in 1868, only 5 years after the line was finished, found Dickie real enough :

> One of the crowning triumphs of Dickie's power is said to have been evinced over the formation of the new Buxton and Whaley Bridge line of railway. He seems to have held the project in thorough hatred, and let no opportunity pass of doing damage. Whenever there was a landslip or a sinking, or whenever any mishap to man, beast, or line happened, the credit was at once given to Dickie.

It has been suggested that the trouble was ended when the engineer interviewed Dickie and offered him a free pass on the line forever !

Between Chapel and Dove Holes the route ran parallel to the horse-drawn Peak Forest Tramway, built in 1797 and owned, by the time the Disley line was built, by the Manchester, Sheffield & Lincolnshire Railway.

Railways were no novelty to Buxton when the first official train ran from Stockport on the afternoon of 30 May 1863, for that morning had seen the arrival of the Midland from Rowsley, via the twisting Wye gorge, far more spectacular than any scenery on the northern approach.

EUSTON CLASHES WITH THE MIDLAND

Relations had been strained between the LNWR and the Midland because of the latter company's advance north through the Peak. Euston resented the Midland's projection of a line from Millers Dale to New Mills to complete another route between London and Lancashire. The Midland rejected the offer of running powers over the SD & WB for several reasons. Curvature of the last $3\frac{1}{2}$ miles of its Rowsley–Buxton line made it unsuitable for conversion to a main line and gradients between Whaley Bridge and Buxton were too severe against up trains. Virtually the whole section is at 1 in 58 to 1 in 70, apart from Chapel and Dove Holes stations, where gradients ease to 1 in 150.

The Midland opened its Buxton route to passengers on 1 June 1863, the LNWR 15 days later. The Midland reached Manchester in 1867, running into London Road station via New Mills, Hyde Junction and the MS & L. The change to Manchester Central on 2 August 1880 necessitated the Midland using Cheshire Lines Committee metals.

In recent years the Buxton–Manchester service was among the first dieselised in the north west. Beeching recommended that the SD & WB should lose its passenger trains, but commuters have fought to retain them, though they are heavily subsidised. Their future was put further in doubt when the Passenger Transport Authority for Greater Manchester—SELNEC—stated that it did not wish to retain the route. Then came the government's acceptance of a major scheme in 1972 for developing Manchester suburban rail services, including an underground to link lines on the north and south sides of the city. It also envisaged an extension of mainline electrification from Stockport as far as Hazel Grove. From there, DMUS were to maintain the link to Buxton, obviously less intensively.

ASHBOURNE & BUXTON

The Cromford & High Peak was vested in the LNWR in 1887, and its later fortunes were tied up with the development by its new owners of a route along the roof of the High Peak from Buxton to Ashbourne, authorised in 1890. North of Ladmanlow the C & HP was abandoned, for it had been made redundant by the much easier graded SD & WB extension, though a short length was retained to the canal at Whaley Bridge. The incline was worked by horse and capstan until its closure in 1952. A line was constructed from Buxton to Hindlow to meet the c & hp, which was realigned between there and Parsley Hay, whence the new line stretched south to Ashbourne.

Work went ahead with vigour and Buxton and Hindlow were linked in 1892, and at the same time the realignment of what was now a branch from Hindlow as far as Ladmanlow was completed. It served quarries and, up to its closure in the 1870s, Goyt Colliery, the only rail-connected pit in the Buxton area. The c & hp was realigned and doubled between Hindlow and Parsley Hay in 1894. After 4 years of activity, Euston's constructional impetus vanished into the Derbyshire mists, for Ashbourne was not reached for another 5 years—until the summer of 1899. The work included a new station at Ashbourne, built jointly with the North Staffordshire. The extension raised no great stir, the mood being caught by Baddeley in 1894 when the line had reached Parsley Hay.

> This extension of the Manchester and Buxton branch is mainly interesting to tourists as saving half of the somewhat monotonous ride or walk over the limestone uplands between Buxton and Dovedale. Parsley Hay, promoted to the dignity of a passenger station, is the latest development of railway enterprise. The route may be described as the antithesis of the 'Dore & Chinley'—all along the tops instead of the bottoms.

The new line gave the LNWR an alternative route to Buxton and Manchester via Nuneaton only 11 miles longer than its shortest link, and also placed Euston in a more competitive position with the Midland and, to a lesser extent, the North Staffordshire route to Buxton via Middlewood, though no serious traffic threat ever developed over that roundabout means of access.

The reason for the development of the line was not passengers but minerals, for there were many quarries in the limestone belt. The Buxton–Ashbourne route may have been seen as a competitive one between London and Manchester in the eyes of some railway officials, but few travellers ever saw it that way. In later years it was very much a local service—so much so that it was claimed to be a line on which every passenger knew everyone else. Ramblers joined the fight to prevent closure, but the battle was in vain, and the service was withdrawn in 1954. The line continued to be available for occasional excursions and emergency passenger services during winter snowfalls for the exceptional length of nine years—until 7 October 1963.

The end of the regular passenger trains had meant the demise of an associated part of the North Staffordshire. This was the original branch between Rocester and Ashbourne, used by the through trains between Buxton and Uttoxeter.

Earlier in 1954, Ladmanlow goods station was closed and the branch cut back to the Mines Safety Research Station Sidings at Old Harpur, reached until 1973 by trains reversing at Hindlow— the terminus of the Ashbourne line since the 1967 closure of the section south to Parsley Hay. The C & HP is well remembered by enthusiasts, a number of whom attended closure ceremonies for various sections. Such closures began in 1963 with the middle section between Steeplehouse and Friden, which included the Middleton Incline.

THE TISSINGTON TRAIL

By the time the High Peak and Ashbourne lines were closed, they ran for much of the way through country that had become part of the Peak District National Park. Its planners had well prepared plans to convert the best sections of both routes into trails for hikers and pony trekkers, where people could enjoy more of the countryside without encroaching on valuable farming land.

The planners acquired $11\frac{1}{2}$ miles of the Ashbourne line from north of the town to a point near Hartington, and also the C & HP, to give walkers a continuous route of 30 miles. The Peak Planning Board paid £2,200 for the Ashbourne trackbed, including seven railway cottages and five stations. But while the purchase price was cheap, the cost of conversion was higher, some £60,000 being needed to create what is now called the Tissington Trail. The trackbed has been covered with 10,000 tons of soil, seeded with grass and planted with trees. Car parks have been created on the sites of four stations. Hartington became the Trail headquarters. The conversion was claimed to be the first in Britain. Most of the cost was met by the government. The Trail was an immediate success from its opening on 5 June 1971 and now the old line is far better known than in its railway days. Once the Trail was complete, work began on the C & HP conversion and on the Midland route between Rowsley and Peak Forest.

CHAPTER XIII

Working the Lines

LABOUR RELATIONS

The North Staffordshire was the only major company wholly based in the West Midlands. While men working for the larger railways took orders from Euston, Derby or Paddington, those of the North Staffordshire had more personal contact with their 'gaffers'. But working conditions were pretty standard. The NSR rulebook was virtually the same as the LNWR's, which was drawn up by Lt H. P. Bruyeres, who controlled the Southern division for many years. He stipulated that a stationmaster had to ensure 'that all the servants at his station come on duty, clean in their persons and clothes, shaved and with their shoes brushed'.

NSR rule no 104 was identical, with one significant omission—the need to shave. In the mid-1860s beards were fashionable. Not that every employee had a beard, for at that time boys joined the NSR at the age of 14, though they were classed as men in many ways and there was concern for their welfare: the GWR Temperance Union at Stourbridge, for instance, recruited a 14-year-old boy soon after he joined the company.

One of the best portraits of a railwayman's life anywhere, and especially in the West Midlands, was given by Arthur Stokes, who spent 44 years as a signalman at Solihull. He joined the GWR at 15 in 1885, working $13\frac{1}{2}$h days ($1\frac{1}{2}$h for meals). Alternate Sundays he worked from nine in the morning until ten at night—without pay. He went first to Bloomfield Crossing box on the OW & W near Tipton. It stood beside a brickworks, whose chemicals turned brasses the colour of a rainbow, he recorded in his excellent book, *50 Years on the Railway: Yarns by a Methodist Signalman* (Cornish Riviera Press, Truro, 1936). The social standing of a railwayman in a local community in Arthur Stokes'

The good old days . . . or were they? Not if we believe an advertisement in the second issue of the *Railway Magazine* in 1897

time was reflected in a foreword written by Sir Josiah Stamp, President of the LMS. He mused that, like many good railwaymen, Arthur Stokes had done much for social and church life.

Not every man who joined a railway company worked for it as long as Arthur Stokes. After Hitler's war, many thousands became redundant because of closures and other economies. Rundown in manpower is a tricky problem, which British Railways have handled with far less trouble than other declining industries —though they have rarely received proper credit for that.

Until the late 1960s the West Midlands was a region of virtually full employment, where the railways had a hard job to recruit men and women as station staff, shunters and guards. The problem cropped up, too, in small places like Northwich, where vacancies for Signalmen and Leading Railmen (shunters) were advertised in 1971. These posts, incidentally, were for staff on what was still called the CLC. In the same paper Australian Railways had a bigger advertisement for men—'with previous railway experience preferred'.

Railway strikes have been few in recent years, but there have been several short periods of working to rule, favoured by freight guards at Crewe during several disputes over pay. They caused only limited disruptions to passenger trains, but traffic was reduced to chaos by a lightning stoppage at New Street Station on Friday evening, 27 June 1969, when it was packed with holidaymakers. The standstill lasted for 2h after the staff walked out, alleging they were not getting extra pay for extra parcels work. Among passengers who were advised to make their own way to catch connections at Wolverhampton, Coventry and King's Norton, were two MPs., who protested against the way travellers were treated by BR.

Occasional periods of unrest must not overshadow ways in which railwaymen and women train to help others: like the forty members of the ambulance class at Rail House, Crewe, who received first-aid awards in 1971. In the same year the Birmingham Divisional Manager, John Pollard, a colonel in the Territorial Army, became an ADC to the Queen; and Jim Eames, a Tyseley driver, attended a lunch with the Queen as a member of Birmingham City Council. Afterwards he dashed off to drive the Royal Train to Cheltenham.

Railwaymen are often entertained by colleagues when they

retire, but a rather more unusual send-off was received by Signalman Cecil Evans, who, before he left his box at Cosford after 16 years, was given a fly-past by RAF training planes. Part of his job had been to tell the RAF of train movements and stop them when planes were using the runway adjacent to the Wolverhampton–Stafford line.

When men retire, BR do not forget them—and some do not forget BR, judging by two cases that received wide publicity in 1970. A Birmingham MP raised the case of 79-year-old Frank Deeley, who was still repaying a £20 handshake, though he had been retired for 9 years and had paid it all back. A deduction of 1s 1d per week was made from his old Midland pension—a sum based on his expected span of life. Mr Deeley's ironic comment was: 'I am apparently being penalised for living too long'.

After retirement, ticket collector Bill Hill of Lichfield and his wife celebrated their golden wedding and visited Trent Valley station, where they had first met soon after Bill returned home wounded from the Somme in 1916. He mused on how the station had changed with modernisation: 'The only thing I recognise now is the signal box. I was the first to operate the telegraph when it was built about 40 years ago'.

ACCIDENTS

The best way to begin a section about unusual crashes, or a few which have influenced operating practices, is to note how primitive safety precautions were 130 years ago. An inspector who investigated a minor accident between goods trains at Whitmore in 1841 found that although it was a 'first class' station at which every train called, it had no signals!

One of the worst crashes in the West Midlands happened on a summer's night—23 August 1858. It involved what was meant to have been a children's excursion from Wolverhampton and intermediate stations, to Worcester; but as it turned out, there were thirty more adults than children among the 1,500 passengers. The excursion left Wolverhampton with thirty-seven coaches and two vans, and couplings broke three times. The return excursion was run in two halves. The first, reduced to the still formidable total of thirty coaches, broke in half at Round Oak and eighteen coaches ran back down a bank of 1 in 75 near

Brettell Lane. When they struck the locomotive of the second train, fourteen people were killed and fifty injured.

The OW & W immediately began experiments with Fay & Newall's mechanical continuous brake to replace the side chains that had proved so dangerous. The Inspector classed the mishap as 'Decidedly the worst railway accident that had ever occurred in this country'.

Next, three LNWR accidents, each different, yet all instrumental in bringing about safety improvements. The need for more interlocking of signals and points was demonstrated when the up Irish Mail was diverted into a siding at Tamworth on 14 September 1870, killing the driver and a passenger. The station was then controlled by two boxes out of sight of each other because of the Midland mainline overbridge.

The second accident involved both companies. It happened at Birmingham in 1892 when a Midland express approaching New Street under clear signals was hit amidships by one from Euston at the junction where the lines joined. The LNWR locomotive fell 30ft into a street from a viaduct. Soon afterwards, work started on an independent double-track access to New Street for the Midland.

Two years later there was another serious accident on the LNWR system when a Manchester–Crewe express ploughed into a wagon blown on to the main line by high winds during shunting at Chelford. Fourteen people were killed, and seventy-nine injured, many seriously.

Several major crashes have taken place on the West Coast route. The down Midday Scot was derailed at Weaver Junction in 1930 while going through the junction at 70 mph—some 15 mph above the limit. Twenty people were killed at Lichfield on New Year's Day 1946 when a fish train ran into the back of a stationary local. Frozen ballast had jammed points—an accident cause said to have been unprecedented.

Two bad accidents have occurred at Winsford. Twenty-four passengers were killed on 17 April 1948 when a mail train ploughed into the back of an express that had left Glasgow more than 3h ahead of it. It had been stopped by a soldier who pulled the communication cord to get quickly to his home near the line, and, after stopping, the express had been left unprotected because of a signalman's error. The other Winsford accident was on

O

Boxing Night 1962 when an express from Glasgow deliberately ignored new signalling on the electrified section and ran into the back of a stationary Liverpool–Birmingham express. Eighteen people were killed and thirty-three injured.

Sutton Coldfield was the scene of a spectacular accident in 1955 when a York–Bristol express, diverted because of Sunday engineering work, took the curve through the LNWR station at about twice the 30 mph limit. The death toll was seventeen.

The Ballad of John Axon remembered the Stockport driver posthumously awarded the George Cross—the highest civilian award for bravery—for staying on his 2–8–0 no 48188 to try and prevent a crash after a steam pipe burst while it was pulling a 500 ton goods train from Buxton. It ran down the steep bank approaching Chapel-en-le-Frith South on 9 February 1957 and piled up on the platform. Fireman Ronald Scanlon, who jumped down on his driver's instructions and pinned as many wagon brakes as he could, received a £50 award.

Some recent accidents have caused concern among the public, who felt that the latest signalling systems were foolproof.

Few rail accidents have caused more public unrest than that at Hixon on 6 January 1968 amid the flat fields of Staffordshire, when the 11.30 am Manchester–Euston express rounded a gentle curve at high speed under clear signals and ploughed into a heavy road transporter carrying a 120 ton electrical transformer that had got stuck on an unmanned crossing. Eleven people were killed and forty-five injured. Concern was immediate because the crash happened as accidents were becoming common on these automatic half-barrier crossings, first introduced in this country 7 years earlier in Staffordshire—at Spath, near Uttoxeter on 5 February 1961. Investigations into the Hixon crash took the form of a formal inquiry—the first since the Tay Bridge disaster of 1879.

The Inspector's report called for modification of more than 200 existing crossings to give drivers longer warning of approaching trains. The first fully modified automatic half-barrier crossing in the West Midlands was installed at Lichfield, on the spur between Trent Valley and City stations, by August 1970. It included a much demanded illuminated sign showing if a second train was due immediately after the passage of the first.

Subsequently, plans were announced for a Hixon by-pass, which may lead to the closure of that crossing.

Two drivers were killed and thirty passengers injured when a Stour Valley local from Wolverhampton overran signals and hit a steel special at Monmore Green on 8 April 1970. The emu driver was blamed. It was said he was going to a football match and the Inspector assumed he had cancelled the automatic warning system without thinking, because of worrying about being late off-duty.

Two children were killed when a school special from Birmingham to Rhyl crashed on the return journey at Waverton on 2 July 1971. Cheshire Police were so moved by the bravery of children in the two rear coaches after they overturned that they presented honours boards to the Birmingham school. The cause was a rail buckled by a heatwave, and a permanent way supervisor was blamed for not taking urgent action on reports sent to him beforehand.

Vandalism has brought a ban on spotting at many stations. One of the first places where the ban was introduced was at Tamworth in 1948 after track and installations had been damaged. Spotters lost of one of their best grandstands in Britain when the footbridge over the north end of Crewe station was demolished for electrification. For years they had used it day and night. Later, spotting was banned at Crewe following vandalism.

PRIVATE SIDINGS

Signalling today is sophisticated rather than complicated, for there is no longer need to provide junctions for dozens of private sidings. For many years they were the very lifeblood of railways, from which every conceivable traffic flowed. They served paper mills, stamping works, obvious plants like gasworks and electric power stations, coalmines, heavy engineering works, ironworks, breweries, toy factories, and brick and glass works. At Great Bridge there was a stonehewer's sidings; at Dudley Port the more tasty Palethorpe's siding, making a trailing junction with the Stour Valley to run no more than a few yards to a landing beside a warehouse. Albion had a private siding belonging to a nut and bolt works.

As firms grew or contracted, sidings were altered, as were their connections with main lines. The LNWR had 170 private sidings on the South Stafford lines, the Trent Valley and branches in 1911, when it was stipulated: 'Alterations in these diagrams, in the names of the firms using them, or in the arrangements for working, to be at once notified to Mr W. A. Jepson, Euston Station'. Mr Jepson was mineral traffic manager.

Private sidings were of tremendous variety. Typical (if that were possible) were those to individual coalmines, like that at Madeley, near Crewe, outlet for one of the most westerly pits in the North Staffordshire coalfield. A single line ran through fields to three despatch sidings lying parallel to the mainline for about $\frac{1}{2}$ mile. There were two exits to south-facing junctions to the Up line, and a third, which, in 1870, continued to a crossover between the Up and Down lines.

Just north of Crewe, sidings of the town coalyard straggled the same route, and again there were three junctions, one a crossover between the running lines. More elaborate was a network developed at Winsford to serve several salt and engineering works. Four private sidings branched away within $\frac{1}{2}$ mile, and they were fed by a common line laid parallel to the down main, with a trailing connection as the only access.

At Bulkington a quarry siding dived under the Trent Valley at right-angles to a connection with the Up slow. A number of private sidings served works that were also served by canals, and this made transhipment of goods from rail to water possible. Some firms had sidings connected to the lines of more than one company. The Aston and Stechford line, which gave access to the Saltley works of the Metropolitan Railway Carriage & Wagon Company. The GWR Guide of 1860 extolled the virtues of an important siding at Stourbridge, noting that a 'branch' from the Oxford, Worcester & Wolverhampton and the South Staffordshire Canal to the foundry and manufactory of Keep & Watkin afforded remarkable facilities for the transport of goods.

OPERATING : LNWR

The railway system of the West Midlands served not only the congested industrial areas but provided several through routes that led to Crewe and New Street becoming junctions from which

exception of the 12.0 noon from Birmingham to the North.

...ade for the greater convenience of the Public, but the Company do not hold themselves responsible for any d
...rom the acts or defaults of other parties, nor for the correctness of the times over other Lines.

TRAINS between BIRMINGHAM, WALSALL, and WOLVERHAMPTON,
OVER THE GRAND JUNCTION LINE to BESCOT AND RUSHALL.
Commencing MARCH 1, 1856.

TRAINS from WALSALL.

Euston, not Birmingham, issued Time Bills for the Stour Valley & South Staffordshire lines in 1856

The Granting 'Tickets to Passengers to places off the Company's Lines is an arrangement made for th...
detention, or other loss, or injury whatsoever, arising off their Lines, or from th...

people can take trains, many direct, to places all over the country. Birmingham is more than a cog in the nation's network, it is a hub; though inferior to London in suburban lines and stations, since workers in the West Midlands have never had to travel far to work and no appreciable commuter network has ever developed.

Reprints of several eulogistic guides to the London & Birmingham and Grand Junction railways by contemporary writers enable enthusiasts to study the leisurely operating of early days. When the Grand Junction opened, Stafford, the main intermediate stop, was served by six daily trains, which took 1h 20m to Birmingham and 3h 45m to Liverpool.

Those early routes quickly proved that they had a strategic value, for in the summer of 1839, a special took the Corps of Riflemen from Birmingham to Coventry to deal with a disturbance after a Chartist meeting. It made the journey in remarkably fast time—19½m—if a contemporary report is to be believed.

As lines opened, desire to attract traffic sometimes took precedence over safety. Neele's *Railway Reminiscences* recorded such a situation on the South Staffordshire in 1849 : there was trouble a few weeks after opening because of a 'very risky plan' of overcoming a carriage shortage by using open wagons with planks as seats to carry people to a Whit Pageant at Lichfield. The experiment was not repeated.

Cattle trucks were next tried but as the rising generation took to 'mooing' at the Passengers while the train was stationary, the dislike to using such vehicles, even at the low rate adopted, caused the plan to be withdrawn. We exploited Lichfield extensively, using its Cathedral as the attraction; excursion trains both for Adults and School Children were well supported. One notice issued by an Excursion Agent, owing to want of proper punctuation, gave rise to considerable amusement at the new light thrown on one of the antiquarian objects in the environs of Lichfield. It stated: 'After viewing the Cathedral, the children will be taken to Barrow Cope Hill; where tradition asserts the three Kings were slain for refreshment and amusement!' These three slaughtered Kings figure in the heraldic escutcheon of the City, and accordingly appeared on the combination of shields that graced South Staffordshire Coaches; it was a rather gruesome piece of heraldry for a railway vehicle!

The rolling English road, which G. K. Chesterton found a subject for excellent humour, had several railway counterparts—in lines and services. One of the most memorable examples was between Euston and Wolverhampton (Queen Street) via Bletchley, Yarnton Curve at Oxford, Worcester and the Tipton curve on to the Stour Valley. From 1854 it was maintained by through trains or coaches, and it survived until 1 October 1861, which meant it was probably the longest through service partly maintained by the West Midland Railway.

The Tipton curve was also used for a time by fast Oxford, Worcester & Wolverhampton trains between Worcester and Wolverhampton, the curve giving access to and from Queen Street rather than the Low Level station.

The Trent Valley opening had a profound effect on passenger operation in the West Midlands. While it brought London and Liverpool to just over 6h apart, it relegated Birmingham and the Black Country to second place in Euston's timetables, because most travellers to and from Birmingham were forced to begin changing at Rugby. People complained until the 1870s when, to suit its own operating requirements rather than public needs, the LNWR split overloaded expresses between Euston and the North West. Liverpool and Manchester were each given their own, and these were able to carry portions for Coventry, Birmingham and Wolverhampton. Birmingham also got three daily expresses from Euston, the fastest taking 5m short of 3h.

In the 1880s, Anglo–Scottish expresses made stops at Rugby, Nuneaton, Stafford and Crewe, and at all of them passengers could obtain luncheon baskets :

> Baskets containing half a chicken, with ham or tongue, or a portion of cold beef, salad, ice, bread, cheese, butter, etc., with either half a bottle of claret, two glasses of sherry, or a pint bottle of stout, 3s.

The last of these stations to have refreshment rooms was Nuneaton, where one was opened in 1881. Unlike the other three, it did not serve hot luncheons to travellers.

Major improvements were achieved by opening the Stechford–Aston line to passenger trains in 1882. It relieved pressure on the Stour Valley by diverting some Wolverhampton expresses away from New Street. They divided at Stechford, the front portions continuing via Aston and the Grand Junction while the rear

Despite the ever-increasing intensity of World War I, Nuneaton's importance as a refreshment stop for West Coast expresses was enhanced by major improvements in 1916

called at New Street and all stations to Wolverhampton. Although nearly 2 miles shorter, the Grand Junction line made little difference to timings because gradients were stiffer.

The Soho–Perry Barr line, opened in 1889, also enabled some expresses between Birmingham and the north to avoid Wolverhampton by proceeding via Bescot and Bushbury. The Soho line was part of the Birmingham 'inner circle' service, which ran until 1939 via Handsworth Wood and Aston.

Growing trade between the West Midlands and East Anglia helped to influence the construction of the Midland & Great Northern Joint Railway. In 1879 a through coach service began between New Street and Norwich, but it ran via Rugby, Peterborough and the Great Eastern.

Companies pandered to the upper-class image and bestowed upon acceptable spas like Buxton and Royal Leamington services that neither their total number of residents or visitors combined could ever make economic. Buxton was a place of great importance in Euston's eyes. Having spent £1,500,000 on building the Ashbourne line, it tried hard to exploit it. From 1 October 1899 a weekday through coach left Euston at 11 am and slipped at Nuneaton, being worked forward to Burton, Uttoxeter and Ashbourne. Hartington was the only stop between there and Buxton, reached at 3.22 pm. The up working left Buxton at 1.20 pm and reached Euston at 6.25 pm.

Queen Victoria often passed through the West Midlands. When she and the Prince Consort returned from their first visit to Ireland in 1849, they stopped at Birmingham to receive an address and meet MPs. After a similar ceremony 4 years later, the Queen lunched at Tamworth, but curtailed her stop to make up time lost on the sea crossing from the Isle of Wight. Security precautions were tightened in the 1860s after letters threatening Her Majesty's life were posted from West Bromwich. The chief constable of Staffordshire always travelled in the Royal Train through the county. Traditionally, the Royal trains changed engines at Bushbury, where LNWR and GWR officials swopped stories.

Operating over the West Coast mainline has been analysed minutely over many years, not least the 1930s, when it was the path of the *Coronation Scot*. Countless fans have logged personal journeys, so how does an author choose a symbolic record? Mine

Stations from which tickets issued.	To OXFORD.		To STROUD.		To BATH.		To CHELTEN-HAM.	
	1st.	3rd.	1st.	3rd.	1st.	3rd.	1st.	3rd.
	s. d.	s. d.	s. d.	s. d.	s. d.	s. d.	s. d.	s. d.
Atherstone	26 0	15 9	—	—	—	—	—	—
Bedworth	25 0	15 0	—	—	—	—	—	—
Birmingham ...								
Camp Hill ... }	25 3	15 3	25 9	15 6	36 9	22 0	—	—
Saltley ...								
Bournville	—	—	25 0	15 0	35 0	21 0	—	—
Brownhills	31 6	19 0	—	—	40 3	24 3	25 0	—
Cannock	33 6	20 3	—	—	43 3	26 0	25 0	15 0
Coventry	—	—	28 0	17 0	38 0	23 0	—	—
Deepfields	29 3	17 6	—	—	39 0	23 6	—	—
Dudley	28 9	17 6	25 9	15 6	38 0	23 0	—	—
Dudley Port	28 0	17 0	—	—	38 0	23 0	—	—
Four Oaks	28 9	17 6	—	—	—	—	—	—
Gravelly Hill	26 6	16 0	—	—	—	—	—	—
Great Bridge	28 0	17 0	25 9	15 6	38 0	23 0	—	—
Harborne	26 6	16 0	—	—	38 0	23 0	—	—
Hednesford	—	—	—	—	42 3	25 3	—	—
Kenilworth	—	—	28 6	17 0	36 9	22 0	—	—
Kineton	—	—	—	—	34 6	20 9	—	—
King's Heath	—	—	25 0	15 0	35 9	21 6	—	—
King's Norton ...	27 3	16 6	25 0	15 0	34 9	21 0	—	—
Leamington Spa ...	—	—	25 0	15 0	36 0	22 0	—	—
Lichfield Junction ...	31 6	19 0	—	—	43 3	26 0	25 0	15 0
Lichfield City	32 0	19 3	—	—	42 6	25 9	25 0	15 0
Moseley	—	—	25 0	15 0	25 9	21 6	—	—
Oldbury	27 3	16 6	—	—	—	—	—	—
Penkridge	33 9	20 3	—	—	43 3	26 0	—	—
Rugeley Junction ...	35 0	21 0	—	—	44 0	26 6	26 6	16 0
Rugeley Town ...	35 3	21 3	—	—	43 9	26 3	26 6	15 9
Selly Oak	26 6	16 0	25 0	15 0	35 6	21 3	—	—
Smethwick	26 6	16 0	—	—	37 3	22 6	—	—
Soho	26 6	15 9	—	—	—	—	..	..
Spon Lane	27 3	16 3	25 9	15 6	37 3	22 6	—	—
Southam & Long Itchington	26 6	16 0	—	—	36 9	22 0	—	—
Stafford	36 0	21 9	32 9	19 9	44 0	26 6	26 6	16 0
Stechford	25 3	15 3	—	—	38 3	23 0	—	—
Stratford-on-Avon ...	—	—	—	—	30 3	18 3	—	—
Sutton Coldfield ...	28 0	17 0	27 6	16 6	38 0	23 0	—	—
Tamworth	29 3	17 6	32 0	19 3	43 3	26 0	25 0	15 0
Tipton	29 3	17 6	—	—	38 3	23 0	—	—
Towcester	—	—	—	—	38 6	23 3	25 3	15 3
Walsall	29 6	17 9	27 6	16 6	38 0	23 0	—	—
Warwick	—	—	25 0	15 0	36 6	22 0	—	—
Water Orton	—	—	—	—	39 6	23 9	—	—
Wednesbury	41 3	24 9	26 6	15 9	38 0	23 0	—	—
Whitacre	—	—	—	—	40 6	24 6	—	—
Willenhall ... } Wolverhampton	30 3	18 3	27 6	16 6	39 9	24 0	—	—
Wylde Green	27 6	16 6	—	—	—	—	—	—

Tourist Tickets are issued at the Birmingham fares from Bournville, Camp Hill, King's Heath, King's Norton, Moseley and Selly Oak, to Tourist resorts south of Birmingham, the passengers being allowed to travel in and out of Birmingham.

When roads were empty and trains crowded . . . Summer 1924, when the LMS alone issued tourist tickets from forty-five stations in the region to 408 destinations

is from a sketchy note I found in a secondhand edition of D. S.
Barrie's *Euston & Crewe Companion*. Undated, but post-1947,
it records a run of the 2.45 pm from Euston, a fifteen-coach formation with an unstated locomotive. After a 3m stop at Rugby at
4.30 pm, Nuneaton was passed at 4.48, Armitage at $5.12\frac{1}{2}$—'dead
slow p.w.'. The log ends abruptly $4\frac{1}{2}$m later at Rugeley. So a
commonplace journey takes on mysticism—one of the inherent
qualities of the fascination of railways.

For many years Coventry had a curious mixed train: the
Belfast boat express on which the city portion—the first two
coaches and a diner—were separated from the rest by a bogie flat
carrying containers for shipment from Fleetwood.

Through the years many attempts were made to establish
through services between South coast resorts and the North West,
but only one ever ran daily—the Pines express.

FORGOTTEN SERVICES

The branches of the region, open and closed, are haunted by
forgotten services. Besides those of the inner circle, there was one
(originally seven weekday and four Sunday trains) which the
LNWR maintained from 1867 to 1917 between New Street,
Kidderminster and Worcester or Hereford. Sometimes through
coaches from Euston were detached at New Street and worked
forward to Smethwick Junction for attachment to GWR trains
from Snow Hill. Some through trains waited at Kidderminster
for nearly an hour. Waiting periods twice that long were sometimes necessary for passengers who used the Princes End branch
to travel between Walsall and Dudley Port (High Level). That
was another service withdrawn during World War I.

Among the most intensive LNWR suburban services were those
already noted over the Harborne branch; those between Wolverhampton and Walsall via Willenhall and the Pleck curve;
between Walsall and Dudley; and especially between Dudley and
Dudley Port, a spur over which in 1915 sixty trains made the
4m journey on weekdays (seventeen on Sundays). A weekday
service of six trains each way, introduced when the Harborne
branch opened, was halved on Sundays, and soon abolished after
strong objections from the well-to-do neighbourhood at Hagley
Road.

Leamington Spa became a natural, if not busy, centre of LNWR local services in areas south of Birmingham. The most intensive working was of twelve daily trains each way to Nuneaton, two continuing to Nottingham. The locals connected with Birmingham trains at Coventry. Leamington's third passenger service—to Rugby—was weekday only and was modest, having eight trains from Rugby a day and one less in the opposite direction.

In Shropshire the LNWR maintained its Coalport branch with a weekday one-class only service of five trains each way, with a mid-evening run between Wellington and Oakengates. A 1915 timetable warned passengers that the last train of the day—9.15 pm from Wellington—called at Malins Lee only to set down. But on Saturdays, it picked up, too!

Beeching reported in 1963. In the following year fresh economies started in the West Midlands, and in 8 years twenty-four passenger services were halved. Services withdrawn since 1964 have been mentioned individually, but they are worth recording collectively because they show the dramatic pattern of decline: between New Street and Leamington via Berkswell and by Coventry; Coventry–Nuneaton; Old Hill–Dudley; Dudley–Lichfield; Stourbridge–Wolverhampton; over the South Staffordshire; Dudley–Dudley Port; Walsall–Rugeley; three between Birmingham and Wolverhampton via the Midland from Castle Bromwich; over the Grand Junction via Bescot; and between Snow Hill and Wolverhampton (Low Level); and Birmingham and Langley Green.

BIRMINGHAM–LONDON BATTLE

The fight between Euston and Paddington for the Birmingham–London traffic was a classic, the sort of contest enthusiasts recall when they remember how modernisation has taken away competition and colour. Quietly sensational from the start in 1852, the battle lasted for more than a century, and will be remembered even longer.

The first incident occurred when a special run on 30 September 1852 to celebrate the opening of the Birmingham & Oxford suffered a number of minor accidents. Passengers got no further than Leamington. The mishaps may have upset some of them, but it did not injure the GWR competitive spirit, or the intro-

duction of a Paddington–Snow Hill link via Oxford of 2 h 45 m
—a creditable 15m faster than the LNWR. Such timings were
restricted to two trains using the route of 129 miles, and stopping
at Leamington and Oxford. From 1 December the GWR eased
the schedule back to that of Euston, because of the wettest
autumn for years, which badly damaged new cuttings and
embankments.

In 1859 Paddington again tried to beat the LNWR with two
daily expresses that undercut the Euston schedule by 10m. But
once again the achievement was short-lived, for when one train
was switched to narrow gauge in 1861 and extended to Birkenhead, 3h 20m was allowed to Birmingham.

In the summer of 1880 an express was speeded up to bring
Birmingham within 2h 42m of Paddington. The next milestone
came in March 1892 with the introduction of the first corridor
train with three classes, which formed the 1.30 pm from Paddington to Birkenhead. Leamington was brought within 2h of London
from 1896, and 2 years later the best Birmingham time was
improved to 2h 27m, a further 2m being saved the following
year when Leamington was given a slip coach.

There was no immediate GWR reply when the LNWR began a
nonstop run of 2h 5m from 2 June 1902, by a single train in
each direction, replaced by 2h expresses from 1 March 1905.
This put Euston firmly ahead in timings until the momentous
year of 1910, when the GWR opened the Aynho cut-off (1 July),
reducing the distance between Paddington and Birmingham from
129.3 miles to 110.6 miles, and putting it on equal terms with
its rival for the first time in 60 years. The Western road was
now 2.3 miles *shorter*, but more severely graded than either of
those via Oxford or Rugby.

Paddington celebrated by introducing 2h expresses. Euston
found it hard to compete, and, instead, tried gimmicks with
short-hand typists to take letters from businessmen on the first
morning and evening expresses between Wolverhampton, New
Street and Broad Street (instead of Euston). A 2h express ran
from Euston early on Sunday evenings. Competition reached
cut-throat standards in 1913 when the North Western matched
the Western with an 8 pm evening express from Birmingham to
Euston.

Time was saved by morning and evening Down expresses

carrying slip coaches. They were of an unusual type with gang-way connections to the main train.

Competition also developed for the comparatively light traffic between Leamington and London. Before Aynho cut-off opened, a Birmingham–Euston express gave a Leamington connection a booking of 1h 50m—about 3m better than the GWR managed with the mileage handicap via Oxford.

MIXED GAUGE TRAINS

Some of the most curious operating on the railways of Britain took place on the mixed gauge frontier at Wolverhampton at the original Low Level station between 1854 and 1869. In a report presented some 3 months after opening, Brunel was at pains to show how well the station worked, with narrow gauge Shrewsbury & Birmingham trains and the Oxford, Worcester & Wolverhampton intermixing with the broad gauge of the Birmingham, Wolverhampton & Dudley. Not all GWR trains used Low Level; some bound for Shrewsbury ran via Queen Street, carriages being attached to trains from Low Level at a platform at Stafford Road Junction. Trains from Shrewsbury ran to Low Level, but the clumsy arrangement ended when the S & B relinquished its share of Queen Street in 1859.

The broad gauge wilted more quickly in the West Midlands than anywhere else, and from 1 November 1868—more than 20 years before the last of the gauge ran west from Paddington—Wolverhampton–Snow Hill–Paddington travellers had narrow-gauge trains, with the exception of one each way. Four broad-gauge goods trains ran daily until April 1869, when the mixed gauge was removed north of Oxford.

Passenger services over the BW & D between Birmingham and Wolverhampton had been mainly restricted to standard gauge for the previous 5 years, and the mixed gauge had been used by many trains from north of Wolverhampton to reach Birmingham, to avoid passengers changing at Wolverhampton Low Level. The OW & W was working standard gauge for some time before the final conversion deadline.

While the broad gauge never reached Manchester, the GWR managed to do so in 1864 with a standard-gauge passenger service from Wolverhampton to London Road. The trains used Queen Street (High Level from 1 June 1885) at Wolverhampton, rather than Low Level, and ran north via Bushbury. Such a service, even though restricted to two daily trains, was a powerful threat to Euston traffic in a sensitive area, but it was abandoned from 1 October 1867. It was replaced from 1 November by a similar service by the roundabout route via Wellington and Nantwich. The switch was made on grounds of revenue : trains were well loaded, but when they ran via Bushbury, the GWR lost all revenue north of there, while those via Nantwich were credited with full mileage to Crewe. The Nantwich line was also used by the GWR for a through coach service between the North West and Bournemouth. Despite commendable efforts, Euston always did better, running through coaches nonstop between New Street and Stockport in 1h 45m.

The opening of the Birmingham & North Warwickshire in the summer of 1908 realised (from 2 November) the GWR dream of a link between Birmingham and Bristol, though with Midland cooperation. A year later the daily trains were increased to three, but the route always remained secondary and its passenger service was withdrawn during World War II. Trains between Birmingham and the West Country and South Wales also used the B & NW. All through passenger services were withdrawn from 10 September 1962, when the Bristol and South Wales trains and the daily Cornishman were switched to the Birmingham & Gloucester.

A GWR casualty of the Kaiser's war was the mainly railmotor service over the Oldbury branch from Langley Green. In 1914 there were thirty trains each way daily, but after 3 March 1915 there were none—a remarkable demise.

A once busy little junction west of Birmingham, Old Hill dealt with locals in four directions. Besides the Birmingham–Stourbridge–Kidderminster trains, it handled locals to Halesowen and to Dudley. Around the turn of the century Halesowen had a pull and push service of fourteen trains each way.

The Halesowen and Dudley branches were once worked by GWR steam railmotors shedded at Stourbridge. They also worked the Town branch and the Kingswinford and Oldbury branches. Railmotors shedded at Tyseley worked the North Warwickshire, again for a restricted period.

The small towns and villages between Wellington and the Severn Valley were well served by locals, the backbone of the services being Wellington–Much Wenlock–Craven Arms. Steam railmotors introduced in 1906 were withdrawn after a year, decisively beaten by the gradients. Diesel railcars did no better when they were tried in 1937 and, to the end, the line was one for robust steam. Wenlock had trains from Shifnal using the Madeley branch, but the service was always sparse—two daily trains at best.

A facet of railways remembered by enthusiasts seeking the past were certain peculiarities of operating, like those at Wellington, where the Wenlock and Coalport locals were run round by gravity. Coaches were pushed into a graded siding and returned to the bay platform after engines had been released.

SUBURBAN ROUTES

The GWR Birmingham suburban services remained constant in character until the end of steam operation in the autumn of 1964. On 4 September rush-hour trains left Snow Hill in steam for the last time, a *County*-class locomotive taking out the Worcester, with the Kidderminster local in charge of a *Castle*. A writer in the *Journal* of the Stephenson Locomotive Society lamented: 'The steam suburban trains will be missed, not least by business-men who preferred the corridor stock to the discomforts of multiple unit travel'. By then, the Paddington–Birkenhead service had only 2 years to run.

Gradually the London Midland Region took over suburban services, among the first being those to Worcester via King's Norton and Stourbridge. The Kidderminster locals connected at Stourbridge Junction with the one-coach diesel shuttle service to Stourbridge Town—a pleasant line running mainly through a wooded cutting into a station that in 1970 retained the atmosphere of a remote GWR branch terminal, even though it could be

Page 237 Cheshire contrasts: (*above*) Crewe. A 1898 view of North Junction, looking towards Manchester. Early Victorian coaches on right, by site of original Manchester & Birmingham station; (*below*) Winsford & Over. For years there was legal resistance to the Cheshire Lines Committee's withdrawal of passenger trains to the wood and stone platform terminus at the end of a meandering branch from Cuddington. Possibly the last one—an RCTS special, 26 March 1960

Page 238 (*above*) North Staffordshire Railway. One of the famous Loop line locals at Cheadle 1905. Original station buildings and unsurfaced platform; (*below*) Cold Meece, the 'secret' station serving a munitions factory that handled millions of passengers yet was never in a timetable. Black Five about to depart with local to Newchapel, 28 February 1958

reached through a pedestrian tunnel under a busy main road outside.

The Shrewsbury and Birmingham diesel service assumed new importance when Shrewsbury and the Cambrian line lost through links on electrification, and passengers had to change at Wolverhampton. The Shrewsbury–Wolverhampton link is part of a longer one to Chester. The final services out of Snow Hill were those maintained by one-coach diesels to Wolverhampton and Langley Green, purely in rush hours. The North Warwickshire trains out of Moor Street have terminals at Henley-in-Arden or Stratford-upon-Avon. Moor Street is also the terminus of locals serving the Solihull area and stations to Leamington Spa.

The closure of Snow Hill did not mean the end of Birmingham–Paddington trains and a service is maintained to and from New Street by several daily Inter City expresses which call at Solihull and several other places. Their average time of 2h 15m is nearly 45m slower than the electrics. To reach New Street the expresses used improved spurs at Bordesley South, Bordesley St Andrew's and Grand Junctions.

MIDLAND OPERATING

The first trains to carry third as well as first and second class passengers into Birmingham were those of the Birmingham & Derby Junction, which the London & Birmingham handled from Hampton. The B & DJ service was started in August 1839 with three weekday trains each way, the fastest taking 2h between Birmingham and Derby. It was augmented by a fourth train within a month, and was still at that frequency when trains were switched to Lawley Street over the new line from Whitacre 3 years later. The service included a mail train each way. The Stonebridge Railway retained two locals, quickly reduced to one.

In 1843 the B & DJ lay fifth in the table of England's fastest services, trains achieving an average of 29 mph exclusive of stops. The best average in England then was 36 mph.

The first through coach service in the West Midlands was established between Euston and Gloucester in 1842—before the creation of the Midland. Maintained by the L & B and the Birmingham & Gloucester, the service ran via Curzon Street. After Lawley Street closed to passengers from 1 May 1851, trains were

P

diverted to Curzon Street via the curve between Landor Street and Derby Junction. Lawley Street was developed on a much larger scale for goods. In that role it did not suffer the handicap of isolation that had made it inconvenient for passengers.

At New Street, the Midland had its own control stretching from Burton to Abbot's Wood Junction, near Worcester, and Redditch. The Midland's Derby–Bristol express service was supplemented for many years by quite an intensive local service from New Street to King's Norton, Redditch or Ashchurch, complemented by one on the Birmingham West Suburban, which claimed Somerset Road as the station for Harborne. A circular service began after the completion of the Lifford Curve in 1892.

The shape of the Midland system was retained by the LMS, carriage sidings at King's Norton handling the division's long-distance stock, and those at Saltley the bulk of stock for suburban use and some holiday expresses. Midland goods traffic was never a problem, since it was able to pass clear of New Street via Camp Hill. During electrification a Newcastle–Bournemouth express completely circled Birmingham, running from Saltley to Lifford, thence to New Street and south over the Bordesley spur to gain the Oxford line. The journey from Water Orton to Tyseley took almost an hour.

The Midland mainline was used for some years by locals to Halesowen via Northfield, five running each way on weekdays. A busier line in its heyday was that from Birmingham to Wolverhampton via Walsall, which at the turn of the century had ten weekday locals each way, increased to a dozen on Saturdays. It was too roundabout to be developed intensely, especially as Walsall and Sutton Coldfield had more direct railways to Birmingham, and the service was reduced as road competition increased. The western section between Walsall and Wolverhampton was closed to passengers in 1931, when the switch was made to the original LNWR route.

Until the working classes could afford to go to the seaside, Sutton Park was a favourite picnic spot, and the LNWR and the Midland ran many specials via Castle Bromwich. Those from central Birmingham started from Curzon Street until 1893, and afterwards from Vauxhall and Duddeston, and Saltley. The Brownhills branch had three weekday trains in late Victorian years, with a late extra on Saturdays.

In Edwardian times the Midland examined the potential of Leamington Spa, and in the winter of 1911 introduced, with the LNWR, two daily trains from Nottingham and Leicester via Coventry. Posters stated that the Midland trains did not have a second class.

NORTH STAFFORDSHIRE OPERATING

While Stoke controlled a comparatively small system, rivals soon realised its power when it came to negotiations; for any company that wanted something from the NSR had to give equal in return. Running powers took its engines and trains—goods and passenger —over a total distance greater than its own system. Not even the mighty LNWR could force its expresses through Stoke without paying a high price. When, by Act of 15 June 1867, Euston received authority to run 'two fast passenger trains' and two goods each way between London and Manchester via Colwich, the NSR received running powers to Cannock, Wolverhampton and Birmingham over the South Staffordshire, which was vested in the LNWR under the same legislation. Euston introduced trains via Colwich and Macclesfield from 1876, and also used the Churnet from 1891 for a through service between Manchester and Nuneaton via Uttoxeter and Burton. Another through the Churnet from Macclesfield to Rugby was worked for 3 months in the same year by NSR locomotives, men and guards.

The workings that took NSR passenger trains deepest into foreign territory were the summer expresses to Llandudno. They started at Derby and Nottingham and ran a greater distance over other companies' lines than their own.

Locally, the NSR pattern of passenger services was dictated by the needs of Euston, which laid down express timings through the Potteries and made sure local trains fitted in. The Loop and its associated services were the most sprightly and intensive of any in the West Midlands, and they were made possible because Stoke was a station where trains arrived and departed but rarely terminated. Unlike many companies, the NSR never had a grand terminal. All its lines of any length were through ones. The Loop trains ran from Blythe Bridge and Longton to Kidsgrove, occasionally Congleton.

NORTH STAFFORDSHIRE GOODS

NSR goods services were quite distinctive from others in the region. The company originally advertised the 'North Stafford' route as the shortest, quickest and best for goods and passengers. Before World War I the image changed to passenger and goods, possibly because local road competition made it harder to attract passengers. The Potteries were alive with mineral and coal traffic for which railways had no rival—and the company made sure it had the resources to exploit that traffic to the full.

NSR locomotive men were stationed at Liverpool and Manchester for many years, being attached to Edge Hill and Longsight sheds to work night goods. When grouping brought the workings, and similar ones from Nottingham, to an end, the men were given the choice of staying at the foreign sheds or returning to the Potteries.

One crack diagram was a mixed goods from Alsager to Wellingborough—with the tender stacked with handpicked coal to avoid buying from the Midland. Such workings were the company's shop window, but by far the most revenue came from trains on its own metals. Besides minerals, farm implements were carried and also hay, not always handled correctly, judging by the 1920 Working Timetable :

> Agents at Stations where Hay and Straw is loaded must exercise greater care in the loading of it. Due allowance is not always made for the settling down and consequent spreading-out of the Hay and Straw, owing to which the ropes become slack and the loads shift.

Pottery, too, was carried in quantity, but it did not always stand up to the robust shunting. Freight workings into the Potteries were on a wider reciprocal base than passenger, and in addition to the LNWR, the Midland, the Great Northern and the GWR ran their own trains and locomotives to Stoke.

TRAIN RUNNING IN CHESHIRE

Although Euston had nothing to do with the Cheshire Lines Committee, it was cheeky enough to 'annexe' the Manchester–Northwich section by showing it in 1915 passenger timetable maps as one of its own main routes. It virtually ignored the rest of the line to Chester. Knutsford–Altrincham–Manchester was served by two afternoon expresses from Euston, which called at Rugby and Crewe and then all stations via Sandbach to Knutsford. They reached Manchester London Road in 4h 45m. There was a single Up train.

Another service with which the LNWR impinged on the Cheshire Lines was more dilatory. Termed officially 'Northwich & Crewe', it was maintained by six or seven weekday trains, about half of which ran to and from Acton Bridge over the Hartford spur.

One of the mainstreams of CLC mineral traffic today is ICI limestone from Tunstead, near Buxton, to works at Northwich. A round-working brake-van trip I made on this link on 25 July 1964 marked the end of steam and haulage by class 8 2–8–0s. The occasion was purely sentimental, for the volume of traffic remains so great that when local passenger services were increased in 1967 between Manchester and Chester via Northwich, there were operating difficulties. Not enough paths could be found between the mineral workings, and the passenger service was cut back. The limestone trains work empty from Wallerscote sidings, beside the West Coast main line, and reach the Cheshire Lines over the Hartford spur. The trains return loaded to Oakleigh Sidings.

FREIGHT—GENERAL

The London & Birmingham promoters based their estimates of income on the 1831 Returns for traffic by roads and canals, calculating the passenger traffic carried by coaches, and goods by vans, stage wagons, market carts and fly boats. They were cautious in forecasting increases likely to result from the advent of a railway:

> Of goods which are also conveyed by canals, the Estimate of Income does not include pig and bar iron, and other metals in a rude form, coals, salt, timber, deals, bricks, tiles, slates, flints, stone, lime, grain, hay, straw, and manure. Neither does it include cattle, sheep and pigs; nor is anything assumed for an increase of passengers, of goods, or of provisions of all descriptions.

Early railways gave precedence to passengers: the Grand Junction was so busy after opening in 1837 that it did not have enough locomotives to start goods services until the following year, when there was a call for goods stations in the main towns.

The Birmingham & Derby Junction continued its goods trains to Curzon Street, via Hampton, until 2 months after the opening of Lawley Street in 1842.

The South Staffordshire began a goods service on 1 March 1850, including a traffic interchange with the Birmingham Canal at Great Bridge. It initially proved to be an interchange in more senses than one, as Neele related :

> The sidings adjoining the Canal basin gave us a lesson in Station Yard working. They were laid unavoidably on falling gradients, and in spite of warnings and cautionary notices, again and again, the wooden stop blocks at the end were broken up, and wagons went into the Canal. A heavy stone buffer block suffered the same fate, and Mr McClean's resident Engineer, Mr Walker, determined to try the effect of dispensing with buffer stops of any kind; the danger of careless running of wagons was patent to the shunters, and there followed a perfect immunity from such occurrences—the danger ensured the safety!

Mergers, amalgamations and take-overs all led to closer relations between companies and the growth of services. The Midland quickly exploited running powers over the South Staffordshire from Wichnor to Dudley, and to Wolverhampton via Bescot—powers obtained in 1867 a month after the South Staffordshire was vested in the LNWR—but ceased to exercise them from Wichnor once it had built its own line to Walsall in 1879, though it continued to run over the SSR from there to Dudley. The Midland developed a busy goods depot at Walsall, served by a short branch opened at the same time. Another freight development by the Midland came in 1865, when it started running to Coventry.

FREIGHT AT CREWE

The 'Oh Mr Porter' jokes about Crewe are aimed at its passenger trains; they ignore its other vital function as a busy freight centre. In 1937, just a century after its creation, Crewe's three marshalling yards were handling some 47,000 wagons in a routine week. They arrived and departed in several hundred trains run in and out of three yards—Basford Hall, by far the biggest with fifty

sidings; Gresty Lane with nineteen sidings; and two groups total-
ling a dozen lines flanking the route to Stoke. Rundown came
in 1972 as more and more block trains came into operation.

These trains were among methods of transport calculated by
the planners of two blueprints, *The Development of the Major
Railway Trunk Routes*, published by the BR Board in February
1965, and *British Railways Network of Development*, issued
jointly by the government and the board 2 years later. The first
plan designated most of the BW & D for closure. The Stechford–
Aston section was to be freight only. The reports did not attempt
to give an overall picture. They did not mention yards like Bescot,
now the focal point of freight traffic for a much wider area than
ever before. Its modernisation, including partial electrification,
cost £1,500,000, and gave Bescot a capacity of 4,000 wagons a
day from official reopening on 18 April 1966.

Birmingham's importance as a centre for imports and exports
led to the creation of Britain's first inland port, opened at Landor
Street on 2 May 1966, after a pilot scheme at Aston. Goods
carried in containers or international rail wagons are cleared
by customs at Landor Street in an operation designed to reduce
delays at ports and to speed delivery by leaving goods untouched
during transit. Two projects associated with the port were an
adjacent freightliner terminal, opened in November 1969, and
a depot for loading containers at Montague Street, across the
London line, opened on 20 January 1969. From Landor Street
goods are sent to more than forty destinations in Europe, North
America and the Middle East. Some go by Channel train ferries.

One object of modernisation was to capture more steel traffic,
an ideal commodity for rail handling, and several concentration
depots were built and block trains introduced. More than
1,250,000 tons were carried in a year by 3,400 trains from North
and South Wales, Yorkshire and Lincolnshire, the North East and
the Potteries.

Coal traffic flows were simplified in 1963–4 when 168 depots
in the Birmingham division were reduced to less than thirty.
Plans for further reductions were abandoned because lorries
entering and leaving extra large depots would cause traffic congestion near town centres.

Oil block trains run to and from refineries in the Birmingham
area. One example is that from Cardiff Docks to Soho Pool.

MODERN OPERATING

Electrification made an immediate and spectacular impact on timetables and a 90m timing was first achieved by the 8.55 am Euston–Birmingham, timed to average 75mph from 6 November 1967.

Birmingham's lack of a commuter service on the scale of London's best suddenly ended in May 1972 when Inter City services were recast for the first time since electrification. A *half-hourly* service throughout week-days began between New Street and Euston: twenty-eight a day. Two were timed at 90m; the rest took 5m longer. All called at Coventry; some at Hampton-in-Arden at peak hours. They terminated at Birmingham with the exception of one to Wolverhampton and another to Shrewsbury.

Birmingham became the focal point of recast cross-country connecting services. Semi-fast electrics that had run between Euston and Liverpool and Manchester via Birmingham since conversion were replaced by through trains and from South Wales, the South of England and the South West.

The Birmingham–Euston service was claimed to be among the most intensive in the world over such a long distance, and it is a dramatic improvement on anything before nationalisation. The best speeds that the LNWR and GWR could manage between the cities was an average of 55mph. Improved track and loco-motive technology of LMS days increased that average, but by only 5mph, and it was left to electrification to take speeds into the seventies. And they are not confined to a few selected trains, as was the case after grouping. Timings between Stoke and Euston of a fraction under 2h are an improvement of up to 45m on steam timings. Recent years have brought a revival of cheap-price excursions: 300 were run from Birmingham in 1971, three times the number of 1968. The problem of local services remains, even though passenger figures rose by a third in the 5 years up to 1971. British Rail, conscious of critics who claimed they never advertised their trains, distributed one-third of a million handbills to houses in the Birmingham area. Publicity was used to boost Birmingham–Glasgow takings, though services were hampered by conversion north of Crewe. A competition launched to find a name for the expresses attracted 3,000 entries and produced the title of *Midland Scot*.

Besides the electrified routes through the Potteries, there is a DMU service between Derby and Crewe, calling at only a handful of stations. The units themselves go farther afield—sometimes to Lincoln or Cleethorpes.

Manchester's link with Buxton remains, and one of the latest services to be developed is that of EMUs from Crewe, which began through running to Altrincham after the conversion in 1971 of the Manchester, South Junction & Altrincham.

DIVERSIONARY ROUTES

It is still possible for enthusiasts to travel over lines no longer used by regular passenger trains. Walsall–Rugeley is sometimes used by Stafford locals (converted to diesel) and expresses between Birmingham and the north. Birmingham–Paddington expresses can run via Coventry and the new spur at Leamington. Birmingham–Leicester services sometimes run via Coventry, and Walsall–Lichfield is used by Derby trains to and from New Street. A summer Penzance–Newcastle is routed via Stourbridge Junction, Galton and Soho. The Grand Junction Bushbury–Stechford is a much-used alternative to the Trent Valley. Expresses sometimes avoid Crewe station by using the freight lines underneath. Sandbach–Northwich is a single line emergency alternative between Crewe and Manchester.

CHAPTER XIV

Fringe Benefits and Frills

PRIVATE LOCOMOTIVE BUILDERS

Railways provided many fringe benefits to the West Midlands. A large private industry grew up to support railways in their heyday and gave thousands of men a livelihood. In the beginning the cart came before the horse regionally, for locomotives were being built before railways arrived. The export of the locomotive, *Stourbridge Lion*, to America helped to increase British influence there at a time when Britain was generally concentrating on building the Empire. Black Country influence was quickly felt in Lancashire: Horseley Ironworks at Tipton built locomotives for the St Helens Railway, no doubt owing to the initiative of the works manager, Isaac Dodds, father of T. W. Dodds, whose wedge motion later caused some havoc through locomotives he built for the North Staffordshire Railway.

That was perhaps one reason behind the NSR's decision to build many of its own locomotives, but even at Stoke it could not claim the distinction of having the only locomotive works, for there was also the California Works, which Kerr Stuart & Company acquired in 1892 from Hartley, Arnoux & Fanning, which had built at least one locomotive. California was greatly expanded in 1909 and turned out 1,500 engines altogether. It collapsed financially in 1930. Of its total output, just two engines worked on the NSR.

Another private locomotive building firm, W. G. Bagnall, at Stafford, remained in production until 1961 when it became the English Electric Castle Works and began making switchgear and other electrical equipment. The Earl of Dudley established locomotive building shops at Castle Mill Works, Dudley, about 1870, for the system that served his ironworks and coalmines. About a

Bagnall—one of the best known names in the private locomotive, carriage and wagon building industry, which grew to be a major one in the West Midlands

dozen engines, tank and tender, were built up to 1915. The works, closed in 1924, were GWR-connected via a branch beside the walls of Dudley Castle.

CARRIAGE AND WAGON COMPANIES

While locomotive building was established at several places, notably Crewe and Stoke, carriage and rolling stock construction was concentrated mainly in the Birmingham area, where it became a major industry. The biggest centre was Saltley, where the LNWR had the headquarters of its southern carriage and wagon division from 1846 to 1865, when the work was transferred to Wolverton and Earlestown respectively. The LNWR originally based 4,800 wagons at Saltley—about half those maintained at Earlestown. The 1865 closure of Saltley was part of a modernisation programme by which the entire locomotive department was placed under one superintendent at Crewe. The old locomotive works at Wolverton were utilised for coaching stock. Machinery was transferred from Saltley and the works dismantled. Richard Bore, who, as the LNWR's first carriage superintendent, had been in charge at Saltley, moved to Wolverton.

Saltley was originally chosen by a London coach builder, Joseph Wright, when it was 'a little village resorted to by artisans of Birmingham as a place of Sunday and holiday recreation'. He developed carriage and wagon works from 1845, first building stock for the London & Birmingham and other early systems. Wright's son, Henry, was an adviser to the LNWR, whose auditors described him in 1850 as 'a gentleman of ability and much practical experience as an Engineer, and formerly in connection with the Soho Works of the late Messrs Boulton & Watt'.

The firm, later Joseph Wright & Sons, was bought by the Metropolitan Railway Carriage & Wagon Company Ltd on 1 July 1862. Eventually Saltley grew to cover 47 of those recreational acres. The company's aims, publicly stated in 1894, were 'The company manufactures railway carriages, tramway cars, wagons, and railway ironwork of every description, and lets on hire coal, ironstone, ballast and other wagons'.

Great expansion came to Saltley with amalgamations on 18 April 1902 which brought in the Ashbury Railway Carriage & Iron Company, Manchester; Brown, Marshalls & Company,

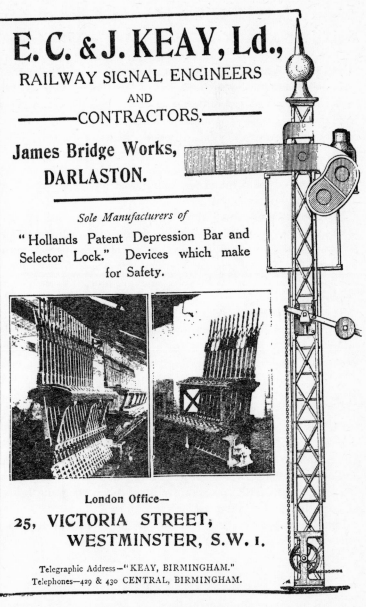

Many firms grew up in the industrial heart of the West Midlands to make every conceivable piece of equipment for railways at home and overseas

founded at Britannia Works, Saltley, on 17 June 1870; Lancaster Railway Carriage & Wagon Company; and the Oldbury Railway Carriage & Wagon Company. Their amalgamation was extended in November 1902 by the addition of the Patent Shaft & Axletree Company. Metropolitan was now a giant, increasing its capital from £1,500,000 to £1,675,000.

In recent years Saltley has declined, chiefly in the early 1960s. A few years earlier the works had employed about 1,800 men, but at the end of 1962 part of it was closed because BR modernisation reduced the demand for rolling stock and there was a drop in orders from many countries.

Metropolitan Cammell remains a big name in rolling stock production, for Saltley's work was concentrated at their Midland Works, nearby at Washwood Heath. The company's rather smaller Old Park Works at Wednesbury was still working on rolling stock in the mid-1960s, but moving more into the general engineering field.

The Metropolitan mergers of 1902 created a giant but not a monopoly, and competitors continued to flourish. They included companies like the Birmingham Railway Carriage & Wagon Company, established beside the BW & D at Smethwick in 1854, straggling both sides of the line; and the Midland Railway Carriage & Wagon Company, of Midland Works, Birmingham, which had a 'branch' at Abbey Works, Shrewsbury.

Besides locomotives. and rolling stock, the West Midlands became the centre of firms that made every conceivable accessory : axle boxes, bolts and nuts, buffer shank forgings, brushware, fastenings, fencing (iron), gauge glasses, lock nuts, lifting jacks, oak keys, paints and varnishes, tie bars, tubes, weighing bridges and machines, wheels and axles.

Blue bricks were an indigenous material often used in railway construction.

A MEMORY OF STEAM

The last steam locomotive repaired for British Rail at Crewe—*Britannia* no 70013—came off works amid ceremony on 2 February 1967 and ran trials along the Shrewsbury line. Five years later main line steam returned to Birmingham when the 77 mile Moor Street–Didcot route became the second longest of five in

Britain reopened to steam preservation societies. None of these routes, stressed British Rail, were very heavily used by ordinary traffic. The first special ran to Didcot on 10 June 1972, hauled by *Clun Castle*, the first of several mainline steam locomotives to be preserved by the Standard Gauge Steam Trust at its expanding Tyseley depot from 1966. The Birmingham & North Warwickshire line was added to steam routes available in 1973, together with Hatton–Bearley provided as a second link for steam specials to Stratford-upon-Avon.

A modest steam venture is being carried out at Chasewater, where a light railway is maintained by the Railway Preservation Society, which was formed at the Station Hotel, Stafford, in 1959. The 2 mile line was acquired in 1965 and runs beside a pleasure lake. A museum of railway relics has been established at Brownhills beside the A5—Telford's road to Holyhead. The Chasewater company runs steam passenger trains on summer Sundays.

MID-RAILWAYANA

A number of West Midland stations of merit were mentioned in a report by the Victorian Society in 1966, which listed sixty in England and Wales worthy of preservation, in whole or part. They included Curzon Street, mainly because of its classical block; Stoke, with its Jacobean Square; its neighbour, Stone; and Waverton, near Chester, a station built regardless of cost for the Duke of Westminster.

An association which maintains the *esprit-de-corps* of the NSR is that formed of its old workers. The line's history has gone on permanent record in a musical documentary recorded by actors at the Victoria Theatre, Stoke. Cheshire Lines memories are kept alive by an association formed in 1949; annual meetings were supplemented by special outings, as in the centenary year, when members proudly toured the system in a two-coach special. A former yardmaster at Northwich recalled : 'We were as strict on the timing of freight trains as passenger'.

Railway relics are preserved in several museums and locomotives are on display at Shugborough and the Birmingham Science Museum, where the locomotive hall was opened on 15 May 1972. It had been built round the main exhibit—no 6235

City of Birmingham (built at Crewe in 1939). The ever-growing demand for relics brought to light many objects that few people knew existed, such as NSR bridge restriction notices, which BR offered for £5. A Manchester & Birmingham poster of 1838, similarly priced by a secondhand bookshop in Manchester, was quickly sold.

Snow Hill's giant clock, which dominated the booking hall for 59 years, has been moved to Wolverhampton and installed on the roof of Wightwick Hall School. But larger chunks of history have been destroyed, including L & B cottages beside the mainline at Coventry, knocked down in 1971 for extensions to the goods station. Stourbridge Library, however, preserves evidence of early road-rail coordination—a Bristol & Gloucester three-part counter-foil ticket covering a stage coach journey to Birmingham as the nearest railhead.

On a Wolverhampton centenary tour on 13 November 1954 a Stephenson Locomotive Society special ran to Victoria Basin—its first passenger train for 100 years *to the day*. More than 40 years after the closing of Halesowen station in 1927, passengers returned there—on a Birmingham University special, run on 2 March 1968.

Page 255 (above) In Derbyshire hills: the LNWR was lavish with the wayside stations it built between Ashbourne and Buxton. Thorpe Cloud, about 1912—wide platforms, milk churns and tin advertisement meant to stand the weather for years; (below) A new junction for the North Staffordshire Railway: Ashbourne, 1899, on the completion of the LNWR route from Buxton. Contractor's locomotive *Tissington* in siding behind footbridge. LNWR train on down platform (right); NSR local in opposite platform. Gaslight left in middle of road widened towards uncompleted level crossing

Page 256 *(above)* One of the most distinctive lines in Britain was the Cromford & High Peak. Ex North London tank no 58860 picking up a train from Buxton at Friden interchange sidings; *(below)* Salt of the earth! Nature throws a weedy veil over the Great Northern Railway aspirations to reach Wales, spearheaded by its branch to Stafford. The scene in summer 1957 soon after the passing of a last special over the route, almost entirely closed some years before

Chronology

One of an author's main tasks is to make a book readable, but one of the difficulties in doing that is dates, the very stuff of history. Essential as they are, they seem to me to place a huge punctuation mark in the middle of an interesting passage. The problem is multiplied in a book of this kind, where mention has to be made of so many railways. This chronology does not include every date concerning every line, but it does give a reasonably complete picture of the development of many lines.

Chapter II Birmingham: 'Premier' Lines

25 July 1831	Warrington & Newton Railway opened.
6 May 1833	Grand Junction Railway incorporated.
	London & Birmingham Railway incorporated.
4 July 1837	GJR opened for passengers (goods January 1838).
9 April 1838	L & B: Birmingham–Rugby opened for passengers (goods 12 November).
24 June 1838	L & B: opened throughout, passengers and goods.
January 1839	GJR extended to own station adjacent to Curzon Street, Birmingham (L & B).
1 January 1846	LNWR formed by amalgamation of GJR, L & B and Manchester & Birmingham.
3 August 1846	Birmingham, Wolverhampton & Stour Valley Railway authorised.
2 June 1862	Aston–Sutton Coldfield opened.
10 August 1874	Harborne Railway opened.
3 October 1887	Soho Pool goods branch opened.
1 March 1888	Soho–Perry Barr opened for goods (passengers 1 April 1889).

	Harborne Junction–Soho Junction quadrupled for goods.
26 November 1934	Harborne branch closed to passengers (completely 4 November 1963).
18 January 1965	Wolverhampton–Walsall–Lichfield–Burton-on-Trent passenger service withdrawn.
6 March 1967	Completion of mainline electrification London–Birmingham–North West.
12 January 1973	West Midlands Passenger Transport Executive sign £3 million a year contract for British Rail to provide commuter services around Birmingham, Coventry and Wolverhampton.
29 January 1973	British Rail announce plans for five-platform station costing £2½ million for the National Exhibition Centre beside Birmingham–Rugby mainline.

Notes. The GJR dominated the formation of the LNWR having absorbed four companies: Warrington & Newton (31 December 1834); Chester & Crewe (1 July 1840); Liverpool & Manchester and Bolton & Leigh (8 August 1845).

New Street station opened 1 June 1854. After extension, platforms for Midland trains were brought into use on 8 February 1885, and the station became LNWR–MR Joint on 1 April 1897.

Chapter III   Birmingham: the 'Midland' Makers

22 April 1836	Birmingham & Gloucester Railway incorporated.
19 May 1836	Birmingham & Derby Junction Railway incorporated.
21 June 1836	Midland Counties Railway incorporated.
4 July 1836	North Midland Railway incorporated.
12 August 1839	B & DJ: Derby–Hampton opened.
4 June 1840	B & DJ: Whitacre–Lawley Street authorised.
1 July 1840	NM: Derby–Leeds opened.
17 September 1840	B & G: Bromsgrove–Cofton Farm opened for passengers.
17 December 1840	B & G: Cofton Farm—Camp Hill opened for passengers.
10 February 1842	B & DJ: Whitacre–Lawley Street opened.
11 April 1842	B & DJ: Lawley Street–GJR spur opened. Goods diverted from Whitacre to Lawley Street.

10 May 1844	Midland Railway formed by amalgamation of NM, MC and B & DJ.
3 August 1846	B & G taken over by MR.
12 June 1847	LNWR–MR Tamworth spur opened.
1 May 1851	Lawley Street station closed to passengers.
30 June 1862	St Andrews–Landor Street Junctions authorised. Opened sometime in 1864.
31 July 1871	Birmingham West Suburban Railway incorporated.
28 July 1873	Stockingford and Kingsbury branches authorised.
30 July 1874	Lifford Canal branch authorised.
1 July 1875	BWSR vested in MR.
3 April 1876	BWSR opened.
1 October 1877	Washwood Heath Sidings opened.
28 February 1878	Kingsbury branch opened.
18 July 1881	BWSR : widening and extension authorised.
1 October 1885	MR expresses switched to BWSR.
1 July 1887	Worcester Wharf goods depot, Birmingham, opened.
22 March 1909	Kingsbury–Water Orton direct line opened for goods (passengers 3 May).
1 January 1917	Whitacre–Hampton closed to passengers.
9 July 1923	Coleshill renamed Maxstoke.
24 April 1930	Whitacre–Hampton closed to regular goods.
1 May 1939	Whitacre–Maxstoke closed to goods.
27 January 1941	New Street–King's Norton via Camp Hill closed to local passenger trains. (Closure confirmed 27 November 1946.)

Chapter IV   Birmingham: Broad and Narrow Gauge

12 June 1844	GWR : Didcot–Oxford opened. Broad gauge [7ft 0¼in].
4 August 1845	Oxford, Worcester & Wolverhampton Railway incorporated.
3 August 1846	Birmingham & Oxford Railway incorporated. Birmingham, Wolverhampton & Dudley Railway incorporated.
31 August 1848	B & O and its Birmingham Extension vested in GWR.
1 May 1852	OW & W : reached Stourbridge from Droitwich.

1 October 1852	GWR : Banbury–Birmingham opened. Mixed gauge.
16 November 1852	OW & W : Stourbridge–Dudley opened goods (passengers 20 December).
1 December 1853	OW & W : Dudley–Tipton opened.
April 1854	OW & W : Tipton–Priestfield opened for goods. Narrow gauge. Priestfield–Cannock Road Junction for goods. Mixed gauge. (Both passengers 1 July.)
1 September 1854	Shrewsbury & Birmingham Railway amalgamates with GWR.
14 November 1854	GWR : Birmingham GWR station (later Snow Hill)–Priestfield Junction opened. Mixed gauge.
1 November 1864	GWR : Birmingham–Wolverhampton passenger trains restricted to narrow gauge.
1 April 1869	GWR : Oxford–Wolverhampton converted to narrow gauge.
6 June 1894	Henley-in-Arden branch opened to passengers (goods 2 July).
25 August 1894	Birmingham & North Warwickshire Railway incorporated.
9 August 1899	B & NW abandons independent route into Birmingham; plans junction with GWR at Tyseley.
30 July 1900	B & NW vested in GWR.
9 December 1907	GWR (B & NW) Tyseley–Bearley West Junction opened for goods (passengers 1 July 1908).
1 July 1909	Birmingham Moor Street station opened for passengers (goods 7 January 1914).
1 January 1915	Henley-in-Arden branch closed to passengers (goods 1 January 1917).
25 December 1931	The Hawthorns station opened at West Bromwich.
1 January 1963	London Midland Region takes over all lines in the Birmingham area from Western Region.
30 July 1962	Wolverhampton LL–Stourbridge Junction closed to passengers.
6 March 1967	Paddington–Birkenhead passenger service ceased.
4 March 1968	Snow Hill South tunnel closed; passenger services switched to New Street. (Line severed 11 November.)

6 March 1972	Birmingham Snow Hill–Wolverhampton LL closed to passengers. Also Snow Hill–Langley Green.
17 September 1972	Birmingham Snow Hill–Swan Village North level crossing: section taken out of use.

Note. The Henley-in-Arden branch track was removed after closure, but the goods depot remained in use with access from the B & NW until 31 December 1962. The B & NW station was passengers only.

Chapter V   Wolverhampton: GWR Lines

3 August 1846	Shrewsbury & Birmingham Railway incorporated.
	Shropshire Union Railways & Canal Company incorporated.
1 June 1849	SUR: Stafford–Wellington opened.
	Shrewsbury–Oakengates opened.
12 November 1849	Oakengates–Wolverhampton opened. Also Stafford Road Junction–Victoria Basin, Wolverhampton.
4 February 1854	S & B begin passenger service Wolverhampton HL–Birmingham (New Street).
1 September 1854	S & B amalgamated with GWR.
13 November 1854	Wolverhampton Junction Railway opened. S & B passenger service switched to Wolverhampton LL and Birmingham (Snow Hill).
14 November 1854	Victoria Basin branch converted from narrow to mixed gauge.
14 November 1858	Kingswinford Junction–Bromley Basin opened.
September 1859	First locomotive built Stafford Road Works.
7 November 1904	GWR bus service started Wolverhampton–Bridgnorth.
11 July 1905	Kingswinford–Oxley branch authorised.
April 1908	Locomotive building transferred from Stafford Road Works to Swindon.
1 July 1923	GWR Bridgnorth bus service transferred to Wolverhampton Corporation.
11 May 1925	Kingswinford branch opened.
31 October 1932	Kingswinford branch closed to passengers. Goods: official date 1 March 1965.
June 1964	Stafford Road Works closed.

1969	Shrewsbury line passenger trains switched from Wolverhampton LL to HL.
27 March 1972	Herbert Street goods closed. Used solely by National Carriers Limited since 1967.
1 May 1972	Wolverhampton–Oxley carriage sidings electrified.

Chapter VI   Wolverhampton: LNWR and MR

3 August 1846	Birmingham, Wolverhampton & Stour Valley Railway incorporated.
2 July 1847	LNWR given authority to lease BW & SV.
February 1852	LNWR opens SV to its *own* goods.
1 July 1852	LNWR opens SV to its *own* passenger trains.
1 November 1872	Wolverhampton & Walsall Railway opened.
1 July 1875	LNWR buys W & W.
13 July 1876	Aldridge–Walsall Wood authorised.
1 August 1876	LNWR sells W & W to MR.
1 July 1879	Wolverhampton, Walsall & Midland Railway (Castle Bromwich–Walsall) opened. Also Water Orton–Park Lane Junction; Lichfield Road Junction–Walsall Junction.
6 August 1880	Walsall Wood–Norton Canes authorised.
1 April 1882	Brownhills branch opened for goods (passengers 1 July 1884).
1 November 1882	Brownhills–Cannock Chase opened. Goods only.
17 August 1901	Wolverhampton & Cannock Chase Railway incorporated. Not built.
31 March 1930	Brownhills branch closed to passengers.
5 January 1931	Wolverhampton HL–Walsall via Wednesfield : passenger service withdrawn.
18 January 1865	Birmingham (New Street)–Walsall via Sutton Coldfield : passenger service withdrawn.

Chapter VII   Black Country Routes

2 July 1829	Shut End railway opened.
3 August 1846	South Staffordshire Junction Railway incorporated.
2 July 1847	Derbyshire, Staffordshire & Worcestershire Junction Railway incorporated.

	Amalgamation confirmed of South Staffordshire Junction and Trent Valley, Midlands & Grand Junction. 'Junction' dropped from South Staffordshire title from 6 October 1846.
1 November 1847	Bescot–Walsall opened.
9 April 1849	Walsall–Wichnor Junction opened.
1 March 1850	Dudley–Pleck Junction and Bescot Curve opened to goods (passengers 1 May).
1 August 1850	ssr leased for 21 years to J. R. McClean.
24 July 1851	Sedgeley Junction–Dudley Port (HL) authorised.
2 January 1854	Sedgeley Junction–Dudley Port (HL) opened.
2 June 1854	Walsall–Cannock and Norton branch authorised.
23 July 1855	Wednesbury–Darlaston; Wednesbury–Tipton; Walsall Wood (Leighswood), and Wyrley Goods branches authorised.
1 February 1858	Cannock and Norton lines opened.
13 August 1859	ssr get extension for construction of Tipton and Darlaston branches.
14 June 1860	Worcester & Hereford and Newport, Abergavenny & Hereford vested in Oxford, Worcester & Wolverhampton and name changed to West Midland Railway from 1 July.
1 February 1861	ssr leased to lnwr.
1 November 1861	lnwr starts working passenger trains to Burton (goods 4 December). To Derby: 1 January 1872.
1 July 1863	lnwr acquires Cannock Chase Railway (Act of 28 July, retrospective).
14 September 1863	James Bridge–Wednesbury opened.
1 September 1866	Swan Village (gwr)–Horsley Fields Junction (ssr) opened.
7 April 1867	Smethwick Junction–Handsworth Junction opened.
15 July 1867	ssr vested in lnwr.
1 March 1872	lnwr starts passenger service: Dudley–Derby.
21 July 1873	Dudley & Oldbury Junction Railway incorporated.
11 August 1876	d & oj: agreement with gwr to work the line.
11 August 1881	d & oj name changed to Oldbury Railway.

7 November 1884	Oldbury Railway opened to goods (passengers 1 May 1885).
1 November 1887	James Bridge–Wednesbury closed to passengers.
1 November 1890	Tipton–Wednesbury closed to passengers.
1 July 1894	Oldbury Railway amalgamated with GWR.
1 July 1895	Tipton–Wednesbury reopened to passengers.
1 August 1907	Spinner's End branch opened to goods.
3 March 1915	Oldbury branch closed to passengers.
1 January 1916	Tipton–Wednesbury closed to passengers for second and final time.
1 January 1917	Galton Junction closed to passengers on LNWR withdrawal of passenger services from New Street to Kidderminster and Worcester.
23 February 1958	Tipton–Wednesbury closed to goods :
30 July 1962	Wolverhampton–Dudley closed to passengers.
4 May 1964	Dudley–Snow Hill, via Swan Village, closed to passengers. Also Dudley–Walsall.
25 May 1964	Norton Junction–East Cannock Junction closed.
6 July 1964	Dudley–Dudley Port (High Level) closed to passengers.
18 January 1965	Wolverhampton (High Level)–Walsall–Burton passenger trains withdrawn.
29 August 1966	Galton Junction–Smethwick Junction spur reopened.
September 1966	Pensnett Railway : Round Oak–Baggeridge Junction closed to goods.

Far too many authorisation, opening and closing dates surround the rise and fall of railways around Stourbridge and Halesowen to make reading comfortable and so they get individual treatment.

RAILWAYS OF STOURBRIDGE

14 June 1860	Stourbridge Railway incorporated.
1 August 1861	Stourbridge Railway : Old Hill–Galton Junction and branch : Cradley–Old Hill goods authorised.
1 April 1863	Stourbridge Junction–Cradley opened. Also Cradley–Corngreaves Siding goods branch.
June 1863	Hayes Lane goods branch opened.
5 July 1865	Stourbridge Town branch authorised (not built).

1 June 1866	Cradley–Old Hill opened.
16 July 1866	Stourbridge Town branch deviation authorised (not built).
30 July 1866	Stourbridge Railway : authority for it to be vested in GWR.
1 April 1867	Old Hill–Galton Junction opened.
1 February 1870	Stourbridge Railway vested in GWR.
31 July 1871	Confirmation of agreement of 10 March 1870 for vesting Stourbridge Railway in GWR—as above.
30 June 1874	GWR receives authority to construct Stourbridge Town branch.
1 October 1879	Stourbridge Town branch opened.
1 October 1901	Stourbridge Town branch extended. New station opened at Stourbridge Junction.

RAILWAYS OF HALESOWEN

17 July 1862	West Midland Railway authorised to build branch from Old Hill to Halesowen & Bromsgrove Branch Railway, and Old Hill–Netherton (later Blowers Green).
5 July 1865	H & BBR incorporated.
1 August 1870	H & BBR : Bromsgrove branch abandoned.
18 July 1872	GWR branch Windmill End Junction–Withymoor Basin authorised.
30 July 1872	GWR and Midland Railway agree to work H & BBR.
13 July 1876	H & BBR name changed to Halesowen Railway.
1 March 1878	Old Hill–Halesowen opened. Old Hill–Dudley South Side of Netherton (later Blowers Green) opened.
10 May 1879	Withymoor Basin branch opened.
10 September 1883	Halesowen–Northfield (Halesowen Junction) opened.
2 August 1898	Halesowen Basin branch authorised.
2 April 1902	Halesowen Basin branch opened.
30 June 1906	HR vested in GWR and MR jointly.
April 1919	Halesowen–Northfield closed to regular passenger trains.
1 August 1921	Withymoor Goods renamed Netherton.
5 December 1927	Halesowen–Old Hill closed to regular passenger trains.

1 September 1958	Longbridge–Old Hill workmen's specials withdrawn.
4 January 1960	Halesowen–Northfield workmen's specials withdrawn.
6 January 1964	Rubery–Northfield workmen's specials withdrawn.
15 June 1964	Old Hill–Dudley closed to passengers.
5 July 1965	Netherton goods closed.
20 October 1969	Halesowen Canal Basin goods branch taken out of use.

Chapter VIII   Through Valleys and Across Plains

Much of this section concerns the progressive widening of the Trent Valley. Dates are given in detail to show how the route was developed as traffic grew.

21 July 1845	Trent Valley authorised.
14 April 1846	Trent Valley purchased by L & B, GJ and M & B.
15 September 1847	Trent Valley partially opened (fully 1 December).
1 December 1847	Greenwich mean time adopted throughout LNWR.
3 July 1871	Lichfield Trent Valley : new station opened. Lichfield : South Staffordshire station replaced by existing one.
14 August 1871	Bulkington–Rugby up slow line opened.
27 January 1873	Nuneaton—Bulkington up goods line opened.
1 June 1876	Nuneaton–Rugby : up slow opened to passenger trains.
18 May 1877	Milford & Brocton opened to passengers (goods 22 January 1882).
1 October 1877	Armitage opened to goods.
29 October 1877	Marshall's sidings, Tamworth, opened.
8 November 1885	Rugby Station–Trent Valley Junction : four lines opened.
30 June 1890	Tamworth (Amington) down loop opened.
26 July 1898	Stafford–Milford & Brocton quadrupled.
1 July 1901	Atherstone–Tamworth part-quadrupled.
6 June 1909	Nuneaton–Hartshill Siding : down slow line opened.
13 February 1910	Attleborough Sidings–Nuneaton down slow line opened.
18 May 1931	Bulkington station closed completely.

| 6 March 1950 | Milford & Brocton closed to passengers (goods 7 March 1960). |
| 2 October 1972 | Atherstone, Polesworth and Rugeley reduced to unstaffed stations. |

RAILWAYS OF RUGBY

9 April 1838	Rugby–Birmingham opened for passengers (goods 12 November).
30 June 1840	Rugby–Leicester opened.
Early 1841	Rugby second station opened.
15 September 1847	Rugby–Stafford opened.
14 August 1848	Rugby station extensions authorised.
1 May 1850	Rugby–Market Harborough opened.
1 March 1851	Rugby–Leamington opened.
22 July 1878	Rugby–Market Harborough doubled.
1 December 1881	Rugby–Roade (Northampton Loop) opened to passengers (goods 1 August).
6 June 1886	Rugby third (present) station opened.
15 March 1899	Annesley–Quainton Road (via Rugby Central) opened to passengers by Great Central.
15 June 1959	Rugby–Leamington Spa closed to passengers.
1 January 1962	Rugby–Leicester closed to passengers.
6 June 1966	Rugby–Market Harborough closed to passengers.
5 September 1966	Sheffield–Marylebone : through passenger trains via Rugby Central withdrawn.

RAILWAYS OF COVENTRY

9 April 1838	Birmingham–Coventry–Rugby opened for passengers (goods 12 November).
18 June 1842	Coventry–Warwick authorised.
9 December 1844	Coventry–Warwick opened.
3 August 1846	Coventry–Nuneaton authorised.
14 August 1848	Exhall–Craven Colliery, and Bedworth–Mount Pleasant branches authorised.
12 September 1850	Coventry–Nuneaton opened.
26 January 1857	Spon End viaduct collapses.
1 October 1860	Spon End viaduct rebuilding and part replacement completed.
5 July 1865	Coventry & Great Western Junction incorporated. Never built.

1 September 1865	Midland began working goods to Coventry via Nuneaton.
26 July 1907	Coventry Loop Line authorised.
10 August 1914	Coventry Loop Line opened.
1962	Coventry new station opened.
10 November 1963	Humber Road Junction (Loop Line) severed.
18 January 1965	Coventry–Nuneaton closed to passengers. Coventry–Leamington Spa closed to passengers.
26 February 1967	Connection to Royal Navy stores depot removed.

RAILWAYS OF LEAMINGTON

18 June 1842	Warwick & Leamington Union Railway incorporated.
1 July 1842	London & Birmingham agrees to purchase W & LU (vested 3 April 1843).
9 December 1844	Coventry–Warwick opened.
27 July 1846	L & B Milverton–Leamington extension authorised.
13 August 1846	Rugby & Leamington Railway incorporated.
17 November 1846	R & L purchased by LNWR.
1 March 1851	Rugby–Leamington opened.
1 October 1852	Birmingham & Oxford opened: Banbury–Birmingham (goods February 1853).
26 January 1864	LNWR–GWR junction opened Leamington (West End).
27 March 1882	Rugby–Dunchurch section doubled.
2 March 1884	Kenilworth Junction–Berkswell opened goods (passengers 2 June). Kenilworth Junction–Milverton doubled.
1 March 1888	Weedon–Daventry opened.
4 August 1890	Daventry–Marton Junction authorised.
1 August 1895	Daventry–Marton Junction opened.
1 February 1958	Western Region takes control: Leamington Spa (Avenue)–Milverton.
15 September 1958	Leamington Spa (Avenue)–Weedon closed to passengers.
15 June 1959	Leamington Spa (Avenue)–Rugby closed to passengers.
9 January 1963	Southam–Napton taken out of use.

10 May 1964	Weedon–Napton & Stockton : official closure date.
18 January 1965	Leamington Spa (Avenue)–Coventry–Nuneaton closed to passengers.
15 May 1966	New junction between ex GWR and LMS lines opened at Leamington.
1 March 1969	Berkswell Junction taken out of use.

RAILWAYS OF NUNEATON

15 September 1847	Stafford–Nuneaton–Rugby opened.
12 September 1850	Coventry–Nuneaton opened.
13 August 1859	Nuneaton & Hinckley Railway incorporated.
14 June 1860	N & H name changed to South Leicestershire Railway. LNWR authorised to construct Leicester–Coventry Loop at Nuneaton.
7 June 1861	Nuneaton–Whitacre authorised.
1 January 1862	Nuneaton–Hinckley opened.
1 January 1864	Completion of through route : Nuneaton–Hinckley–Leicester.
1 November 1864	Nuneaton–Whitacre opened (goods 1 December).
15 July 1867	South Leicestershire vested in LNWR.
1 August 1873	Ashby & Nuneaton Joint opened to coal traffic (goods 18 August, passengers 1 September).
1 September 1873	Nuneaton (Midland) replaced by new station 150yd west.
19 July 1880	Nuneaton (Midland Junction)–LNWR station : spur opened.
22 June 1881	Griff Colliery branch opened.
2 June 1924	Nuneaton (Midland) renamed Nuneaton, Abbey Street.
13 April 1931	A & NJ line closed to passengers.
31 May 1961	Griff Colliery branch closed.
18 January 1965	Coventry–Nuneaton closed to passengers.
19 July 1971	A & NJ closed completely : Abbey Junction–Market Bosworth.

STAFFORD & UTTOXETER

| 29 July 1862 | Stafford & Uttoxeter Railway incorporated. |
| 23 December 1867 | S & U opened : Stafford–Bromshall Junction. |

1 August 1881	S & U purchased by Great Northern (Act : 18 July).
4 December 1939	Stafford–Uttoxeter closed to regular passenger services.
5 March 1951	Stafford Common (Air Ministry sidings)– Bromshall Junction closed completely.
23 March 1957	Last special (Stephenson Locomotive Society) run before lifting east of Stafford Common in November 1959.

Chapter IX   Shropshire Networks

COALBROOKDALE

This section includes details, generally excluded elsewhere in the chronology, of the opening and closing dates of halts. The reason for their inclusion is that they reflect how hard and unsuccessfully the GWR tried to develop local passenger traffic.

1767–8	World's first cast-iron rails laid on tramroads in Coalbrookdale.
1802	Trevithick locomotive tested on Coalbrookdale line.
3 August 1846	Shrewsbury & Birmingham Railway incorporated.
	Shropshire Union Railways & Canal Company line authorised between Stafford and Wellington.
2 July 1847	Shifnal–Ironbridge authorised.
	SUR & CC. Railway and canals leased to LNWR.
1 June 1849	Shrewsbury–Oakengates opened.
	Stafford–Wellington opened.
12 November 1849	Oakengates–Wolverhampton opened.
20 August 1853	Wellington & Severn Junction Railway incorporated.
1 June 1854	Madeley Junction–Coalbrookdale opened.
1 September 1854	S & BR amalgamated with GWR.
1 May 1857	Ketley Junction–Lightmoor opened.
17 June 1861	Wellington–Coalport opened.
1 August 1861	Wellington & Severn Junction leased to GWR and West Midland Railways.
1 November 1864	Lightmoor–Coalbrookdale opened.
	Junction opened between Wellington & Severn Junction and Wenlock Railway at Coalbrookdale.

1 July 1892	Wellington & Severn Junction vested in GWR.
12 August 1907	Lightmoor Platform opened.
24 February 1908	Hollinswood–Stirchley opened. Goods only.
22 March 1915	Shifnal–Lightmoor closed to passengers.
13 July 1925	Shifnal–Lightmoor reopened to passengers.
21 September 1925	Shifnal–Lightmoor finally closed to passengers.
1 December 1932	Doseley Halt opened.
29 January 1934	New Dale Halt opened.
12 March 1934	Green Bank Halt opened.
6 March 1936	Ketley Town Halt opened.
2 June 1952	Wellington–Coalport closed to passengers.
6 February 1956	Lightmoor Platform converted to unstaffed halt.
5 December 1960	Stirchley–Coalport closed completely.
23 July 1962	Wellington–Much Wenlock closed to passengers. Ketley Junction–Ketley closed completely
6 July 1964	Hadley Junction–Stirchley closed completely.
7 September 1964	Stafford–Wellington closed to passengers.
31 July 1965	Lightmoor–Horsehay reopened to goods.
1 August 1966	Stafford–Newport (exclusive) closed completely (official closure July 1967).
22 November 1969	Newport–Donnington (exclusive) closed completely.

MARKET DRAYTON

7 June 1861	Nantwich & Market Drayton Railway incorporated.
7 August 1862	Wellington & Drayton Railway incorporated.
20 October 1863	N & MD opened.
30 July 1866	W & D amalgamated with GWR.
16 October 1867	W & D opened.
1 July 1897	N & MD amalgamated with GWR.
9 September 1963	Wellington–Nantwich closed to passengers.
8 May 1967	Wellington–Nantwich taken out of use.

SHREWSBURY & CREWE

20 August 1853	Shrewsbury & Crewe authorised.
27 July 1857	Deviations authorised at Shrewsbury.
1 September 1858	Shrewsbury–Crewe opened.

20 April 1863	Whitchurch–Ellesmere opened for goods (passengers 4 May).
18 January 1965	Whitchurch–Ellesmere closed to passengers (goods 29 March).

Chapter X   Cheshire

30 June 1837	Chester & Crewe incorporated.
	Manchester & Birmingham incorporated.
4 July 1837	Grand Junction opened Birmingham–Warrington for passengers (goods January 1838).
1 July 1840	Chester & Crewe absorbed by GJR.
1 October 1840	Chester–Crewe opened.
10 May 1842	Stockport–Sandbach opened.
10 August 1842	Sandbach–Crewe opened.
20 February 1845	First locomotive completed at Crewe.
21 July 1863	Northwich–Sandbach authorised.
14 July 1864	Macclesfield, Bollington & Marple Railway incorporated.
28 June 1866	Macclesfield, Knutsford & Warrington Railway incorporated. Line not built.
11 November 1867	Northwich–Sandbach opened for goods (passengers 1 July 1868).
March 1870	Hartford north to east spur opened by LNWR.
27 June 1872	Sandbach & Winsford Junction Railway authorised. Not built.
1 October 1872	Whitchurch–Tattenhall Junction opened.
26 July 1878	Chester & Crewe deviation opened south of Crewe Works.
1 June 1882	Over & Wharton branch opened.
5 August 1891	Lancashire, Derbyshire & East Coast Railway incorporated.
6 July 1895	LD & ECR : Chesterfield–Warrington section abandoned by Act.
2 March 1942	Cledford Bridge Halt closed.
4 October 1942	Mickle Trafford Junction restored.
16 June 1947	Over & Wharton branch closed to passengers.
16 September 1957	Whitchurch–Tattenhall Junction closed to passengers.
4 January 1960	Northwich–Sandbach closed to passengers.
12 September 1960	Manchester–Crewe electrification completed.
1 January 1962	Liverpool–Crewe electrified.

| 4 November 1963 | Whitchurch–Tattenhall Junction closed completely. Diversion route until 8 December. |
| 7 August 1972 | Thomas Street coal depot, Crewe, closed (formerly NSR). |

CHESHIRE LINES COMMITTEE

14 June 1860	Altrincham–Northwich authorised.
11 July 1861	Northwich–Helsby Junction authorised.
12 May 1862	Altrincham–Knutsford opened for passengers (goods 1 May 1863).
29 July 1862	Cuddington–Winsford authorised. Hartford Junction–Winnington authorised.
1 January 1863	Knutsford–Northwich opened for passengers (goods 1 May 1863).
21 July 1863	Northwich–Sandbach branch authorised.
5 July 1865	Mouldsworth–Chester (Northgate) and junction at Mickle Trafford authorised. Also Northwich Salt branches.
17 December 1867	Northwich Salt branches opened.
1 September 1869	Northwich–Helsby Junction opened for goods (passengers 22 June 1870).
1 June 1870	Cuddington–Winsford opened. Also Winnington branch.
1 January 1874	Winsford branch closed to passengers : first time.
2 November 1874	Mouldsworth–Chester (Northgate) opened for goods (passengers 1 May 1875).
1 May 1886	Winsford branch reopened to passengers.
1 December 1888	Winsford branch closed to passengers : second time.
1 February 1892	Winsford branch reopened to passengers.
1 January 1931	Winsford branch closed to passengers : finally.
June 1947	Hartford spur closed to passengers.
16 June 1957	Northwich west-south spur opened.
6 January 1964	Mouldsworth–Helsby closed to passengers.
5 June 1967	Winsford & Over branch closed to goods (physically 11 February 1968 when Winsford Junction (CLC) box closed).
15 April 1968	Closure of Marston branch—last of the salt branches, taken out of use progressively from 1963.
6 October 1969	Chester Northgate closed to passengers (goods 5 April 1965).

R

Chapter XI   North Staffordshire Railway

13 May 1776	Froghall–Caldon Low tramroad authorised. Opened for goods 1777.
26 June 1846	Main lines authorised: Burton-on-Trent and Willington–Crewe. Macclesfield–Colwich. North Rode–Uttoxeter. Stone–Norton Bridge. Harecastle–Sandbach. Newcastle branch.
2 July 1847	Authorised: Marston Junction–Willington deviation (from 1846 Act). Etruria–Shelton. Apedale branch. Extension of Newcastle branch to Pool Dam line.
3 April 1848	Stoke–Norton Bridge opened for goods (passengers 17 April).
22 July 1848	Ashbourne branch authorised.
7 August 1848	Stoke–Uttoxeter opened.
11 September 1848	Uttoxeter–Burton opened for passengers (goods 11 September 1849).
9 October 1848	Stoke–Crewe opened. Also Harecastle–Congleton.
1 May 1849	Stone–Colwich opened.
13 June 1849	Congleton–Macclesfield opened to passengers (goods 18 June).
13 July 1849	North Rode–Uttoxeter opened. Also Marston Junction–Willington.
13 June 1850	Etruria–Shelton opened for goods (passengers January 1862).
1850	Knutton–Pool Dam opened for goods.
21 January 1852	Lawton Junction–Wheelock opened for goods (passengers 3 July 1893).
31 May 1852	Ashbourne branch opened.
6 September 1852	Newcastle branch opened. Also goods to Knutton Junction.
7 November 1853	Apedale branch opened.
1854	Pool Dam–Newcastle Basin opened.
24 July 1854	Potteries, Biddulph & Congleton Railway authorised.
3 August 1859	PB & C opened for goods (passengers 1 June 1864).
13 August 1859	Silverdale–Pool Dam converted from private to public railway. Knutton–Silverdale authorised. Shelton–Hanley authorised.

28 June 1861	Talk o' th' Hill branch authorised. Had opened for goods 1860.
20 December 1861	Hanley branch opened for goods (passengers 13 July 1864).
February 1862	Newcastle–Silverdale opened for goods (passengers 7 April).
13 July 1863	Leek branch authorised. Also Burton goods branch.
14 July 1864	Macclesfield, Bollington & Marple Railway incorporated.
25 July 1864	Newfields and Tunstall (Pinnox) goods branches authorised.
29 July 1864	Silverdale–Market Drayton authorised. Separate Act authorised Audley line, and Bignall Hill, Chesterton, Grange and Jamage goods branches.
5 July 1865	Loop line (Hanley–Kidsgrove) authorised.
29 January 1866	Chesterton branch opened.
16 July 1866	Longton, Adderley Green & Bucknall Railway incorporated.
1 November 1867	Leek branch opened for passengers (goods 1 July).
1 April 1868	Burton goods branch opened.
2 August 1869	MB & M opened for passengers (goods 1 March 1870).
1 February 1870	Market Drayton branch opened.
24 July 1870	Bignall Hill and Jamage goods branch opened. Also Audley line to industrial traffic : no goods stations until some years later.
29 March 1872	Grange branch opened.
1 November 1873	Loop line extended Hanley–Burslem. (Tunstall 1 December.)
1 October 1874	Loop line extended to Golden Hill. Newfields branch opened.
1 June 1875	Tunstall branch opened for goods (passengers 27 July 1892).
September 1875	LAG & B Railway opened. Goods only. (Park Hall–Adderley Green closed January 1895.)
15 November 1875	Loop line completed to Kidsgrove.
28 June 1880	Audley line opened for passengers.
1 October 1881	Audley line diverted to Keele Junction.
7 August 1888	Cheadle Railway incorporated.
7 November 1892	Cheadle Railway opened to Totmonslow.

6 March 1899	Leek & Manifold Valley Light Railway authorised. Also Waterhouses branch.
1 January 1901	Cheadle Railway completed.
27 June 1904	L & M Railway opened for passengers (goods November).
5 June 1905	Leekbrook–Ipstones opened.
1 July 1905	Ipstones–Waterhouses opened. Also Caldon Low goods branch.
21 August 1907	Trentham branch authorised.
1 April 1910	Trentham branch opened.
25 March 1920	Froghall Caldon tramways closed.
11 July 1927	Biddulph branch closed to passengers.
28 July 1930	Sandbach branch closed to passengers.
27 April 1931	Audley line closed to passengers. Tip of Talk branch closed in same year. Rest in 1955.
26 November 1933	Cheadle branch deviation opened.
12 March 1934	Leek & Manifold Railway closed completely.
30 September 1935	Waterhouses branch closed to passengers.
5 August 1941	Cold Meece branch opened. Passengers only.
1 January 1949	Burton branch closed to passengers (goods 6 May 1968).
Summer 1954	Jamage branch closed.
1 November 1954	Ashbourne branch closed to passengers. (Completely 1 June 1964.)
7 May 1956	Market Drayton and Leek branches closed to passengers.
1 October 1957	Trentham branch closed completely.
28 June 1958	Cold Meece branch closed.
3 August 1959	Newfields branch closed.
7 November 1960	Churnet Valley closed to regular passenger trains. Workmen's trains ran over limited sections until 4 January 1965.
29 October 1961	Grange branch closed.
18 June 1962	Madeley Chord opened. Goods only.
7 January 1963	Audley and Bignall Hill lines closed completely.
17 June 1963	Cheadle branch closed to passengers.
17 February 1964	Tunstall branch closed.
2 March 1964	Loop line closed to passengers. Waterloo Road–Birchenwood closed completely 3 January 1966.
15 June 1964	North Rode–Leek closed to goods.
6 July 1964	Last section of Longton, Adderley Green & Bucknall Railway closed completely.

18 July 1964	Tunstall branch closed.
18 October 1964	Chesterton branch deviation opened.
25 January 1965	Oakamoor–Uttoxeter closed to goods.
14 June 1965	Wedgwood Halt becomes station.
27 June 1966	Harecastle deviation opened.
16 May 1967	Market Drayton branch closed completely, apart from Madeley Chord–Brampton.
7 October 1967	Apedale and Pool Dam branches closed (except for Holditch Colliery line).
1 April 1968	Congleton–Biddulph closed completely.
21 June 1968	Chesterton branch closed. (Beyond Hem Heath since 1964.)
5 January 1970	Macclesfield, Bollington & Marple closed completely south of Rose Hill.
4 January 1971	Sandbach branch closed completely.
1 June 1971	Birchenwood–Park Farm Bunker (Goldenhill) reopened for goods.
1972	Leek Brook Junction–Leek closed completely.

Chapter XII   In Derbyshire Hills

2 May 1825	Cromford & High Peak Railway incorporated.
29 May 1830	Cromford Wharf–Hurdlow opened.
6 July 1831	Hurdlow–Whaley Bridge opened.
21 February 1853	Extension Cromford Wharf to MBM & MJR at High Peak Junction opened.
31 July 1854	Stockport, Disley & Whaley Bridge Railway incorporated.
9 June 1857	SD & WBR opened.
17 August 1857	Junction opened between SD & WBR and C & HP.
25 March 1861	C & HP leased to LNWR.
15 June 1864	Whaley Bridge–Buxton opened for passengers. (goods 1 July).
16 November 1866	SD & WBR transferred to LNWR.
3 January 1869	Hurdlow–Dowlow deviation completed and Hurdlow Incline closed.
16 April 1877	Hopton Incline gradient eased to allow adhesion working. Stationary engine removed.
1 July 1887	C & HP vested in LNWR.
25 June 1892	Ladmanlow–Shallcross abandoned, including Bunsall and Shallcross Inclines.

27 June 1892	Buxton–Parsley Hay opened for goods (passengers 1 June 1894). Dowlow–Old Harpur realigned.
4 August 1899	Ashbourne–Parsley Hay opened.
9 April 1952	Whaley Bridge Incline closed.
2 August 1954	Old Harpur–Ladmanlow closed.
1 November 1954	Ashbourne–Buxton closed to regular passenger trains.
12 August 1963	Steeplehouse–Friden closed, including Middleton Incline.
9 April 1967	Cromford–Steeplehouse closed, including Sheep Pasture Incline.
2 October 1967	Parsley Hay–Friden closed.
21 November 1967	Parsley Hay–Hindlow closed.
5 June 1971	Tissington Trail walk opened by Peak Park Planning Board.

Bibliography

I have quoted from contemporary documents, minutes, travel guides and newspapers because they give a vivid picture of how people felt about railways as they were conceived and built. Especially valuable has been C. R. Clinker's chronology, *The Railways of the West Midlands, 1808–1954*, published by the Stephenson Locomotive Society. Other books consulted, apart from those mentioned in the text, were

Barnes, E. G. *The Rise of the Midland Railway 1844–74*

Bradshaw's *Railway Manual, Shareholders' Guide & Directory*. Various years

Branch Line Society. *Passenger Train Services over Unusual Lines* (annual publication)

British Railways. *Your New Railway* (1966)

Casserley, H. C., & Dorman, C. C. *Railway History in Pictures: The Midlands*.

City of Birmingham. *Official Handbook* (1950)

Clinker, C. R. *Register of Closed Passenger Stations & Goods Depots in England, Scotland and Wales*

Coalbrookdale Company. *Coalbrookdale 1705–1959*

Countryside Commission. *Disused Railways in the Countryside of England & Wales* (1970)

Daniels, G., & Dench, L. *Passengers No More*

Dow, G. *Great Central*, Volumes I–III

Ellis, C. H. *British Railway History*, Volumes I & II

Galt, W. *Railway Reform* (1865)

Greville, M. D. *Chronological List of the railways of Cheshire 1837–1939*

— *Chronological List of the railways of Lancashire 1828–1939*

Griffiths, R. P. *The Cheshire Lines Railway* (1958)

Hadfield, C. *The Canals of the West Midlands* (1966)

Harrison, W. *History of the Railways of Manchester* (1882)

Hibbs, J. *The Omnibus* (1971)

— *History of British Bus Services* (1968)

Hodges, W. *A Treatise on the Law of Railways* (1855)

Holcroft, H. *The Armstrongs of the GWR* (1953)

Ironbridge Gorge Museum Trust. *Ironbridge Gorge*

Kellett, J. R. *The Impact of Railways on Victorian Cities* (1969)

Lee, C. *Passenger Class Distinctions*

Lewin, H. G. *Early British Railways*

— *The Railway Mania & Its Aftermath* (1936)

Lewthwaite, G. C. *Branch Line Index*, 2nd ed. (1972)

'Manifold'. *The Leek & Manifold Valley Light Railway* (1965)

Millward, R., & Robinson, A. *Landscapes of Britain: The West Midlands* (1971)

Murray, A. *The British Isles* (1967)

Parris, H. *Government & the Railways in Nineteenth Century Britain* (1965)

Railway Clearing House. *Railway Junction Diagrams, 1915*

— *Handbook of Stations, 1925*

Railway Year Books. Various dates

Reed, B. *Crewe to Carlisle*

Rimmer, A. *The Cromford & High Peak Railway* (1967)

Rolt, L. T. C. *George & Robert Stephenson*

— *Red for Danger*

Savage, C. I. *An Economic History of Transport*

Webster, N. W. *Britain's First Trunk Line*

— *The West Midlands: A regional study*

West Midlands Economic Planning Council. *The West Midlands: Patterns of Growth*

Whishaw's. *Railways of Great Britain & Ireland*

Wingate, H., & Gillham, J. C. *Great British Tramway Networks*

Journals of the Branch Line Society, Historical Model Railway Society, Industrial Railway Society, Railway & Canal Historical

Society, Railway Correspondence & Travel Society, Stephenson Locomotive Society, Wirral Railway Circle

Magazines: *Modern Railways, The Railway Magazine, Railway World, Trains Illustrated.*

Reports of Transport Users' Consultative Committees.

Acknowledgements

One name—my name—appears on the title page, but many people have kindly helped in the preparation of the book. If there be any praise, they share it. If critics place blame, that is mine alone.

R. W. (Bob) Miller, my co-author of other railway histories, drew the draft master map and helped to check the manuscript. So, too, have C. R. Clinker and Dr J. R. Hollick. I also owe especial thanks to Charles Farmer; James Lovelock; Harry Wilkinson, deputy divisional librarian, Prestwich; and several railwaymen—W. Avery of Shrewsbury, J. J. Davies of Fishguard, J. Dentith of Chester, J. Edgington of Euston, H. Forster of Manchester, and J. Williams of Birmingham.

I received willing help from the British Transport Historical Records; libraries at Birmingham, Coventry, Dudley, Lichfield, Nuneaton, Rugby, Stafford, Stourbridge, Tamworth, Walsall, Wolverhampton; Record Offices of Cheshire and Nottinghamshire; the Ironbridge Gorge Museum Trust; the Peak Park Planning Board, Telford New Town Development Corporation; and the Chasewater Light Railway Company. I am indebted to J. Ned Williams, leader of the group that wrote *By Rail to Wombourn*, for permission to quote extracts.

Photographic sources I have acknowledged at the beginning of the book, but I would like to add extra thanks to W. A. Camwell, D. Ibbotson and G. K. Fox, for placing collections at my disposal, and to Park Pictures (Manchester) Limited for printing work and advice.

Whitefield,
Lancashire
1973

Index

The Chronology is not indexed as major dates affecting every line are given in chapter sequence. They include those of authorisation, opening, closure and other major changes (page references in bold face numerals denote illustrations and maps)